Creative Change

CREATIVE CHANGE

A COGNITIVE-HUMANISTIC APPROACH
TO SOCIAL WORK PRACTICE

Howard Goldstein, Editor

with Harvey C. Hilbert
and Judith C. Hilbert

Tavistock Publications
New York and London

To Jenny Sue
To Jacob David
and Bernard Schmidt
and
To LaVerne Keller

First published in 1984 by
Tavistock Publications
in association with Methuen, Inc.
733 Third Avenue, New York, NY 10017
First published in the UK in 1985 by
Tavistock Publications Ltd
11 New Fetter Lane, London EC4P 4EE
© 1984 Howard Goldstein, Harvey C. Hilbert, Judith C. Hilbert

Typeset by Activity Limited, Salisbury, Wilts
Printed in the USA

Library of Congress Cataloging in Publication Data
Main entry under title:

Creative change.

   Bibliography: p.
   Includes index.
   1. Social case work——Addresses, essays, lectures.
2. Cognition——Addresses, essays, lectures.   3. Social work
with the socially handicapped——Addresses, essays,
lectures.   4. Social work with minorities——Addresses, essays,
lectures.   I. Goldstein, Howard.   II. Hilbert, Judith C.
(Judith Cicero)   III. Hilbert, Harvey C.
HV43.C74   1984   361.3'2   84-16194
ISBN 0-422-78650-0 (pbk.)

British Library Cataloguing in Publication Data
Goldstein, Howard
   Creative change.
   1. Social service
   I. Title   II. Hilbert, Harvey C.
   III. Hilbert, Judith C.
   361.3   HV40

ISBN 0-422-78650-0

Contents

List of Contributors

MICHAEL BLAUNER, a candidate for PhD in social welfare, is a lecturer in the field of hospital administration at Cleveland State University. As a practitioner, researcher, and consultant he is associated with national associations for arthritis and Alzheimer's disease and is a founder of a hospice.

AUDREY BOHNENGEL-LEE PhD, has had extensive experience with the chronically ill and is now a medical social worker at University Hospitals in Cleveland, Ohio where she is responsible for social services for renal transplant patients.

HARVEY HILBERT MSSA, is a disabled Vietnam veteran who has worked with the readjustment problems of other veterans. He is co-director of Rainbow Associates, Cleveland, Ohio, a counseling, research, and consultation center.

JUDITH CICERO HILBERT PhD, ACSW, has taught social work practice at three universities. She is co-director of Rainbow Associates, Cleveland, Ohio, where she specializes in research and practice with battered women.

KINLY STURKIE MSW, PhD was on the staff of the Arkansas Alcohol/Child Abuse Demonstration Project, 1979–82. He is now Assistant Professor, Department of Social Work, Clemson University, South Carolina.

MARCIE C. TAYLOR PhD, is a researcher at Western Reserve Psychiatric Habilitation Center, Cleveland, Ohio. She has had extensive experience in all aspects of the field of mental health including direct practice, program development, staff education, teaching, and administration.

WILLIAM F. VANEK MSSA, is occupational specialist for Alcohol Services of Cleveland Inc., Cleveland, Ohio and is in private practice. His work with chemical dependency and stress management includes direct practice with individuals, families, and groups and consultation to teachers, police, and industry.

SUSAN VAUGHN PhD candidate, is Assistant Professor of Social Work at the University of Montevallo, Alabama. She has worked with low income clients in both rural and urban settings and now teaches and supervises students in the rural social work practicum she has designed.

Acknowledgements

In many ways, this book is an offspring of Judith Hilbert and Harvey Hilbert. Together they created the idea for the structure of this work and contributed their remarkable creative energies and their time to its emergence. And, of course, their own chapters, reflecting their sensitivity and talents as social workers and scholars, add considerable substance to these pages. I am personally grateful to them for their support, help, and presence as friends and colleagues during the more difficult times in this book's evolvement.

Likewise, I am indebted and deeply grateful to Audrey Bohnengel-Lee, Michael Blauner, Kinly Sturkie, Marcie Taylor, William Vanek, and Susan Vaughn, not only for their fine contributions to this volume but for their willingness to join in this venture. That we now share these pages together will, I hope, stand as a visible and enduring bond, a symbol of our friendship and collegiality.

Bonnie Kolberg deserves special thanks not only for her fine secretarial support but for the calm, dependable way in which she always came through.

Linda, my wife, comrade, and friend, was my staunch partner in this project. A superb author in her own right, she provided the editorial help, the criticism, the metaphors, and always, the inspiration that kept things going. Most important, she was with me. And last, there is the memory of "Harriet," and the presence of "Rosie" — caring companions, both.

Now having identified the specific people who in their own ways contributed to this endeavor, we cannot overlook those who, unknowingly yet so meaningfully, shared in this effort. I am speaking here of the clients, Mary, Mr S., Jay, Johnny G., Gracie, the Boykins and Jacksons, and the others, named and unnamed, who are what this book is all about. Inevitably, they are our teachers; it is their lives that are the sources of our learning about what existence really means.

Preface

Two purposes are expressed by this book. A glance at the table of contents will indicate what might seem to be the more apparent purpose: that is, to propose a fresh approach to practice with those marginal client populations that seem to resist the best-intentioned efforts of social workers and other helping professionals. These clients include the poor and dependent families whose chronic problems can appear to be overwhelming; violent and abusive families that have become a frustrating concern of communities and social welfare systems; the chronically ill and dying patient; the alcoholic and his or her entrenched and dismal patterns; the mentally ill patient to whom hospital and community are a series of revolving doors; and the most current problem group, the Vietnam veterans. These clients do not, of course, exhaust the categories of "hard-to-reach" or "difficult"; however, we assume that the principles of practice outlined in these pages are, within reason, applicable to other clients — whether voluntary or involuntary.

The second purpose overarches the first and, basically, it is what this book is all about. Incorporating the examples of direct practice noted above, the intent is to present a model of practice that synthesizes recent knowledge derived from the cognitive sciences, moral philosophy, and theories about how people learn and change. It is an open-ended model since the best of what we know about these fields is still in an emergent state. What is even more exciting about what we have come to learn in recent years about brain, mind, and behavior is the anticipation of what we have yet to discover.

We use the term "cognitive-humanism" to represent this synthesis. It expresses the premise that when we enter into a client's flow of living we become involved, not with abstractions such as a diagnosis, a clinical category, or a statistic, but with the very real, perplexing, and often enigmatic problems of living. These existential problems (even as we ourselves experience them) are not subject to positivistic, linear, cause-effect explanations; rather, they epitomize the complex dialectics of living: the ongoing interplay between thought, feeling, and action, between action and value, person and person, person and community, and so on. In ordinary life, these transactions are not so neatly distinguished by commas, conjunctions, and categories insofar as they inevitably involve the very singular ways in which people perceive their circumstances and create their very own realities and meanings. In this regard, the term "cognitive-humanism" embodies other pairings: science and art, theory and philosophy, knowledge and value, mind and spirit, fact and intuition, for example.

In our view, the practice that flows from this orientation is necessarily more reflective and dialectic than it is technical. To the extent that it is possible, the helper joins with the client as a collaborator and colleague in a search for the meanings that are crucial to the client's existence. The routes that are pursued and the terrain that is covered are determined by the client's constructions of reality, by his or her values, and, not the least, by his or her faith and beliefs. Along the way, careful attention is given to the distortions, confusions, and misconceptions in the client's manner of perceiving, thinking, and interpreting that may block the achievement of worthwhile solutions to problems of living.

For the sake of perspective, a few words about the origins of this book are called for. Although it is virtually impossible to trace the heritage of any lasting idea, it seems safe to say that a particular direction was set many years ago: it was at a point in time when I could, at last, begin to trust my uneasy conclusions that at least some of what I had been taught in becoming a professional was standing between myself and my clients — if not actually obstructing my understanding of them. Many of the theoretical frameworks and prescriptive (as well as proscriptive) methods that had defined my role as a human-relations expert actually served to distance me from the common sense world in which both the client and I had to work out our respective lives. Moreover, it became increasingly questionable that it was wise or helpful to sort my clients into various categories of clinical aberrations: they weren't "sick," "dysfunctional," or "psychotic." Rather, they were people who were often troubled by their confused thoughts and misconceptions, by their tendency to fall back on ineffective solutions, by baffling moral and value conflicts, by feelings of powerlessness and demoralization, and frequently at the root of things, by their futile struggle to retain a shred of dignity and personal worth. Perhaps to outside observers these people looked mad, disturbed, or absurd. As they saw themselves, however, these clients were just trying to maintain a semblance of control and integrity the best way they could.

These reflections resulted in a book (*Social Work Practice: A Unitary Approach* Columbia: University of South Carolina Press, 1973) which proposed a social-systems orientation combined with a Dewey-based, educative, problem-solving approach to practice. But further study of how people adapt and cope with their problems of living provided the persuasive evidence that the fulcrum of learning and change actually is the individual's shared and unique conceptions of his or her past, current, and future reality. It is how the person defines self, relationships, and the social system in relation to what he or she expects life ought to be like that should be the starting point for problem-solving and change. This perspective does not ignore the need for environmental change, reform, or social action; however, it underscores the need to be certain that the people who may be beneficiaries of such projects are active participants and decision-makers in the process.

These ideas were worked out in the book *Social Learning and Change: A Cognitive Approach to Human Services* (Columbia: University of South Carolina Press, 1981) which is, by and large, the parent of this book. Where the former book offers a more comprehensive and detailed theory of practice, *Creative Change* shows how these theories find application in practice with various personal and social problems. Frequent references to the former book are included here for the readers who wish to increase their understanding of particular concepts or topics. It will also be noted that this volume more strongly expresses the conviction (clearly apparent in the clients' lives depicted in these pages) that metaphysical questions — matters of spiritual, ethical, and moral values — play a signal role in our clients' existence and must therefore be given careful regard in the helping experience.

This book comprises two major sections followed by a final chapter that integrates the two. Altogether, they express the basic premise that work with human problems that is in any way attuned to the actualities of living must be woven of: (1) a social and moral theory about the nature of humankind; (2) a consonant theory of mind and behavior; and

(3) a coherent set of practice principles that give life and direction to these premises.

The first two chapters provide the philosophical and theoretical foundations for cognitive-humanistic practice that include the nature of the inner and interactive self, a theory of cognition, and a framework for change. The next eight chapters, written by specialists in their respective fields, demonstrate these principles in action. In Chapter 3, Kin Sturkie offers an approach to working with abusive families that synthesizes family theory, cognitive theory, and the mediating factor of the worker's personal style of practice. Audrey Bohnengel-Lee, in Chapter 4, deals with the challenge of working with the chronically ill and dying patient and the inevitable threats to the helper's own sense of mortality. She shows how these patients can be helped to redefine their existence in personally meaningful terms and points to the role of faith and spirituality in this process. In Chapter 5, Bill Vanek portrays the dialectic that characterizes the relations between body and mind in the case of the alcoholic. He shows how both the physiologic-addictive and the cognitive meanings of alcoholism must be addressed in the helping experience. Judy Hilbert, in Chapter 6, offers a theoretical and operational outline for practice with battered women that incorporates the roles of hope, fear, values, and choice in the attempt to help these women re-create a more secure and authentic life. The focus shifts in Chapter 7 to the plight of the poor, the dispossessed, and the dependent family in the rural culture. Here, Susan Vaughn shows how the perceptions and interactions of these clients, their culture, and their community provide the context for fostering growth, adaptation, and the restoration of a sense of power and integrity. In Chapter 8, Mike Blauner shows how cognitive-humanism applies to work with groups. With the self-help group as his focus, he carefully details how the professional role must be worked out in a way that encourages and enhances the group's autonomy and values. Marcie Taylor, in Chapter 9, uses rich case examples to portray the dreadful paradoxes that the mental patient faces as a hospital patient and as the ex-patient attempting to find a place the community. The inescapable significance of this person's inner reality is emphasized as the starting point of change. In Chapter 10, the last of the practice chapters, Harvey Hilbert, by addressing the paralyzing ambiguities that the Vietnam veteran confronts, depicts the pivotal role of ethical and moral choice in the cognitions and actions leading to principled decisions for living. The final chapter recapitulates and animates the philosophical and theoretical ideas that introduce this volume by drawing from the rich array of real-life examples in these pages.

It should be noted that although the contents of this book are written within (and therefore cannot avoid reflecting) a North American perspective, the cognitive-humanistic framework is eminently germane to social-work practice in other nations and cultures. The principles contained within this framework are universally applicable since they are, by their very nature, devoid of a cultural bias. The relevance of this approach to international social work is apparent in the grounding premise that work with people must be rooted in *their* belief systems, *their* personal and social values, *their* traditions, *their* moral and spiritual outlooks, as well as other cultural or political factors that characterize life in specific societies.

PART I
Foundations

Chapter 1

A Cognitive-Humanistic Approach to Practice: Philosophical and Theoretical Foundations

HOWARD GOLDSTEIN

A CASE IN POINT

Jean is seventeen. She is also pregnant. Even before her Italian-Catholic parents divorced a few years ago she was a problem in school, often truant. She dabbled with alcohol and drugs, and ran with the "wrong" crowd. Her mother's subsequent marriage to a Black engineer only intensified Jean's resentment and heedless behavior. She is deliberately indifferent to her stepfather and treats her mother with disdain. Her mother is exhausted, resigned to the idea that Jean will always get what she wants. At seventeen, Jean is not only pregnant but is unalterably convinced that she knows what she wants.

Bob, the father of the unborn child, is twenty. Jean is his first and only love; the two years he has pursued her have been stormy, marked by frequent fights and temporary reconciliations. Bob's Catholic mother was also married before. For the past ten years Bob has lived with his mother and Jewish stepfather who adopted him when it became evident that his natural father had detached himself from his son.

In contrast with Jean, Bob has always been bent on doing the right thing. He avoided even the more commonplace adolescent problems and held part-time jobs since he was sixteen to earn his own spending money. He tried college for a few semesters but got little out of the experience since he had no clear career goals. Unlike Jean, Bob really cannot express what he feels. This distance from his own emotions leaves Bob frustrated and hamstrung when faced with the need to make a decision of any kind.

3

Thus at twenty he has no idea what he wants to do about Jean's pregnancy.

Ironically, the shattering discovery that Jean was pregnant came after Bob had finally worked out a decision about his life. With a blossoming sense of self-assurance, he decided to drop out of college, work full time, pay off his debts, and take whatever time was necessary to think about his future. Without the burden of homework, he was able to spend every evening with Jean — this to the delight of her parents who saw Bob as a stabilizing influence in her life.

Over the next few months, Bob's outward confidence changed to surliness and, because he didn't know what else to do, he finally admitted to his parents that Jean had missed her period and was probably pregnant. He added that he and Jean had been quarreling, that she wouldn't tell her parents about the pregnancy, but that the two had agreed that an abortion was the only solution. This news stunned his parents and there was a furious exchange, full of recrimination and anguish.

Once Bob and Jean had sought medical services and confirmed the pregnancy, Jean immediately changed her mind about the abortion. Obstinately, she said that she would do nothing at all. It therefore fell to Bob to inform Jean's parents of their daughter's pregnancy. Their reaction was one of feeble anguish; they accepted it as a "phase" Jean was going through, and more or less agreed that she and the baby could live with them if she so wanted. And they certainly wouldn't hold Bob responsible.

As things stand now, all of the actors in this drama are stuck — frozen into roles none had planned for or expected. The idea of becoming a father overwhelms Bob; it just doesn't fit and he doesn't want the baby. Yet he can't give up Jean. Bob's parents have asked him to move out "for his own good" but Bob sees this request as "You're throwing me out!" He has found his own apartment but has done nothing about unpacking his belongings or making the place livable. In the meantime, Jean has graduated from high school as if she were a virginal senior. She is outwardly content and seemingly at peace as long as Bob comes to see her every day. But within the climate of anger, hurt, and foreboding, no one talks about what's going to happen: there are no plans for marriage, no plans for prenatal care or delivery, no plans whatsoever for anything. With the life of the unborn child ripening, all the other lives remain dormant.

What is the point of this case? Why begin this book with an account of rather unexceptional people who are enduring a problem that is becoming so commonplace in present times as to be accepted as a condition of growing up? Yet, though problems of this sort threaten to become rather banal in our society, the anguish and suffering that these people endure are, to each of them, very special, unique, and to some extent very private. In these ways, this case is like and at the same time unlike other cases; thus it serves as an analogy for the kinds of conflict, confusion, dissension, and demoralization that counselors, psychotherapists, and other helpers confront with some frequency in the course of their daily practice. For what we see here is a breakdown of coping and communication, an inability to find a reasonable and self-verifying solution, the burgeoning of a problem that threatens to wipe out self-esteem and the worth of relationships that have been so carefully nurtured.

More to the point, the purpose in presenting this sketch is to add the human ingredient to the abstract question that shapes the theme running through this and the succeeding chapters. The question is this: as helping professionals who in one way or another become involved in our clients' lives, how do we begin to make sense of or find some order and meaning in the torn and twisted circumstances that we encounter? What is it that we need to know and understand so that we as helpers can make the kind of difference in our clients' lives that will enable them to work out the changes they are capable of making? Putting this question in another way, how do we achieve the kind of understanding that will assure that, however we carry out our helping role, this process will protect (if not enhance) the worth, values, and dignity of our clients, will be keenly relevant to their needs and goals, and will free these people to search for, define, and risk fresh, creative, and ethical solutions to their problems of living?

These aims represent the principles of a cognitive-humanistic approach and will be developed and enlarged in the following pages of this chapter. We will consider, first, some of the general explanatory frameworks (psychological, socio-cultural, ethical/moral, and spiritual) that are pertinent to human problems as well as their functions, relationships, and limitations. These ideas will be linked to certain cognitive assumptions about mind, behavior, emotion, and meaning. We will see how these assumptions become shaped into a conception of a self that is purposeful, conscious, reflective and, most important, capable of redefining and resolving the obstacles that block the path toward a more rewarding and confirming existence. We will conclude with a set of premises that support the actual framework of cognitive-humanistic practice that will comprise the next chapter and its application to specific client populations and problems in the succeeding chapters.

UNDERSTANDING AND MEANING: SOME PRELIMINARY ASSUMPTIONS

The simplest answer to the preceding question, "How do we begin to make sense of and find some order and meaning...?", is that we should attempt to study the actual human circumstances as they present themselves to us and for what they have to tell us in their own terms. This means that whether we are concerned with the upheaval that Bob and Jean are undergoing or any other human dilemma, it is necessary to enter into these circumstances in an active way and to allow the situation itself to yield its own substance and meaning. In some ways, this requirement runs counter to some conventional ways of defining a personal or social problem. Typically, the helper is seen as the expert who studies what he or she deems significant and who organizes these findings into a preconceived diagnostic or categorical scheme. In contrast with this formal, systematic approach, we propose that, as far as is possible, preconceptions or generalizations that might distort or bias a straightforward perception of the client's situation as it actually is should be set aside (Goldstein 1983).

To what extent can this ideal be achieved? Is it possible to forget the dependable models of knowledge that we have been taught and the common knowledge we have gained through our own experiences of ordinary living? Admittedly, it is doubtful that we can put aside what we already know or that we can apprehend another's experience in its pristine form. This being the case, it becomes important to take another look at the major frameworks of theory and knowledge that guide our understanding of personal and social problems to see if and how they might be used to gain a more accurate grasp of the human situation. In other words, if we can be more aware of the distortions in the lenses we are using to perceive a particular occurrence, we are more likely to use them with greater care and humility.

Four frames of reference

Generally speaking, the helping professional employs any or all of four major frames of reference to organize his or her approach to the understanding of a client's circumstances. It should be noted in advance that these orientations do not have equal valence nor are they of the same order of explanation. Each, as will be seen, derives from rather different assumptions about human nature. For this reason, each framework poses different types of questions that are addressed to different aspects of the total person.

The first is, of course, the *psychological* frame of reference. It attempts to embrace and comprehend the inner life of the person, the dynamics of mind, emotion, and intellect that, it is assumed, will explain the individual's behavior and personality. This framework may raise questions about one's motivations (e.g. what Jean has at stake in keeping the baby), about persistent characteristics or traits (e.g. the meaning of Bob's patterned avoidance of feeling or decisions), self-concept (e.g. how the parents define themselves in relation to their children's problems), and other factors that illuminate mind and behavior. The second orientation may be termed *socio-cultural* insofar as it is concerned with the social milieu in which the client's life and problems are embedded. Questions in this instance would focus on the community, the culture, and social groups. They would inquire about their standards and expectations (e.g. are they punitive, supportive, or indifferent to Bob's and Jean's plight?), deficits or strengths in institutional systems, questions of status and role, family values, and other variables linked to assumptions about people as social creatures. The third and fourth orders of understanding are somewhat more elusive since they do not conform to the logic and rationality of the preceding frameworks. In fact, if they enter into the helping experience at all, they will probably reflect the personal rather than the professional concerns of the helper. The first of these frameworks accounts for the *ethical and moral* issues and dilemmas that are assumed to lie at the core of personal and interpersonal conflict. Here the concern is with personal definitions of rightness or wrongness, goodness or badness that represent the fixed and enduring convictions of the person and his or her social order (e.g. Jean's position about abortion), with the question of personal obligation to self and/or to others (e.g. Bob's commitment to his own needs in relation to those of his parents, Jean, or the unborn child), with the matter of sexual freedom, and so on. The last, the *spiritual* frame of reference, directs us to the most obscure level of existence since it marks a departure from any measure of objectivity that might be found in the preceding frames. Spirituality is consonant with the deepest subjectivity of the person since it embodies one's personal symbols and icons, the deeply-held and enduring beliefs that have more to do with one's otherworldly, transcendent commitments than with the more mundane affairs of living. Thus, to appreciate the meaning of, say, Jean's Catholicism, we would have to know something more about the metaphors of her devotion (the experience of being and believing) than the extent of her participation in the rituals of her religion (the experience of doing).

This very brief overview certainly does not reflect either the range, complexity, or depth of these various orientations; it is designed primarily to underscore the point that the initial attempt to comprehend even the more apparent aspects of our clients' lives will, in some way, be altered by our own theories, values, and beliefs; we are inclined to search for only the conditions of living that we consider to be most significant. It is also important to observe that these four frames of reference do not exhaust the array of perspectives on the human state that one might call on to explain a particular phenomenon. It is safe to say that the psychological orientation is probably the most dominant in the helping professions; for example, even if attention is given to ethical/moral or spiritual factors, it is likely that they will be explained in psychological terms. Beyond these constructs, biological, economic, environmental, political, and anthropological paradigms might also be applied even to Bob's and Jean's predicament.

One additional point should be made to clarify further the process of understanding. Any and all of these frames of reference express not only the point of view of the individual who employs them but also the values and disposition of the society in which they are promulgated and learned. Prevailing social and behavioral science theories are not the products of pure research that is pursued for its intrinsic value; rather, such theories are, in many ways, indicators of how a society defines particular social problems, the importance it attaches to these problems, and what it wants to do about them. That these orientations are culture-bound makes them no less powerful than if they were rooted in demonstrable scientific evidence. And they are rendered even more persuasive and indelible when they are incorporated and supported by those institutions that are responsible for defining which behaviors are problematic or deviant and how they are to be treated or controlled (Goldstein 1981: 212–22). This point will be well-developed in the later chapter on the mental patient.

A PROPOSAL

The most authentic understanding of a client's circumstances depends on the extent to which the observer is open and receptive to these conditions as they actually are. However, the subjective nature of our personal and cultural biases will inevitably limit and distort what we are able to perceive. What I want to show is that the pursuit of understanding and meaning as a rationale for our interventions in our clients' lives is never final or conclusive; no matter how much we think we know about our clients, certain enigmas and puzzles are bound to persist. It is for this reason that some grand theories that purport to tell us all that we need to know about human behavior or certain simplistic cook-book approaches are so enticing; if nothing else, our acceptance of these prescriptions and recipes not only simplifies life but lessens the discomfort that comes with uncertainty.

Given these barriers to understanding, can we comprehend our clients' personal reality in a way that at least approximates to how things really are for them? A simple yet valid answer to this question is, of course: "Why not just ask the client?" But although such questions are necessary, they are not entirely sufficient: even if the client willingly answers this question (which is not always the case), all we have to deal with are the "facts" as the client construes them. These "facts" are by no means insignificant. But what we have still to grasp are the *meanings* that are contained within or lie behind these facts. For example, what do they imply about the individual's self-image or self-esteem? How do they define his or her worth and role within relationships and community? What are the clients' conceptions of their own goodness and responsibility and the strength of their hope and faith? Above all, what are the purposes that these "facts" serve in enabling the clients to justify their beliefs about "Why things are the way they are" so as to maintain a degree of dignity and rectitude? Suppose Jean was asked why she wants to keep the baby and she replied: "To have someone to love and someone who will love me." What might this answer mean? Is it that she sees herself basically as unlovable or that her parents really haven't loved her, or what? And what does she mean by "love"?

Since our way of viewing reality is, as previously noted, circumscribed by our own world view or inner frame of reference, what is required, first of all, is that we attempt to be aware of the limitations of what we can actually perceive and know. (After all, do we not ask this of our clients when we urge them to reflect on and reconsider their own unquestioned conclusions?) Beyond this principle, we propose that the familiar orientations that we have at hand can be employed in ways that are more relevant to the actual nature of the client's life; they can be used to understand both facts and meaning in terms that are more existential than abstract. However, since we want these frameworks to increase our knowledge about and awareness of the whole person rather than the sum of the individual parts, it becomes necessary, if only for the sake of clarity, to give these familiar frameworks rather unfamiliar titles. Thus, the psychological frame now becomes the *person of the mind*; the socio-cultural, the *person of the community*; the ethical/moral, the *person of principle*; and the spiritual, the *person of faith*. Although each of these frames of reference addresses an arbitrarily defined aspect of the self, we will see that they do not lose sight of the individual as an irreducible whole. Perhaps the following preliminary sketches of each of these orientations will help make the point.

Person of the mind

The wish to understand the person of the mind should direct our attention to the many lineaments of consciousness that are at the core of what we will later define as the *self*. Of concern, in this instance, is the client's inner life that is distinctly unique while at the same time shaped by all that one shares with others as a social being. How we interpret and make sense of the symbols of this inner world depends on whether we assume that they tend to be either reactive or proactive cognitions. Putting this in elemental terms, are the client's thoughts, feelings, and images seen largely as products of or reactions to events of the past, or are they appreciated as the active and intentional means by which the individual attempts to make sense of and cope with the present and future? Since it is the latter assumption that guides our approach to problems of living, our interest would be in the cognitive processes that direct the individual's purposive patterns of coping, goal-seeking, and adaptation. These intentions would be expressed in personal modes of thinking and reasoning, in the personal symbols that underly one's conceptions of reality, in the idioms that are part of one's ethnicity or culture, and in the myths and metaphors that help make existence more vivid. The autobiography that one has shaped would also be a matter of interest: what does the past look like from the vantage point of where the client now is? How is this narrative used to explain the present or to predict the future? And, without exhausting this inquiry, we would like to know where and how the client places the responsibility for how his or her life has turned out and how this is dealt with.

Person of the community

The attempt to understand the person of the community broadens our understanding of the individual as we now see him or her as a social being as well as an entity. Mind and social nature are united when we see that the image of who and what we are emerges out of the meanings that we give to our interactions and relations with others and the environment. Thus a greater awareness of the person of the community does not just add to but expands and enriches our awareness of the person of the mind. The term "community" is not used here to refer necessarily to a geographical space but rather to the more ambiguous boundaries of the society, the culture, the group, and the family to which we feel we belong. We are interested then in the nature and quality of our identifications, relationships, and kinships, the values that are shared or rejected, and among others, what the community can or cannot provide in terms of sustenance, support, security, or provisions. As Langer observes in referring to the relationship between the individual and his or her environment, the latter has *gross control* as it determines what is given; the former has *fine control* as it determines what is taken (Langer 1967: 26). Thus our understanding of the person of community calls for attention, simultaneously, to three factors: the quality of community life and what it can or cannot provide; the nature of the individual (or the person of the mind); and the character of the transactions between the two.

Person of principle

It is probably more accurate to speak of *verstehen* rather than understanding when it comes to the attempt to appreciate the person of principle (and, of course, the person of faith that follows). In contrast with the hypothetical and more or less conventional constructs used to define the person of mind and community, we must now deal with a more metaphysical way of thinking as we try to grasp the elusive questions of human principle and spirituality that, to a great extent, round out the total person. Putting this another way, as imponderable as the mental and social nature of the person may be, one's moral and spiritual selves are even less subject to classification or analysis. Thus we speak of *verstehen* — or the more intuitive mode of grasping these symbolic impressions — rather than the more intellectual mode of understanding as the means by which we might begin to know something about these selves.

The designation "person of principle" is used to refer to the rooted, ingrained beliefs and tenets, the ethical and moral standards previously mentioned, that ultimately guide and justify one's behavior during critical moments of living — those moments when serious choices involving deeply personal questions of what is good, right, or obligatory need to be made. Since the term "person of principle" may suggest only positive meanings, it needs to be said that this title does not necessarily connote intrinsic rightness or goodness: although the individual may be convinced that his or her actions are unquestionably ethical and proper, other observers (or victims of those actions) might protest that they are unprincipled and unconscionable. We will see some examples of this sort of twisted morality in some of the ensuing chapters — particularly those dealing with physical or emotional abuse.

Ethical and moral values are, of course, inseparable from the person of the mind and community. How one thinks and reasons, particularly when faced with a critical choice, are affected by one's tacit and unquestioned beliefs about goodness, rightness, and obligation, and the kind of behaviors that will express these convictions. These values are learned, tested, and validated in one's intimate community — the early family, the closely-bound group, and the surrounding culture, for example.

What we wish to grasp in knowing the client, then, are the premises and values (scarcely rational) that guide his or her orientation to the world of interpersonal relationships, the needs of others, and the sense of obligation and responsibility toward others. The words we use to affirm our beliefs in truth, justice, honesty, or other virtues are one thing; how we act on them may be quite another. Perhaps, then, we can best realize the nature of the person of principle at points of active conflict — when guilt results from actions that violate one's moral code, when shame accompanies behavior that contradicts one's ethics, when one feels victimized or oppressed because one's values have been repudiated by others, and certainly, when one's actions exploit or hurt others.

Person of faith

We approach the second metaphysical concept, that of the person of faith, with some caution — largely because it is so boundless and profound in scope. The intent at this point is not to offer some discourse on this critical dimension of living, but, more modestly, to encourage the helper not only to respect the client's spirituality, but to appreciate the

12

meaning it holds for the client's full-blooded existence. It is curious that helping professionals (except perhaps some pastoral counselors and Jungian therapists) shy away from questions of faith and soul and the spiritual dimension of their clients' lives. Whether this tendency is the consequence of the wish to present a scientific posture or for reasons of personal discomfort, it succeeds in ignoring beliefs, creeds, and faith that, in some instances, have as much to do with some clients' suffering and joy as do the more palpable environmental and interpersonal factors in their lives. It is also curious because many of the models of counseling and therapy not only have their early roots in religious and spiritual ideas, but also bear a very striking similarity to current spiritual healing practices in other cultures (see, for example, Ari Kiev's book, *Magic, Faith, and Healing* and the recent work by Sudhir Kakar, *Shamans, Mystics, and Doctors*).

If we say nothing more about faith and the spiritual life, it is important that we give heed to its role in how people live and find meaning within their real worlds. In some respects, spiritual beliefs both complement and contradict what the intellect tells us. Our rational mind forces us to confront the horrors, the anguish, and the threats that are so evident in our daily contact with the events of the world; newspapers, television, and other media bombard us constantly with instances of brutish behavior and exploitation, with stories of cancer-producing ingredients in the air we breathe and food we eat, and always, the deadly peril of the outbreak of war. If one's spiritual beliefs are not too easily dismissed as "delusions" and "opiates," they can be respected for how they offer a measure of relief from the painful facts of living, or how they offer hope — the image of a better world here or in the hereafter — that makes it possible for one to muddle through and make some sense of the more dreadful conditions of human life. In even more proximate terms, an enduring faith, a belief in a particular destiny, or trust in a divinity may be all that some people have to fall back on when reason and intellect are no longer sufficient resources. We will see a bit later that catastrophes such as serious illness, the death of a loved one, or the failure of a deep relationship may not be resolved by these transcendent beliefs, but at least they may be rendered meaningful and tolerable by an abiding faith.

Now we can consider how these ideas shape the assumptive foundations of a cognitive-humanistic approach upon which will be built more elaborate theoretical and operational propositions. Understanding of these four "persons" or selves hinges first on the study of the inner

13

processes of thought, reasoning, imagery, and the intimately personal as well as the socially learned and shared ideas that link mind and behavior. This understanding, involving the persons of mind and community, is the *cognitive* dimension of knowledge that is one basis for professional actions. It allows us to apply what we know and have learned about human thought and behavior in a way that does not drastically alter or reshape the client's own reality. The conceptual frameworks that we use in this instance are open, waiting to be filled by the client's reality; meaning therefore derives not from our own theoretical presuppositions but from the client's own story.

Second, we must have regard and respect for the moral and spiritual forces that less reasonably and rationally guide one's way through the demands of living. They embody the persons of principle and faith, and stand for the metaphysical or *humanistic* level of understanding. On this dimension, theoretical frameworks are of little value since we are dealing with intimately first-hand symbols, values, and creeds that resist uniform classification. Here, however, we must be conscious of the weight of our own values and beliefs since the awareness of another's deepest convictions will likely evoke our own — particularly when we find that the two are in conflict. I must add, parenthetically, that a willingness to meet clients in this humanistic realm will no doubt result in a "therapeutic" experience for the helper, who, in grappling with other sorts of world views — some, perhaps, rather alien — will need to reconsider his or her own.

Thus, we have the foundations of what we call cognitive-humanism — cognitive referring to the personal and social processes of the mind that account for human behavior in commonsense terms, and humanism accounting for the moral and spiritual values that imbue mind and behavior with meaning and purpose. The hyphen that separates the two terms symbolizes the dialectic or the enduring interaction between the two.

MIND, ACTION, AND MEANING

To this point, we have considered the concepts of cognition and humanism in somewhat philosophical terms. In more operational terms, cognition, first of all, refers to the conscious processes of the mind that include, for example, the ability to store and retrieve information, to perceive, think, create ideas, interpret experience, and so on. These are not merely intellectual functions. We will see that consciousness has

14

many levels and that the emotions play a significant role as the meaning-givers to our thoughts and perceptions; the distinction that tends to be made between the "cognitive" and the "affective" is indeed artificial.

However, since there is little agreement about the nature of the mind (is it something separate from the brain? A function of the brain? The brain itself?), cognition, as a process of the mind, comes to be used and defined in various ways. On one extreme are the artificial-intelligence theorists who believe that we will one day be able to map the structure of the mind in such a way that it can be schematized and duplicated in an advanced, precocious computer. On the other are those who see the mind as boundless, ineffable, and capable of transcending itself in mysterious ways.

The concept of humanism is subject to more numerous and ambiguous definitions. As Wertheimer (1978) concludes after his survey of humanistic psychology, " 'Humanistic psychology' is a phrase that has been used with so many different, and such vague meanings that it is highly unlikely that an explicit definition of it could be written that would satisfy even a small fraction of the people who call themselves 'humanistic psycholog-ists.' "

As a prelude to further development, a few propositions will show how the two concepts will be used in these pages. As already suggested, we reject the notion that human nature is ultimately determined and fixed by what one has undergone in the past or by particular forces in one's environment. To the contrary, we would point to the inventive and imaginative ways in which people are able not only to redefine and grapple with their experiences of living, but also how they are even capable of overriding their genetic inheritance. Although there are no guarantees about how things will turn out, we are free at any point in time to make the small and large conscious choices that bear on the quality of life we believe we deserve. Now there is no question that many of us behave *as if* we were shackled to our past traumas or to certain strictures in our surroundings or relationships. But this behavior is also a choice of sorts — the choice to look backward or outward for the cause of our bondage rather than inward to our values, aspirations, and our capabilities for changing some things in our lives. If one's history or environment unalterably molds one's life, it is not because it must, but because one requires it to do so.

This is not a naive or overly idealistic outlook on the human state that turns its back on poverty, discrimination, disability, or oppressive economic conditions that, in themselves, need to be rectified. Nor do we assume that all people are equally capable of choosing and acting. But even

15

under these burdens there are some choices to be made that, if nothing more, will serve to ensure a trace of personal dignity and worth. How is it that in the face of some catastrophe, one individual will give up or recoil while another will take it on as a challenge to be overcome? Why is it that one person will fall back on his or her misery as a justification for being, whereas another will use it as a spur to success? Ultimately, one must decide whether one is to be temporarily hindered or trapped by sorrow. Neither decision is particularly attractive; but the former view holds some hope of escape while the latter implies resignation and the inevitability of suffering.

Statistical evidence notwithstanding, we cannot generalize about, nor predict how, any single person will react to a particular hardship; although the results of research on various social problems can tell us a great deal about the possible behaviors of, say, large numbers of children of schizophrenic, alcoholic, or abusive parents, of single parents or welfare recipients, these findings can do little more than alert us to some probabilities. In the final analysis, our speculations about our clients must be tested against their own personal images, the inner meanings, that only they know and can tell us about.

The concept of cognition, then, directs our attention to the conscious mind of the person we wish to understand. It provides a means of grasping the peculiar and selective way any one person looks out at his or her world of experience, how these perceptions are organized, thought about, and explained, and, perhaps most important, how the individual depends on these explanations and interpretations as a justification for his or her actions. Correspondingly, the humanistic perspective urges us to regard the less rational mind — or the realm of identifications, values, and spirit — with at least equal respect.

One final point of qualification: the emphasis given to the conscious mind may, by this point, lead the reader to wonder whether the role of unconscious processes is being ignored. Arguably, many of our actions over the course of an ordinary day surely reflect the absence of consciousness; some are not only mindless but thoughtless as well. Indeed, we are able to drive through a maze of traffic, respond to musical rhythms, nimbly return our tennis opponent's serve, put the coffee on in the early morning darkness, and do other things seemingly without the aid (and often without the need) of awareness and thought. But as Konner (1982: 191) notes, there is an important difference between the term "unconscious" when it is used as an adjective and when it is used as a noun. In its most familiar form as a noun, it represents a region of the topography of the mind which, according to psychoanalytic theory, contains repressed drives, memories, and affect. As such, it is a metaphor for the hidden forces that determine our unwitting actions. As an adjective, however, "unconscious" is a term that qualifies the state of the mind when neural, reflexive, and autonomic systems take over.

What this means is that over varying periods of time, the mind seems to shift back and forth across the borders of consciousness — from the utter depths of hypnotic sleep on one extreme of the continuum of awareness, to the other, where vigilance is finely tuned, when, say, we are peering out the window while waiting in the early hours of the morning for the arrival of the son or daughter who promised to be home at midnight. And along this continuum, awareness may take many other forms: as images, sensations, feelings, as well as thoughts, concepts, and ideas. In this view, the mind is understood in processual rather than in topographical terms: whatever consciousness may be, it is fluid and variable and not something that sits on the borders of an inexplicable region called unconscious where the latter has the final say about the nature of the former.

THE SELF

Having spoken of the individual as an active and determining agent of his or her existence, it is time to say something more about what this agency means and how it relates to our approach. There are many explanatory metaphors that could be used to refer to this agency; for our purposes, the concept of the *self* is pertinent insofar as it embodies both the singular and shared characteristics of the person. It is a venerable concept dating back to the work of William James (1896) who detailed and developed the idea of the self as comprising several constituents. Other major self-theorists, among them Sullivan, Fromm, Rogers, Combs and Snygg, and Gordon Allport, have added to the definitions of this concept — e.g. the essential nature of the person, the individual known to the individual, the individual's identity, and the continuity of personal experience.

In *Figure 1* we see a paradigm of the self that incorporates the cognitive functions of the mind (Goldstein 1981: 181).

The first thing to be said about the idea of self is that even though it is a metaphor, its meaning, like those of all powerful metaphors, is not far removed from the actualities of living; essentially, one's self becomes known and understood only in the context of and in its relation to some

17

life event. This life event may be something that the person is actually dealing with. But it is no less meaningful if it is something imagined (but "real" to the person), if it is a memory recalled from the past, or something anticipated in the future. To speak, therefore, of someone's "aggressive" or "passive" self without direct reference to the kinds of situations in which this self finds expression does little more than create a pointless abstraction. Since "who we are" is revealed in some ways in relation to "where we happen to be" it is doubtful that we can fully

FIGURE 1 A paradigm of the self

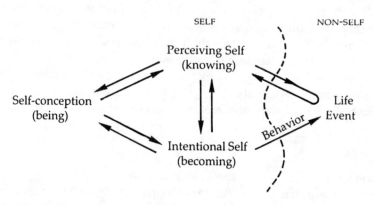

appreciate the total self of another person. For example, the client we thought we understood so well over the course of many individual counseling sessions blossoms into quite another person in group counseling or when we happen to meet him or her by chance at the theatre. Simply, different circumstances evoke different aspects of the same self.

This does not mean that the individual is not conscious of his or her own unitary, coherent self. Despite the various and sometimes incompatible roles one plays out over the course of any day, the ordinary person is able to conserve a core sense of unity and continuity; without this sense of wholeness, fragmentation and disorientation would take over. Moreover, the extent to which one is aware of this core of being frees one to try new experiences, risk new solutions, and carve out new paths. More important, the awareness that one has survived such ventures enriches the esteem of the core self that was.

What this implies is that the self is both a state and a process. The former embodies the more or less enduring characteristics of the person that allows him or her to lay claim to a particular identity; the latter refers to the person in flux — moving into the future, coping with obstacles, maturing, and reorganizing and redefining the notion of "who I am." The state of the self is never fixed or final; should one deny the possibility of change, the difficult process of accommodation to the status quo would, in itself, force certain changes in the self.

Self and non-self

With this view of a dynamic self in mind, let us consider the particular aspects of the self contained in the paradigm. We note first a division between the self and the non-self. An irregular broken line indicates that this border is not always distinct or unambiguous; simply, we are not always certain about the distinction between what is Me and what is not Me. Ordinarily, the second and third person forms of our language ("You are ...," "It is ...") allow us to distinguish ourselves from the people and things around us. For that matter, we are even able to distance ourselves from our own feelings and thoughts — especially those that abrade our moral values or spiritual commitments; unwelcome erotic or malicious impulses may, in all honesty, be dismissed as a momentary possession of sorts by some mysterious force — like "The devil made me do it!"

At the same time, we also can meet with the kinds of experiences that seem to dissolve the borders that enclose our separateness. In the intimacy of love relationships, in the state of "I-Thou" that Martin Buber celebrates, we may experience a fusion of sorts that, for the moment, denies our differences. Likewise, powerful spiritual states may take the form of a sense of communion — a feeling of unity with God, with nature, or with the greater universe. Thus the observer cannot mark out the boundaries of another's self; we learn this only from the mind of the other.

Three interacting aspects of self are identified in the diagram which, for heuristic purposes, signify that most serious human experiences involve the interplay and reciprocity of self-consciousness, motives of some sort, and awareness of the outer world. Quite simply, our meaningful actions involve various combinations of how we define ourselves, what we intend, and how we see and interpret what is going on.

Self-concept

One's self-concept is, in most critical circumstances, the most powerful aspect of self. The term defines itself: it is the innate cognitive portrait that we create of ourselves over time that embraces our accumulated flaws and scars as well as our ideals, worth, and success. We are also aware of the continuity of self since our sense of who and what we are in the present reflects our recollection of what, in the past, we had been or ought to have been, and looking forward into the future, what we want to be or should become.

One's conception of self develops out of a number of impressions. There is the image that we hold about our bodies — the only physical proof we have that we do in fact exist. This image is made up of what we know or would like to believe about such attributes as attractiveness, strength, health and well-being, desirability, and other conditions that influence how we present ourselves to others. Clearly, these images are not absolute, but depend on and are balanced against the standards and norms of the culture we inhabit.

Our identifications also contribute to the self-concept. These have to do with the sense of belonging and integration — the extent to which we are sure we are a part of something else. In addition to gender identifications, self-identity may incorporate the values and beliefs of family, community, culture, religion, and class as well as those of specific social groups. Our identifications are most evident at the times that we are asked some variation of the question: "Who are you?" Depending on how the inquiry is interpreted, the response might, for example, include: "Well, I'm a teacher and, in fact, I just got tenure. I live in the suburbs, I'm married and have two children. I'm active in the Democratic party."

The term "self-concept" carries with it the implication of a mind capable of reflecting on itself; thus one's self-concept is constantly subject to the scrutiny and judgment of its reflective tendencies. In an odd sense, then, we can say that we are able to pull back and evaluate our evaluations of self. Not infrequently, this is the cognitive aspect of self that is called on in the helping experience — the assumption being that if clients authentically can come to see themselves in more positive or less self-demeaning terms they will then take a healthier approach to their problems of living.

This often troublesome ability to reflect on our essential values, standards, and motives results in the last of these attributes of the self-concept. This may be called self-image, self-esteem, self-worth or any other term that refers to the individual's basic estimations of self at a particular point in time. This valuation of worth may be balanced against a number of standards: whether one has or has not met certain valued social expectations; personal ideals; and personal measures of achievement and success. At a more fundamental level are the more plaguing questions which, if pursued, may blemish our self-image with feelings of shame or guilt. This risk emerges when we venture into the domain of our moral obligations, our ethical principles, and our spiritual covenants — that is, when we judge ourselves against the essence of our deeper beliefs and faith.

An inventory of this sort scarcely does justice to the idea of a self-image: it is not a collection of variables that can be arranged and rearranged into a definite structure. Ordinarily, we do not give much thought to questions of self-esteem. But at the times in life when we do undergo personal failure, rejection by the one we desire, or some violation of our basic values, we discover quite painfully how vulnerable the image of ourselves can be. This sort of threat is also evident in how far we will go to save face, to avoid the possibility that we might be proven to be wrong, or to otherwise shield an attack on our integrity and self-esteem. Indeed, it is the sensitive helper who is responsive to the fitful nature of the client's sense of self-worth, while at the same time helping this client risk new perceptions of self that are less distorted, over-demanding, or in other ways blocking the path to self-emergence.

Intentional self

What is described as self-concept is not an isolated phenomenon; rather, as *Figure 1* shows, it is linked to and seeks expression through the intentional and motivational inclinations of the individual. Conversely, the quality of one's goal-seeking tendencies is dependent on the strength of the self-concept: what I want to be reflects what I believe I am — and vice versa.

Three types of intentional strivings can be noted: those that attempt to fulfill basic human needs; those that expand the self to embrace relationships, objects, or values; and those that attempt to transcend the self to achieve more exalted goals. Although these intentions appear to resemble Maslow's hierarchy of needs (Maslow 1954), they do not necessarily emerge in a hierarchical fashion. Conceivably, to achieve a greater good, one may put one's basic security and needs at risk.

More specifically, our essential energies are directed towards achieving the conditions that will ensure our survival. In addition to food, shelter, and security, they include the need for caring and affection and, above all, some confirmation of one's existence. More expansive motives are evident in the need to create an identity by our willingness and desire to become part of something significant. We may be invested in the material things of living: expressions such as "my money," "my career," or "my house" indicate that these are one's objective symbols of personal worth, identity, or achievement. Or we may expand our selves to include significant relationships, loyalties to certain causes, or the values of a cherished group. Here the notion of "who I am" as an individual obtains from the belief about "who we are" together. The third type of intentionality is manifest when we pursue the lofty objectives that promise no certain reward. In this instance, the goal is seen as valuable in and of itself; its pay-offs are incidental to the importance of pursuit. Common examples of this uncommon purpose include the altruistic search for fellowship with others, commitment to an ideology or belief system, and, not the least of these, the truly creative endeavor — the need to be or do what no-one has been or done before.

Perceiving self

The third link of the whole self, what we term here the perceiving self, is the medium by which we can better understand the other two. We will consider this concept briefly here. Because of its central role in the active processes of change, it will receive greater attention in the next chapter. Basically, this aspect of self can be seen as the function of consciousness; it is the cognitive link that not only connects the inner self with the outer world but in some ways reveals one's conception of self and one's motives. Putting this another way, what I think and feel about myself may well affect how I look out at my world; when I am feeling dejected, what is going on around me appears somewhat more dismal than when I see myself in brighter terms. Likewise, my needs and motives at a particular moment will strongly affect what I pay attention to and what I ignore in my environment.

The term "perceiving self" is used in place of the more common concept of perception so as to make the point that this critical function is not an isolated physiological event (e.g. visual or auditory) that can be understood apart from the attitudes, predispositions, and needs of the total self. As Bruner (1973) points out, there is no such thing as "immaculate perception." The extent and nature of our openness to the world is subject to our plans, attitudes, and predispositions. In fact, much of the self-perpetuating character of human suffering and failure is the consequence of the unrelenting need to look at the world in a rather

22

biased or twisted fashion in order to prop up and justify some necessary notions about what the world is "really" like in the first place. Exasperatingly, the depressed person searches out misery to validate his or her gloom; and the overly-compulsive are on the lookout for disorder so as to justify the importance of their meticulousness and control.

Two other features of the paradigm of self need to be considered, both representing the self's ongoing transactions with life events. The arrow directed outward from the intentional self stands for the actions that result from the way the initial perception was processed. This does not necessarily connote overt behavior; silence or indifference may be more potent reactions than more active responses. The feedback loop linking the outer event with the perceiving self underscores the dialectic in the way we normally deal with experience. Simply put, specific stimuli do not just impinge on ourselves, nor do we just respond in a conditioned, automatic manner. Rather, an elliptical process goes on that has no single beginning or end. Within this process, we may take the time to evaluate the immediate consequences of our perceptions. If some correction seems necessary, qualitative changes in our thoughts and actions follow, and the process goes on. It is this ongoing process that is an important medium of change — particularly when we ask clients to reconsider their conclusions about a certain happening by inquiring, for example, about the details of who did what, when, for what reasons, and so on.

To recapitulate, the willingness to give equal value to the various facets of the person (the persons of mind, community, principle, and faith) allows these facets to be understood in ways that do not lose sight of the integrity of the whole. Moreover, this proposition forestalls the possibility of reducing our understanding to limited psychological or socio-cultural equations that offer only a one dimensional view of the multidimensional person. The paradigm or metaphor of self was presented to illustrate the idea of the person as the agent and maker of his or her own existence — and, within certain limits, the one who determines what quality of life means.

What we call self-concept reflects the nature of the person's identifications with other social groups and therefore shapes the person of the community. And because it is the repository of one's ideals, values, and standards against which ideas about self-worth and self-esteem are balanced, it embraces the person of principle and the person of faith. Of no less importance are the intentional and perceiving aspects of the self. The former is the volitional expression of the self that translates needs and aspirations into directive, goal-seeking forms. The concept of the perceiving self, as we shall see, serves as the link between the inner self and outer world: it is the medium by which reality is experienced and defined. It is through a sensitivity to the three aspects that we can begin to understand the person in the process of being (self-concept), becoming (intentionality), and knowing (perception).

PRINCIPLES OF COGNITIVE-HUMANISTIC PRACTICE

The philosphical and theoretical ideas we have considered thus far lead to some principles of practice that, on one hand, confirm the human and social values expressed by traditional forms of practice. On the other hand, however, these principles differ in some qualitative ways from certain traditional approaches that lock human problems and behavior into a fixed system or structure, that depend on set methods or techniques, or that impose abstract diagnoses, definitions, or objectives on the client. Such a technological orientation to change implies that there is such a thing as "effective practice" and that it can be achieved if one just acquires the proper evaluative, interviewing, and interventive skills. The fallacy of this assumption is well stated by Wilkes who says:

> No one disputes that there are human problems to be solved; the dispute is about whether these are *all* there is. For what happens when I approach the world with the measurements of science in my hand? I abstract and select from the environment all those aspects of it that my instruments will deal with and I omit anything the yardstick does not reveal. Everything that is of interest to me as a human being — the unique, the incomprehensible, the complicated, the mysterious — is left out. Farrer [1948] calls this process the respect for fact to the exclusion of the respect for being, and he views such a state of affairs with the gravest disquiet: "it portends the death of the soul." In the human studies we are faced with the whole human being and our task is not the limited one of measuring intelligence, or measuring the distance between some arbitrarily chosen baseline and some equally arbitrarily chosen moment when evaluation takes place. This is no more than the triumph of method over content. The object of our study is *this* individual, body, mind, and spirit, and for study we need "a cupboardful of yardsticks" all of which will be broken "against the requirements of truth." The method is whatever enables the participants to form accurate pictures of the way the other person thinks and lives. Thus we may understand what we try to describe. (Wilkes 1981: 9)

This type of understanding imposes some troubling demands on the helper. Since psychological and socio-cultural "truths" are not always absolute, our speculations about what is going on in the mind of the client or in his or her social relations and identifications will necessarily have to remain tentative and open to change as our knowledge of the person deepens. The challenge is even more severe when we attempt to grasp the metaphysical dimensions of the client's life. Although some of the ethical bases of decision and choice, or the spiritual ideals one lives by, may indeed conform to some conventional systems of belief, we must leave room for the possibility that other closely-held images that guide the client's way of life may be rather exceptional — that is, if we can resist the tendency to judge them as bizarre according to our own "proper" outlook.

One demand that this perspective places on the practitioner is the need to live with a fair amount of ambiguity — a particularly difficult demand if one needs to define one's self as an expert professional. But this demand is softened a bit if we can accept the substantial fact that the only real expert is the client. No matter what the problem or circumstances may be, the ultimate decisions about and the responsibility for the way life is to be lived falls within the client's domain alone. Quite simply, we cannot process people into new forms and shapes: as helpers, we may offer our ideas, disclose new alternatives, and even provide guidance and direction, but it is the client who will and must decide if and how these revelations are useful. Stripped of its theoretical and methodological attire, the aim of the professional helper is to make the kind of difference in the client's life that frees and empowers the client to pursue that which is meaningful and beneficial. But "meaningful" and "beneficial" are empty terms which can only be filled in and given meaning by the client.

If there is any merit in these assumptions, they logically should lead to the major principle that understanding of the client becomes possible when we are willing to receive and respect his or her way of defining self and world. We must regard these renditions of a personal reality as not only real to the client, but as beliefs that, in many ways, validate his or her own existence, dignity, and worth. This does not mean that receiving this definition implies blanket acceptance, approval, or condoning; neither does it imply negative judgment. Rather, it speaks to the well-worn precept: "Start where the client is" (Goldstein 1983). In itself, the helper's intent to receive and understand is the powerful first step toward progressive change: first of all, it lessens the possibility of threat and conflict; second, by confirming the client's view of reality, the client is invited to take responsibility for its consequences and meanings — that is, how well this outlook serves him or her; and finally, this intent places

25

the client's values and principles into more open view as possible guides to how the helping experience progresses. Now let me show how this basic principle embraces and proposes yet other principles of a cognitive-humanistic practice.

Purpose

Behavior that might otherwise be seen as peculiar or pointless begins to take on meaning when we begin to understand that, as far as the individual is concerned, it does have a particular purpose and intent. We could, of course, scour the client's biography for certain episodes or traumas that might explain present behavior. Whatever we might discover would allow us to make our own inferences about these actions. It stands to reason, however, that more authentic understanding will be revealed if we can learn the client's intentions and goals. We are not assuming that the answer will readily be forthcoming or that it necessarily will be logical or comprehensible. Nonetheless, clients' views will not only tell us something about where and how they see themselves in the here and now but also where they believe they are heading. And more important, this search for purpose begins to inform clients that they are the agents of their actions and thus bear responsibility for them.

Reasoning

No matter how odd one's behavior may appear, we assume that behind these actions are some kind of thought processes. A distinctly human trait is the need to believe that our actions indeed rest on some rational ideas: even a flagrant, impulsive act will be explained by the actor in what, to him or her at least, are surely logical terms. Without excusing this person for the consequences of such behavior, what is critical is not whether the explanation is rational or relevant to some notion of "reality testing," but how the client's premises and presuppositions support this explanation. What we want to know is how this rationalization reveals something about the client's self-concept, what the client is perceiving or ignoring in relationships or environment, what this behavior attempts to achieve or avoid, where responsibility is placed, and other conceptions that say something about the self and one's relations with the world. Equally important is what we might learn about *how* the client thinks — the particular cognitive style that characterizes how one processes perceptions and information. For example, one person may rely on a rather convergent, oversimplified, or concrete way of thinking that

26

reduces a complicated occurrence to absurdly prosaic terms. A second may use highly intellectualized thought processes thereby distancing one's self from the emotional level of the experience. And a third person may reflect the kind of distorted thinking that serves to change the meaning and implications of the act. Altogether, this knowledge begins to offer some valid guides for how we might begin to engage the client in the kinds of rethinking and relearning that are basic to productive problem-solving.

Critical faculties

If we assume that, as humans, we are capable of reflecting on ourselves and our actions, then, as part of our attempt to understand the mind of our clients, we need to learn something about these processes. Here we are concerned with more than just thoughtwork; our interest is in the client's values and standards (or their absence), and the ethical and moral principles that feed into their way of thinking, acting and feeling. We need to grasp some sense of not just what the client believes he or she has done, wants to do, or fears doing, but what these intentions mean relative to the client's principles of living, be they personal, social, or spiritual. Some clients will speak openly about their moral or spiritual conflicts since these tensions are what often prompt people to seek help. As likely, others may be more guarded and will reveal these critical conflicts in the language they use (e.g. "I know I'm probably wrong for thinking this way ..." or "I should be a better parent but I don't seem to be able to."). The last statement is a particularly common instance of inner conflict of an ethical or moral nature since it speaks to the existence within the person of two "I"s — one *I* setting the standards that the other *I* cannot meet. Finally, the weight of these critical faculties may be disclosed either by the peculiarity of their absence or by the client's excessively righteous protests that he or she has done no wrong.

Fallibility

The over-righteous reaction just noted touches on one of the most feared possibilities — the inescapable fact that we might be wrong about something. Unlike computers or other machines, humans are capable of error; in truth, learning, change, and growth are premised on the fact that we are not pre-programmed, purely instinctive, or determined creatures and that, at any point in time, we are free to reconsider and cast off the erroneous beliefs that get us into trouble. Yet, many of us will rely on any

27

kind of absurd excuse to avoid admitting error; to be mistaken or just plain wrong somehow afflicts one's self-concept and sense of worth with unbearable doubt and suffering.

The task, then, is to help the client discover that there is no compulsion to repeat the same blunders in coping with problems of living and that being wrong does not need to be equated with incompetence. But this discovery will not follow kind words of reassurance. Rather, we need to appreciate, first, what the client has at stake in the beliefs and conceptions that are so closely held. Does this investment express a shaky sense of self-esteem, a commitment to certain familial or cultural values, or perhaps an identification with prized spiritual images? The principle in this instance, then, involves the ethical questions that arise when we enter into the belief systems of our client; here we need to achieve a fine balance between our intent to help clients become aware of the error of their ways and the need to be the protectors of the beliefs that are central to their integrity.

Meaning

Inseparable from our need to make some sense out of our client's intentions, reasoning, and reflections is the aim of understanding this person as a creator of his or her meanings — one who, like us, devises themes and motifs that give life its necessary pattern, form, and purpose.

As we are well aware, life does not present itself to us with ready meanings or instructions; what we make of life (both literally and figuratively) depends on how we define it. Thus, part of the ongoing turmoil of living is the constant pursuit of meaning so as to avoid the dread of strangeness and detachment. We need constantly to reaffirm our convictions that our lives are somewhat worthwhile, that we are doing something more than merely surviving. We need to believe that there is some value in what we are doing, or, if our immediate circumstances seem rather vacant, that we are in some way moving toward a more meaningful future. And within our relationships with others, we need to find some confirmation of our worth and significance. Clearly, the attempt to explain meaning results in a tautology: meaning is found in whatever is meaningful.

The principle in this instance is that we enter our clients' lives only by way of the paths of meaning. We learn much of what is meaningful for clients by their autobiographical narratives — the story that they create our of their selective recollections of the past. We learn about critical themes of living from the idioms the clients use to express cultural and familial influences on their lives. Hopes, goals, and aspirations will also tell us what life means. Perhaps we learn the most from the metaphors that slip into the client's speech — the symbols and illustrations that embellish literal language with the real significance of what life is all about to the client.

Choice

Ultimately, our understanding of our clients evolves as we come to see how the principles of thought and action considered thus far converge in some form of active choice. Quite simply, human purpose, reasoning, meaning, and so on, come together in the decision one makes to take one direction over another, to select one goal instead of a second or third, to say yes or no.

Not uncommonly, we tend to think of the act of choosing as something reserved for the more momentous occasions in our lives — for example, the selection of a mate, a career, a home, or the decision to have a child. By contrast, the countless options that confront us daily and that we must choose from may seem trivial, having few implications beyond how the minor event will turn out. Yet these seemingly insignificant choices begin to build into a pattern and style of living that, in a way of speaking, the individual falls victim to. We find that in working with families, for example, that it is not just the "big" or "presenting" problem that is the source of distress; on a more insidious and habitual level, the problem is embedded in the practiced rituals by which family members have abdicated choice about the "small" things. If we were to put the major problem aside for the moment and ask about the basic routines in a family's way of living we might discover that Dad, for example, chooses to refrain from giving an opinion because "It's just not that important," while Mom chooses to take over everyone else's responsibilities because "It's so much easier."

We are concerned not only with *what* choice people make but also with the ethical basis upon which the choice is made. Is the choice made with only the ends in mind and with little regard for the means? Or is the individual guided by certain ingrained moral precepts that, with consistency, guide his or her way of dealing with others? In the first instance, one acts as one wishes, particularly if one believes that the outcome will be "good" for everyone involved: the mother referred to above may, in the desire to keep peace in the family (the ends), deprive her children of the opportunity to learn responsibility (the means). In the second case, one's choice, say, always to be fair or honest (the means), often will override a concern with possible outcomes. Certainly these are not absolute distinctions; yet, more so than not, how does the client justify the alternatives chosen as well as those that are rejected?

Finally, we must take account of the implications of the act of choosing and the choice itself for the client's way of life. In many instances of practice, we face people who choose not to choose and who need to be helped to learn what the penalties of passivity really are: if they abdicate the power of choice, self-esteem suffers; if they are too fearful to choose, then hopelessness is the consequence; and if they submit to the authority of others, then they must admit to their helplessness. Fundamentally, a chunk of one's self-concept is at risk each time a serious choice is faced. First, choice implies the giving up of a trace of security; choice may mean change and, despite the misery of life as it is, change often is undesirable since that misery is, if nothing else, predictable. And second, however thoughtfully we arrive at the choice we decide to make, there are no assurances that it will work out according to plan. Thus, there is the risk of personal failure, the horrendous possibility that we might be proven wrong — or even worse, foolish.

Our clients' choices — active or passive, gratifying or regretted — tell us much about themselves in our pursuit of understanding.. We learn something about their sense of personal responsibility, the place of ethics and morals in their lives, the extent to which they are aware of alternatives within their own powers or in their environment, and most important, whether they are conscious of their freedom and obligation to choose and define their own destinies.

SOME FINAL COMMENTS

Ideally, the objectives of a cognitive-humanistic approach are more concerned with the means and process of the helping experience than the specific outcomes. Certainly there is the enduring hope for a better quality of life, a greater sense of self-worth, and the achievement of all that the client believes is worthwhile. But these ends are achieved only when the client discovers his or her own power and autonomy — the strength to pursue valued goals in a principled way that assures a degree of harmony between the metaphorical persons of mind, community, principle, and soul.

This is accomplished in a helping relationship that, in its classical sense, is described as educative rather than therapeutic. The intent is not to treat or cure, but to enable the client to learn something about self, others, and living and to create or discover fresh alternatives. This calls for a collegial relationship in which open dialogue is concerned with a search for meaning within the client's subjective reality. In this relationship, the helper and client may, as required, exchange the roles of teacher and learner.

For these reasons, the helping person (irrespective of his or her official title) does not meet the client as an expert or technician. In active and open ways, the helper is a humanist and colleague — a knowledgeable and caring participant in the client's pursuit of a better life as he or she defines it.

Finally, despite the many philosophic overtones in the preceding pages, the helping experience is not an abstract, ephemeral event. To the contrary, it is firmly rooted in the hard facts of the client's life as they are and not in the speculative inferences we make about them. For this reason, this approach is not restricted to the so-called voluntary client, one who can ask for help, spell out the problem, and demonstrate the capacity for "insight." If we truly value the importance of the client's own reality then we should be able to start wherever the client may happen to be. And with the reluctant client, this may be at the level of the person's confusion, fear, and even outrage about finding him- or herself unwillingly cast into the role of client. If the purpose of the helping process is the achievement of greater self-esteem and autonomy — which Kaufmann (1973: 2) defines as "Making with open eyes the decisions that give shape to one's life" — then it must begin with an unrelenting regard for the client's self within the context of his or her perceived reality.

REFERENCES

Bruner, J. (1973) *Beyond the Information Given: Studies in the Psychology of Knowing*. New York: Norton.
Farrer, A. (1948) *The Glass of Vision*. London: Dacre Press.
Goldstein, H. (1981) *Social Learning and Change: A Cognitive Approach to Human Services*. Columbia: University of South Carolina Press; pbk edn 1984, New York and London: Tavistock.
—— (1983) Starting Where the Client Is. *Social Casework* 64(5): 267–75.
James, W. (1896) *The Principles of Psychology*. New York: Henry Holt & Co.
Kakar, S. (1982) *Shamans, Mystics, and Doctors*. New York: Knopf.

Kaufmann, W. (1973) *Without Guilt and Justice: From Decidophobia to Autonomy*. New York: Dell.

Kiev, A. (1964) *Magic, Faith, and Healing*. New York: The Free Press.

Konner, M. (1982) *The Tangled Wing*. New York: Holt, Rinehart & Winston.

Langer, S. (1967) *Mind: An Essay on Human Feeling*, Vol. I. Baltimore: Johns Hopkins University Press.

Maslow, (1954) *Motivation and Personality*. New York: Harper.

Wertheimer, M. (1978) Humanistic Psychology and the Humane but Tough-minded Psychologist. *American Psychologist* 33: 739–45.

Wilkes, R. (1981) *Social Work with Undervalued Groups*. London: Tavistock.

Chapter 2

A Framework for Cognitive-Humanistic Practice

HOWARD GOLDSTEIN

The intent of this chapter is to show how the ideas of mind, action, and meaning described in the previous pages may be translated into useful principles of practice. We will look at how the awareness of the functions of perception and cognition will deepen our understanding of the way people cope with ordinary and critical problems of living. In more practical terms, we will consider how these functions of the mind may be subject to development or modification so as to enhance these coping patterns. In this view, change will be defined as a creative problem-solving process. We will consider the issue of motivation in a cognitive-humanistic perspective with particular regard to its role in the beginnings of the helping experience. Finally, we will outline the successive phases of the cognitive-humanistic model which progressively enable clients to raise and sharpen conscious awareness, to reframe and redefine their realities, and to transform this understanding into active patterns of living that are in accord with their essential values, beliefs, and commitments.

To sustain our perspective, it would be useful to review some of the major premises of cognitive-humanism covered in the first chapter:

(1) A more reliable and accurate understanding of our clients and their problems is achieved when we are able to comprehend their subjective worlds. Only as we are able to set aside our own theoretical biases and social stereotypes can we begin to appreciate how things really are from the client's point of view.

(2) A corollary of this intent is the need to resist the inclination to categorize our clients in diagnostic or any other terms or to otherwise

classify, objectify, or stigmatize them as if they were members of a special class rather than ordinary humans like ourselves. From a humanistic standpoint, we must appreciate that we are entering the client's world and not the other way around — a world that is in the constant state of flux and emergence. Simply put, if we wish to honor the client's dignity and individuality we cannot reduce him or her to the limits of a label, or extract the client from the intricate design of his or her way of life.

(3) The behavior of our clients begins to take on even greater meaning when we see that it has some purpose and aim. Although people are reactive to acute signals and events, the flow of living itself is constantly going forward into the future toward and for the sake of some personally valued end. Proactivity rather than reactivity best characterizes human motive and intent.

(4) Correspondingly, the intent is to help our clients come to terms with their essential values and aspirations, to deal with distortions in perception and thought, to discover fresh and creative opportunities, to encourage risk-taking, and to foster an autonomous and ethical approach to living — all of this in accord with the client's beliefs, heritage, and value system.

THE PERCEIVING SELF: THE SOURCE OF THOUGHT AND ACTION

We first need to give a moment's thought to the question, "How do people really understand one another?", in order to appreciate that the ability to communicate one's ideas, to achieve a modicum of consensus about something, and to comprehend another's experiences are indeed things of considerable wonder. If we assume that any one particular event does not present itself to us in a finished and uniform manner, then it would follow that each of us will attend to that event in somewhat different ways; how each of us will think about that event will be governed by our respective styles and patterns. And most important, even if by some coincidence you and I do happen to perceive and think about the same event in the same way, it is most likely that each of us will ascribe rather different meanings to it since our respective frames of reference arise out of our special experiences and histories.

So we ask again, how do people communicate with, relate to, and understand one another with some degree of harmony and congruence? Basically, we do have enough in common as human beings and social creatures to allow us to understand one another on certain levels. First, we share similar sensory and neurophysiological systems, which assures that we will process messages in more or less the same fashion. Second, if we inhabit the same locale, we usually share not only the same language but also the rules that determine how the language is to be used and understood. Third, we can, to some extent (as the Symbolic Interactionists say) exchange roles and symbols so that I can put myself in your shoes, so to speak, when I wish to understand what you mean. And finally, we tend to adhere to certain normative standards — courtesies, if you will — which would prompt me to preserve a modicum of good will by acting as if I did understand your ideas even if I didn't.

These factors apply to the more ordinary exchanges between people. In deeper relationships, where something more than amiability is at stake, true communication can occur only if two additional conditions are met: first, there needs to be some degree of similarity in our respective perceptions — that is, we must agree that, in many ways, we are playing the same game, in the same field, and according to the same rules; second, if we do happen to disagree about the nature of a particular reality, the respect we hold for one another is sufficient to allow for differences to exist without risk to our ongoing relationship. If neither of these conditions is met then some type of disconfirmation will follow — personal, in the form of painful self-doubt, or interpersonal, in the form of charges of madness or badness.

It bears noting that the two conditions noted above are equally or even more relevant to the helping relationship. The wisdom, experience, and skill that the worker has to offer are certainly important — but they are not sufficient to assure that a relationship, one that is responsive to the values and beliefs of the client, will indeed evolve. To be sure, helpers do want to understand their clients. Understanding in depth is, however, not without considerable uneasiness; to enter another's system of beliefs means learning a new language, so to speak, and coming face to face with another's values and purposes that, at the outset, may seem incomprehensible. Such understanding requires that we live with some degree of ambiguity and that we hold our own assumptions about what is "real" in abeyance for a time. In the final analysis, there are few greater gifts that we can give to a fellow human being than the undisguised and unconditional intent to know "How is it for you?" Again, this regard does not connote a blanket acceptance of the client's reality as being "right" nor does it suggest that this reality should be accepted or condoned on any terms. Rather, the principle of respect and commitment creates a climate within which difference and challenges can arise without danger to the relationship.

This commitment also has some important implications for how we first approach the problem the client brings along (or in the case of the involuntary client, the problem that someone else sends along). Although we are not disinterested in the problem itself, our overriding concern is with the client's definition of it, what it means to him or her, what (if anything) the client sees as possible remedies and goals, and other personal visions that take us the first step toward understanding. As important, we need to learn something about how or whether the client has grappled with the problem. No one is excused from particular problems of living — particularly in the precarious and, at times, absurd world that we inhabit. Yet why some people fare better than others has much to do with how they come to terms with their valued purposes and goals, their ability to think through, imagine, and discover other alternatives and their readiness to venture active and novel solutions.

This conception of the client and his or her problem leads to another principle of cognitive-humanistic practice: the problem that a client presents is of lesser consequence than the *solution* that he or she has attempted to resolve it; hence "what is wrong" can best be understood when we learn something about the errors or failures of perception, thought, meaning, and action that tend to perpetuate rather than resolve the problematic state.

COGNITIVE STYLES, PATTERNS, AND PURPOSES

If the premise is correct that people behave in certain ways because they think in certain ways and vice versa, then it would seem that all one would have to do is change either thought or action in a more appropriate direction and all would be well. In some instances, problems can be resolved in this straightforward, simple fashion particularly when all that is needed is some specific piece of information that the individual did not have or perhaps never knew existed. The unsuccessful job-seeker, for example, who finally learns something about proper dress, how to write a resume, and how to conduct oneself in an interview is a case in point.

The following chapters will show, however, that the more entrenched problems of living that people wrestle with are more likely to resist even the best-intentioned and sensible advice or guidance. The reason for this sort of evasion or blindness is not some pathological condition; rather, this sort of "resistance" often expresses a basic human need to cling to our own version of reality — what we believe we know and can explain — sometimes at any cost. We need only to reflect on our respective ways of looking at and defining the world about us to see how insistently attached we are to our personal truths — even in the face of contrary facts that others accept as self-evident. Why else is our need to be "right" sometimes a crusade of sorts? Why at times do we feel so strange and alienated when no-one else sees things the way we do? And why are criticism or disagreements between ourselves and others so terribly painful? As already suggested, the elemental answer to these questions is that the personal reality that we have so carefully nurtured may be disconfirmed; and since the "I" is at the core of our reality, this implies a disconfirmation of ourselves.

One's personal version of reality, or cognition, is sustained by a variety of mental strategies. As we will see, these strategies often work in circular ways and as self-fulfilling prophecies — particularly at those times when we feel our essential beliefs being threatened. This sort of circularity — the tendency to attend to only those things that will confirm what we already believe is true — is painfully evident in practice with troubled couples and families; each member's story, fabricated from his or her own personal logic, is so persuasive and coherent as to repel any question about its veracity. For example:

Wife: I'm telling you, there is no question that given the chance, John will be unfaithful. I know this because at least half of the time I call him at work, he's not where he is supposed to be. Now I know about this woman there and when you put two and two together, well...
Husband: I've always known that there is no way to please a woman. But I really try to make her happy. Like I brought home a couple of tickets to the concert she wanted to go to — but how do you think she acted?

But these examples are merely extreme versions of the way any one of us tries to make some sense out of living. What we are beginning to learn about the working mind confirms that it is something more than an information processor or an exact mirror of what is "out there." The mind is intentional: it is constantly seeking to create patterns of order and meaning out of what might otherwise be regarded as random and meaningless in the individual's experiences. Quite simply, each of us needs to know, to explain, to understand, to demystify, and to reduce confusion to manageable proportions if we are to survive as reasonable people. But whether such understanding emerges out of lengthy musings or as a sudden flash of insight, the cognitive process that enables either to occur is most complex and still very elusive. For our purposes and for the sake of some clarity, let us simplify this process by considering three major

FIGURE 2   Paradigm of processes of perception and cognition

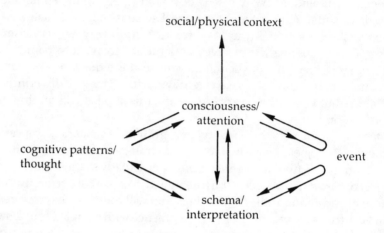

functions — attention, thinking, and interpretation. *Figure 2* depicts the interdependence of the three functions.

This paradigm can only presume to show how, within a particular place at a particular time, we come to make sense out of a specific experience. Attention refers to the way we perceive things; cognition refers to how we think about and organize our gained impressions; and interpretation, based on the frames of reference (schema) that we carry in our minds, is the meaning that we give to these ideas. The three functions stand in reciprocal, interdependent relationships with one another — each influencing the others. Note again the feedback loop (see *Figure 1* in previous chapter) which indicates that these cognitive functions are typically in the process of flux and change. Let us consider the elements of this paradigm in more specific terms.

Consciousness/awareness

Consciousness is defined here as the primal and subjective "knowing" that occurs at the moment that an image of something is created by the mind; it is the immediate sensation that precedes words and intellect. This awareness is alerted by the sensory and neural systems that involve the brain and its functions as well as the raw emotions that are simultaneously aroused. Yet it would be misleading to assume that this response is purely automatic or reactive. Unlike a machine or electronic device, these alerting functions are contained within a vital being who, in most instances, is engaged in the demands and business of everyday living; depending on the circumstances, the individual will determine what he or she will be receptive to in the environment, and what, if anything, will be selected out of the multitude of stimuli.

The profusion of studies and literature on the differential functions of the left and right hemispheres of the brain provide but one source of support for the idea that we are able to experience different types of consciousness. Although all the evidence is not in, there are very convincing empirical grounds for assuming that each hemisphere processes incoming impressions in its own special ways. In right-handed people, verbal, analytic, and rational processes are located in the left brain (in the case of left-handed people, the opposite pertains). Here, gained impressions are categorized into words and concepts, reduced to their parts, and organized into linear and temporal forms. These functions enable us to know things in explicit ways and to tell ourselves and others what we have perceived in somewhat logical terms. The right brain complements the left as it creates images, sensations, or pictures rather than words; it is more intuitive than objective, deals with wholes and relations rather than parts, is free of the logical constraints of time, and is more diffuse than explicit. Putting this another way, the left brain provides us with a sense of objectivity, logic, and order about our perceptions, whereas the right brain offers possible meanings, intuitions, and a sense of the relationships among the events we are perceiving. Ordinarily, there is an ongoing process of exchange (laterality) between the two hemispheres which, for example, allows the verbal left brain to explain the intuitive insights of the right. But this is not always the case — particularly if we give greater weight to our "rational" faculties than to our intuitive capabilities.

It should be apparent that even these pre-cognitive operations have important implications for our work with clients. For example, even before we can begin to do something about clients' thinking and problem-solving abilities, we need to get some sense of how they "see" things in gross terms. Are they, perhaps, not attending to some critical details in what is going on around them? Maybe they are selectively ignoring certain aspects of their experience, or are paying attention only to irrelevant details. Another type of distortion can occur when one insists on being "objective" and literal. In this case, the tendency of clients to depend only on what their intellectual and analytic faculties tell them may alienate them from the more meaningful but subtle emotional and metaphorical nuances in their relationships. It should be noted that such perceptual distortions may themselves be the source of the client's dilemma; in any case they would have some serious effects on the thought and interpretive processes that follow.

Cognitive patterns/thought

Our attempt to grasp how another person thinks, and therefore why he or she acts in what may appear to be bewildering ways, requires that we attempt to be open to the metaphors that are so much a part of one's way of thinking. The concepts and symbols that people use to explain themselves and their experiences typically represent various levels of meaning. There is, of course, the literal level on which we use the conventional terms that permit us to communicate with one another. But what people really mean is often distilled on the metaphorical, emotionally-laden level of ideas and words. Consider the client who complains of loneliness — certainly a common and understandable term. We can rightly infer that, if nothing else, this client may feel physically or emotionally separated from others. But can we really appreciate what "lonely" represents if it happens to be a metaphor for other meanings? Are these clients really alone? Or do they have a number of acquaintances whom they feel don't really understand them? Perhaps they really do see themselves as totally abandoned. Or does this metaphor serve as a justification for their actions that they can't otherwise explain ("Since I'm so lonely, the only thing I enjoy is eating a lot")?

Research shows that some people think exclusively in visual or pictorial ways, others think only in verbal terms, while most people tend to alternate between the two forms of thought (Taylor 1979: 214–15). Some people are *field-dependent* in the way they think while others are *field-independent*. The former tend to rely on the clues and guides within their social environment for directions about how and what to think about something. The field-independent thinker, in contrast, tends to reason and think without a great deal of reference to the opinions of others or the constraints in his or her environment (Hunt 1982: 286). Cognitive styles may also be *convergent* or *divergent*. Convergent thinkers (sometimes called "concrete" or "unimaginative") strive to reduce their impressions and explanations of the world to closed and limited categories (e.g. "I drink because I am an alcoholic," or "He doesn't have

40

any problems. He's just going through a phase."). Divergent thinkers, on the other hand, are able to entertain and imagine any and all possibilities and define reality in any number of forms as they think about and organize their impressions. The divergent imagination (sometimes called "creative," other times "neurotic") is by its very nature unconventional; it can create all sorts of analogs and metaphors which may lead to a personal reality that is exceptionally rich and diverse (Goldstein 1981: 157–64).

The point to be made is that human thought rarely, if ever, follows the rules and ideals of formal logic. The procedures of logic require that one starts with a self-evident statement and then proceeds carefully to work out the derivative truth. This is rarely the case in human thinking since thought is more often based on some unquestioned personal premises that constantly need to be validated; hence our thinking tends to prove that we are "right" rather than to discover what may be "true."

We begin to see that how people think about and process their impressions presents many opportunities for error, self-deception, or miscalculation that will get in the way of the individual's ability to achieve a worthwhile existence. If clients mislabel their impressions, depend too much on others for direction, or are too convergent or narrow in their way of thinking, then their conclusions will turn out to be ineffective and circular. Further, if one's self-concept is wedded to the need to be "right" (or more important, to the fear of being "wrong") then one's thinking will be rather rigid. This does not presume that there is one proper or desirable way of thinking — nor that we can determine for the client how he or she *ought* to think and solve problems. The only measure of "effective" thinking that seems valid (no matter how bizarre, erratic, or different it may appear to others) is the extent to which it furthers one's sincere and authentic pursuit of meaning — given that this meaning results in actions that are personally rewarding and at the same time ethically concerned with social consequences. We will see that even seemingly "weird" thinking may be the means and ends of a favorable solution — particularly when one needs to break out of the rut of habitual or banal thought.

Schema/interpretation

We have assumed that the mind is not a receptive information processor. Rather, the mind is purposive and intentional as it searches for order and meaning by transforming seemingly random experiences of living into patterns that are personally and socially comprehensible. This is the power of human thought. But there is yet another power of the mind, a meta process if you will, that somehow governs how we pick our way through, organize, and ultimately give meaning to the hodge-podge of stimuli that seem to enter into the course of daily living. This meta faculty has been acknowledged in various ways by many thinkers. Perhaps the most enduring view is the idea of the soul as the origin of all vital meanings. In modern terms, Chomsky (1976) refers to the concept of "deep structure" as the basic meaning level of language. Polanyi (1966) speaks of the "tacit dimension" of the mind which allows us to understand what we already know. Sartre (1965) calls this power of the mind the "true self." Within the cognitive-humanistic perspective, we refer to this interpretive function of the mind as the "schema," a concept originally proposed by Immanuel Kant, the eighteenth-century philosopher.

However we refer to this work of the mind, we are saying that the meanings that we give to our perceived experiences are shaped by certain basic and long-standing (and usually unquestioned) premises and categories of beliefs. We carry with us our own firmly-embedded perspectives on the world — our assumptions about how things really are, how they really came to be, what they really ought to become, and ultimately, what they really mean. Again, one's self-concept is very much a part of one's schema: if, as noted earlier, "what I believe is Me," then, in this case, it is safe to say that "what I know is true is really what *I am*." To contradict another's basic premises, then, is tantamount to disconfirmation of that person's conceptions of self.

On thinking about the power of the schema in this way, we begin to see other cognitive problems that can get in the way of harmonious and effective living. In some instances, one's frame of reference may be so hide-bound and unyielding as to create a very narrow and stereotypical outlook on the world. An extreme example is the bigot, the ideologue, or the cultist. In existential terms, we find many clients who believe one way but act in another — possibly to seek approval, or out of the fear of being too self-assertive. In these instances, one is bound to suffer the dreadful sense of meaninglessness when personal values, ethical commitments, or spiritual beliefs are sacrificed for a false end.

Thus cognitive-humanism is not focused on inferential abstractions about what is wrong with the client's mind nor does it attempt to locate earlier causes in the client's life that are assumed to have effected the

42

present difficulty. Rather, it is concerned with clients in their immediate and projected worlds of meaning and how they go about attempting to create and sustain an existence that offers the promise of growth and the realization of their hopes and potentials.

It may be argued that this focus is too narrow and that it overlooks other aspects of human living. What about the role of emotions? And while a cognitive perspective might explain "here-and-now" behavior, what does it have to say about the past conditions in the client's life that may be related to the more immediate problem? Emotions and history are by no means ignored by cognitive-humanism. But we want to show that their roles and meanings need, however, to be appreciated as subjective, felt experiences rather than as objective variables that somehow cause the client to be as he or she is.

Emotions and cognition

Notions about how the mind works have suffered from the erroneous assumption that so-called "affective" states are somehow separate and distinct from the "cognitive." Piaget, the great cognitive theorist, dismisses this idea:

> There is no affective behavior and cognitive behavior. Behavior is always both. Thus, only an analysis, an abstraction for the study of their respective mechanisms separates these two aspects which in reality are always presented *simultaneously*. Hence, if one acknowledges affectivity and cognition (perceptual or intelligent) as two aspects of behavior, it makes no sense to wonder which causes which or even which precedes which. One aspect does not cause another aspect or precede another aspect. They are complementary because neither process can function without the other. (Piaget, *quoted in* Weiner 1975)

Our emotions have little meaning and substance until we are able to name them or explain them in some comprehensible fashion — the process of cognition; at the same time, our thoughts and ideas about anything will remain sterile and literal until we become aware of what our feelings have to say about them. So we must move beyond sensations, to name and define our feelings (as perhaps anxiety, joy, fear, or desire), before they can tell us more about ourselves and our circumstances. Thus counselors who say that they focus largely on their clients' feelings are by no means ignoring the dimension of thought. Certainly there is great relief in getting one's emotions out in the open; yet one can muddle along only so far on a feeling level. To make sense of one's plight, and to act to change things, these emotions will have to be converted into constructs that are

43

meaningful to the person. Clients who can now recognize, for example, that "I guess I'm really scared about taking that job," or "I never realized what I really felt about my wife leaving me," have equipped themselves with a new kind of consciousness that allows them to contemplate alternatives that did not exist as long as they were mired in the confusion of raw, unintelligible emotions.

Finally, emotions are the anchors of our basic moral, ethical, and spiritual values. No matter how convincingly we may intellectualize and rationalize our ideas about such values as commitment, honesty, fidelity, or trust, the extent to which these or other principles of living are truly part of ourselves is measured by the anguish that is spilled when they are violated or the sense of wholeness we feel when they are fulfilled.

Personal history and cognition

Our attention to the proactive, goal-directed nature of human behavior cannot disregard the past. But we do distinguish between the past as a determining force in its own right and one's history as a purposeful, selective pattern of recollections that persists in the mind of the individual. In the latter view, the individual is understood as an autobiographer of the unfinished chronicle of his or her life — one who is constantly in the process of recalling, interpreting, and at times, revising personal or shared history.

In this perspective, the question of what may have actually occurred in the individual's past loses its importance. Whether one was *really* rejected by one's parents or *really* had no friends is secondary to two related questions: (1) how these presumed events are interpreted by the person; and (2) how the meanings that are given to these experiences may be employed to explain or justify the person's current way of life. Even if serious past events can be documented — say, a serious illness or a parent's death or divorce — they, too, are equally subject to the same questions.

We are learning that memory is a rather tricky faculty. Try as we may, we cannot reproduce the actual nature of events in our past lives. For one thing, the specific event was perceived by another person — for example, the child or the adolescent that we no longer are. Also, the picture that we carry with us is necessarily incomplete; one of the purposes of our selective memories is to exclude certain details so as to prevent the mind from being overloaded or oppressed (Taylor 1979: 235). Moreover, what we recall from the past usually has much to do with what is going on in the present. We draw from our histories in order to locate workable solutions to current problems, to see if what we had learned before will explain a novel perception in the present, and so on.

In more existential terms, we select and order our recollections in order to reaffirm our personal realities as well as what we presume our mission and plan in life ought to be. This is seen in the concept of *life themes* (Csikszentmihalyi and Beattie 1979: 45–63) which refers to the human tendency to be absorbed over time with a central question or problem — one that infuses one's approach to living with meaning and purpose. The choice of a particular career, the tendency to avoid or to seek out certain kinds of relationships, the desire to model oneself on someone special, or other such motives form a cognitive system, an outlook on life, that leads to a characteristic design for living.

Our personal histories are therefore not objective relics of the past, like old diaries or photographs that we can ruminate about in a detached fashion. To the contrary, our recollections are an integral part of our present insofar as they feed into our cognitions about who we are in relation to what we have been; they form the logic and justifications for how we are; and they provide the biographical content that shapes our themes of living and governs what we are doing and where we are heading.

THE PRACTICE OF COGNITIVE-HUMANISM

The succeeding chapters of this book will offer abundant illustrations of the various applications of this approach with particular client groups. Here, in the concluding section of this chapter, I want to crystallize the many ideas covered thus far by showing how they provide the guidelines and the principles for a humanistic helping experience. These principles are specifically concerned with the goals of practice, the question of the client's motivation for help, and an overview of the phases of practice with special emphasis on the critical beginnings of the helping process.

The goals of helping

Simply stated, the intent of cognitive-humanism is to foster the kinds of conditions (in the client's mind, environment, and relationships) within which clients (individuals, families, or groups) may be helped to determine their own valued goals and to find the means of achieving them in effective and autonomous ways. It is assumed that if the proper means can be worked out, the client will determine the appropriate ends.

The specific implications of this general statement become clearer when we consider how the client, the problem, and the process of change are seen in this perspective.

It is worth saying again that we do not see the person or family in some kind of difficulty (whether so defined by self or by others) as sick, as a victim, as deficient or helpless, or as a clinical case. Rather, these are people who, in their respective ways, feel beleaguered and trapped by harmful conditions that may be self-created or imposed by others (Wheelis 1969). In either or both cases, it is assumed that at the root of things, these clients want, at the very least, some relief from suffering, or at best, the opportunity to regain a fragment of lost dignity and the freedom to make more rewarding choices about the quality of their lives. In many instances, even those who are seriously disabled by a condition as uncontrollable as senescence, a crippling or fatal illness, or a sudden disaster will cling to the hope that they will be granted the right to make their own choices and definitions about what their lives ought to be.

Clients who find themselves unable to understand or to cope with their dilemmas struggle with feelings of hopelessness and demoralization. Any of a number of obstacles may block the path toward a rewarding solution. Oftentimes, anguish follows when the client insists on resorting to worn-out and inappropriate solutions; to be sure, one tries to do the best one can with what one knows. Yet futile attempts not only fail to resolve the problem, they in fact compound it. The grimly tolerant spouse of the alcoholic, who is sure that indulgence and kindness will help his or her mate cut down on drinking, is a case in point. In other instances, helpless frustration results when the client is convinced there are only two alternatives to choose from—both unthinkable (e.g. *either* to leave a painful relationship *or* to endure it as it is). Having closed off one's options prematurely, this person cannot entertain the possibility that a third alternative exists — namely, choosing to cast off the other two and to start afresh in the search for a more gratifying solution. But perhaps the most common obstacle is the fear of change itself; it is frequently less frightening to live with familiar pain that is predictable than with the uncertainty of untested and unproven alternatives.

We propose that clients will find their way out of this disheartening state of bewilderment as they come to develop their own creative problem-solving potentials. The adjective "creative" is used here neither in an offhand fashion nor to dress up the term "problem-solving." The creativity that a client might wield in grappling with rather ordinary

46

problems of living may be considerably less breathtaking than the efforts of the ingenious scientist, the poet, or the artist; nonetheless, it does contain the same elements of inspiration. Should we not applaud the new-found ability of the retiree to fashion a fresh and rewarding life style? What about the welfare mother who discovers within herself some new talent — or even former "child abusers" who find they are able to deal with their children in healthier ways? These examples and others to be found in the succeeding chapters will rarely capture public attention. But they do meet the criteria for creativity: they give life to novel forms of thought, imagination, and feeling (the process of creativity), and these in turn foster solutions and consequences that previously did not exist (the product of creativity).

There is no set prescription for how this creative change may be achieved. In fact, it can be argued that doctrinaire approaches should be discarded since the intent is to enable clients to step beyond their own social or personal constraints, to put habitual ways of thinking aside, and to begin to find some merit in their own imagery, in their rare visions, hopes, and core values. The client is helped not only to think in more divergent ways but also to attempt more assertive actions even though they may seem risky or possibly subject to criticism by others. But even before the client can embark on this sort of creative problem-solving venture, he or she must come to learn that everyone has the right, the freedom, and more important, the obligation to hope and strive for a better life.

This last point is the most critical and decisive issue since *creativity always depends on purpose*. The impetus and pressure for any inventive endeavor — whether it represents the lofty realms of Einsteinian discovery or the more lowly and prosaic attempts to work out a new budget — depend on the extent to which the individual is in some way gripped by a special objective, an unremitting curiosity, or the compulsion to find an answer. Only when one is conscious of such a motive will one begin to consider that there may be a novel and bold solution to the challenge. Assisting the client in discovering and defining a purpose that holds special value for him or her is thus a special principle of helping.

Although standard techniques cannot be prescribed, we know enough about human problem-solving and creativity to provide us with a framework which outlines the order and rationale of the helping process. The work of John Dewey and the later educational theorists tells us that to be effective, problem-solving must unfold over time in a series of stages:

47

✓ (1) before the problem can be tackled in a productive way, its existence must be sensed — even if only on some elemental level of awareness; (2) it can then be located, defined, and identified in a way that suggests the directions that might be taken; (3) possible alternative solutions can now be discovered or imagined; (4) a range of consequences can be anticipated; and (5) the solution can be tested and evaluated (Goldstein 1981: 379–99). As will be seen shortly, this framework finds expression in the stages of creative practice.

The question of motivation

The statement that purpose is the impelling force of creative problem-solving may seem to imply that the client must demonstrate a motivation to change before we are able to help. Does this mean that the cognitive-humanistic approach is relevant only to those clients who actively seek help, and inappropriate for those others who "resist" or "deny" the need for assistance? This question can be answered by a closer look at what the concept of motivation really means.

Motivation is easily defined since it clearly connotes the idea of movement toward or an active interest in something. A question arises, however, when we attempt to decipher what its opposite, "unmotivated," means, particularly when the term is used to judge or evaluate certain clients. Since every living being, unless comatose, is at least motivated to survive, the term, as it is applied by counselors to the unwilling client, often means, "This person is not motivated to do what *I* believe he or she ought to do." This judgment is sometimes embellished by such appraisals as "insufficient anxiety," "lacking in insight," "poor reality-testing," or just plain "resistant." We must doubt the reliability of such judgments since they are often based on rather sparse data, emerging out of intake interviews or early sessions when rather little is known about the client's basic intentions. We can surmise that clients who are confused, fearful, or otherwise in doubt about having to present themselves to a professional will tend to disclose far less about themselves than the more eager applicant.

Let us assume, for the sake of argument, that a common human characteristic is our unwillingness to make radical changes in how we perceive, think, and act. We make the point again that few of us wish to relinquish our cherished beliefs and convictions. Now the apparent attitude of the voluntary client who acknowledges pain and problems and who actively seeks out assistance may seem to belie this assumption.

But more often than not, the tacit admission, "I need help," disguises a more elemental (and very natural) wish for someone else to change, a hope for some sort of spontaneous cure, some simple advice, or other sorts of quick and magical answers. The experienced helper knows that even the most eager clients will at some point in the process undergo considerable strain and ambivalence, if not the impulse to escape, once they come face to face with the realization that they must make some changes in how they think about and deal with their lives.

The difference between clients who are commonly defined as "motivated" and those that are dismissed as "unmotivated" is therefore not a matter of whether one wants or does not want to change. Rather, it is a matter of whether, at the outset, the individual believes that there is a need for or the possibility of some kind of betterment or relief; if so, what the client thinks or hopes it might be; what, specifically, he or she wants to have happen; and what the client thinks he or she is ready to do to achieve these ends. We will call these criteria *availability*, *expectation*, *motive*, and *incentive* (Birch and Veroff 1966; Goldstein 1981: 422–30). We want to show that the difference between voluntary and involuntary clients is that the former have already met at least the initial criteria (they have located a type of assistance and believe something positive will come of it) while the latter have not.

Availability means something more than ready access to existing social or psychological services. Even if the best of services are in place and are directly offered to the individual, this does not mean that this person necessarily will recognize them as potentially useful or helpful. For example, in settings where social services are ancillary to other programs (e.g. health centers, correctional centers, residences for the elderly), the referral for psychological or social assistance may well strike the client as peculiar and having little to do with his or her real concerns. Even those who find their way to a clinic or agency at someone else's urging or command may be ignorant of what this place can do for them. In these or other similar situations, we would be wrong to assume anything about the client's knowledge or readiness to tackle a problem until we provided the opportunity for the client to disclose, clarify, and work out if and how he or she feels these services have any connection with the particular problem.

When the client does recognize that a particular agency or professional has something pertinent to offer, our next concern is with the client's expectations. What, if anything, does the individual think will happen?

How will talking actually achieve anything? What is his or her role in the process? What will the helper do? How will this thing proceed? What about cost, time, and other factors that might well interfere with one's usual routines of living? If one has had no prior association or is unfamiliar with the helping professions, or knows only what one has seen on television or in the movies, one is likely to have a distorted view of this novel experience. And, if the individual's prior experience with other professionals was something less than gratifying, then expectations about this encounter will probably not be high. In any case, if the client is not really sure a problem exists, or at least, what the problem really is, how will he or she know what to expect of the helper? And, if clients themselves feel dreadfully demoralized about their life's circumstances, could their expectations be other than dismal and hopeless? The point to be made by these few questions is that the helping process cannot proceed with any sort of harmony or understanding until the expectations of the participants are brought to light and are talked through — at least to the point where the client finds it possible to grant even a limited, short-term commitment to the venture.

The unraveling of expectations opens the way for the preliminary clarification of ends and means. Only when the questions about hope, procedure, and ground-rules are temporarily settled, can the helper and client give some thought to the next stage of problem-*setting* — that is, determining something about the client's troubles, what might be achieved in the change experience, and what they will need to do together to achieve these ends — at least in preliminary terms since these issues will arise again and again. This brings us to the issues of the client's hopes and goals (motives) and the actual changes the individual will need to work out if he or she is to realize these goals (incentive). The difference between the two is not a hair-splitting one: one person may dearly wish to be free of a drug habit (motive), but may feel that the suffering and deprivation it would be necessary to endure (incentive) would be too painful; conversely, another client may have the incentive to be more forceful and direct in a marital relationship, but may fear that, among other possibilities, the outcome may turn out to be the end of the marriage. In other instances, conflicts between such means and ends may reflect certain moral and spiritual grievances, as when a child must be relinquished, suicide or other questions about death and dying must be faced, or the wish to be free of a worn-out marriage might involve steps that violate one's religious beliefs.

The concepts of availability, expectation, incentive, and motive only help dissolve the dubious distinction between "motivated" "unmotivated" clients but also question whether these terms are ti relevant. More important, they urge us to put the so-called "presentuig problem" aside for a time while we attempt to gain some understanding of the client's perceptions and interpretations of what the helping experience is all about. If we are to start "where the client really is" we cannot assume, first of all, that he or she really is a client — that is, someone who sees some value in the helping experience, who grants the worker the right to intervene in his or her life, and who cautiously begins to wrestle with the tentative questions of possible goals and the means required to achieve them.

BEGINNINGS

Much of what has been said thus far recommends that we dwell a bit on the nature of the beginnings of the helping experience. If we are to understand the client's subjective reality and grasp the rooted premises and themes that guide the individual's active way of being, then how do we begin to fashion the climate in which this awareness can occur? How do we start to foster a relationship that, from its very outset, is marked by a humanistic spirit?

Even in ordinary circumstances, when people first meet the occasion is often fraught with uncertainty and some amount of clumsiness since it does take time for people to work out the rules about how they will relate. Given the natural factors that tend to create distance between people until a measure of trust develops, two attitudes or ways of seeing are called for. The first asks practitioners to refrain from imposing any assumptions (theoretical, moral, or judgmental) and, instead, give careful attention to the natural way in which clients present themselves and their common-sense world. The second attitude is an extension of the first; that is, the endeavor to meet clients on their own grounds and within their own worlds of experience. Michael Whan (1979) puts this quite eloquently when he says:

Whenever a social worker and client meet, part of the time they spend together usually involves the social worker listening to various accounts by the client concerning his past and present experiences. The client re-presents and articulates particular segments of his world in narrative form: he tells his *story*. Such stories serve as his "supreme fictions", his way of relating and presenting

51

himself to others. In telling and listening to a story, both client and worker are concerned to understand the unfolding drama of the client's life.

These individual tales reflect our culture, not only its folklore, religion, and literature, but also its philosophies.... Calling a person's story "fiction" is meant in two ways. Firstly, a tale is "a fiction in a philosophical sense," since very little of what is related can be verified in any strict empirical way. And secondly, the various plots and ascribed meanings we discern in the story are attempts at imaginative and empathic understanding through the use of allegory, analogy, and metaphor... story helps create an awareness of time and history. However, the past is always reflected on, remembered, and spoken about in the present. Because of this, it may be we can never tell the same story twice. We are always telling it from a different point in time. (Whan 1979: 489–99)

As the story unfolds, we listen to the language the client uses to portray his or her life, to the emotions that give it weight and substance, and to the idioms and metaphors that create a special personal and cultural texture. This story is not a whimsical tale, however, designed only to amuse or as a reminiscence. Rather, it is a very purposeful account in which the teller is the main character in the story that spins out his or her script of how things came to be — often in a way that grants the teller vindication and reprieve and, at the same time, protects his or her pride.

We know that when life is more or less secure, these "fictions" are unquestioned since they mesh with and even support a consistent and comfortable way of living. When life goes wrong, however, these "fictions" become justifications for falseness and pretense. We can say that the secure mind bases its conclusions on authentic beliefs; the insecure and troubled mind tends to search out beliefs after the conclusions have already been formed. The troubled client's story not only rationalizes his or her past but also attempts to manipulate the present as a way of, for example, obscuring painful facts, in order to plead helplessness, to control the relationship, or to test the helper's interest.

In itself, a sensitive awareness of the client's reality does not open an easy path to spontaneous improvement. Paradoxically, the helper's perceptiveness may, in fact, create a dilemma of sorts to the extent that this awareness reveals the frailties and vulnerabilities of the client's outlook. Since the best-intentioned client wants to "get better" without having to give up too much of what he or she prizes, the exposure of the individual's beliefs may create the seeds of conflict and struggle — or at least the possibility of an endless debate about whose "truth" is the truest.

A solution that fits our humanistic thesis is proposed by Saposnek (1980). He uses the uncommon analogy of Aikido, one of the martial arts, to illustrate how helpers can avoid struggle for control and at the same time create the conditions in which clients will discover for themselves the need to question their own beliefs. Paralleling the effective Aikidoist, the effective helper

> never confronts or clashes with the challenger. Instead, he accepts, joins, and moves with the challenger's energy flow in the direction in which it was going. Through such blending, resistance ceases to exist because the Aikidoist offers nothing for the challenger to resist.... By offering little or no resistance back, the therapist can utilize the client's potential resistance as free energy that he can guide into more beneficial directions. Hence the therapist may talk the same jargon as the client...or agree with the hopelessness of the situation, or even with the futility of therapy.   (Saposnek 1980: 227–37)

The willingness not just to receive, but even to encourage the client's circular and self-justifying account, first of all bypasses the struggle for control and creates the ground for the development of trust. Most important, it also shifts the locus of responsibility for change from the helper to the client. Rather than the helper taking the responsibility to change the client, this sort of acceptance carries with it the expectation that the client alone is accountable for the way his or her beliefs work. Thus, with sincere interest and curiosity, the helper is free to ask the many versions of the question: "I have some idea how things are for you. But since you see things in the way you do, how does it work for you? Where does it get you? Are you content?" Only as the client gradually discovers the futility and absurdity of his or her own guiding premises will the screen separating client and worker begin to dissolve. It is then that expectations for a more reasonable "better way" are aroused and incentives and motives become more conscious forces.

THE CREATIVE PROBLEM-SOLVING PROCESS

The task now is to enable the client to find alternatives to the distortions, misconceptions, and other cognitive problems that get in the way of healthier solutions to his or her predicaments. As we have seen, the basic problem may be perceptual insofar as one happens to be selectively inattentive to one's inner feelings or outer experiences. It may also be conceptual insofar as the individual's thinking and processing are inadequate or confused. The problem may also be interpretive if certain life experiences continue to be confusing or meaningless to the client. Inevitably, these distortions find their way into the client's way of coping and so a circular, self-defeating process comes into being.

53

Since our cognitions strive for symmetry and coherence, how we perceive, think, interpret, and act typically form a seamless whole. Yet, the ability to identify whether the client's difficulties lie in one area more than another offers the helper a point of entry and a particular focus. These points also correspond with the stages of the process of human problem-solving previously described. In the following overview we will consider how the intent to sharpen and raise consciousness conforms with the first stages of problem-solving during which the difficulty is sensed, located, and defined — at least in preliminary terms. Helping the client to redefine his or her reality is in accord with the intent to discover other alternatives and consider their consequences. And what we call risking the creative solution corresponds with the final phase of problem-solving in which the solution is tested and evaluated.

It should be noted that this is not a process that unfolds in a logical fashion. There are times when thought does progress in a systematic fashion, usually when we are working on a problem where the desired solution is known in advance — say, in the attempt to start a faulty motor. Personal and social dilemmas, however, defy this sort of logic because usually the ultimate solution is not yet known — or even envisioned. For that matter, we propose that there are times when logic ought to be put aside. We need to encourage the client to free the mind, to dream, to make illogical leaps of intuition, to imagine, to project any and all sorts of fantastic possibilities so as to allow fresh and unaccustomed possibilities to come forth. The helping process can truly be an adventure that follows any path and pursues any ideal.

Sharpening/raising consciousness

This primary phase, also called discrimination-learning (Goldstein 1981), attempts to enable the client to find release from the perceptual and attentional problems that block one's awareness of a richer or more dependable reality. It is this phase that is often overlooked in the rush to do something about the "big problem" that the client brings.

Since clients are, so to speak, stuck in their own story, they will offer, perhaps eagerly, gross impressions and conclusions about their problem and even its probable causes — the set of "truths" that they more or less take for granted. As already stressed, the helper must be sensitive to the fact that the client clings to his or her beliefs for what are seen as vital reasons. Thus the helper does not challenge the sincerity of the client's beliefs but, with active curiosity and a caring interest, asks the client to

54

enrich and develop the narrative with more and more details. In more specific terms, the helper may use any or all of four types of inquiry that are essential to creative thinking: the helper asks for *generalizations*, for *specifics*, for the client's *abstract impressions*, and for *concrete examples* (Perkins 1981).

The search for generalizations strives to broaden the scope of the client's view of his or her circumstances — in effect, to urge the client to expand the self-imposed boundaries of sense. As an example, let us consider an institutionalized young boy who complains that he cannot return home because the weekends he spends with his parents seem to turn out so badly. The client gives an impression of what it's like at home: "Well, let's see. Mother is always hanging over me like she's waiting for me to do something crazy. And Dad...I don't know. He's angry or something or on edge — maybe like he wants to get mad at Mother but doesn't want to start a fight."

Now the quest for specifics asks the client to look at what these people are actually doing and, in this regard, what they might have in mind. The helper picks one of the reported troublesome events — say a harsh exchange between the boy and his mother — and asks the client to detail carefully how it unfolded — e.g. what seemed to lead up to it, who said what, who responded, and so on.

As they pick their way through the particulars of the event, the client may come to see that the problem of his weekend visits is a bit more complex than he originally thought. For example, the youngster might now observe that his mother gets mad at him only when father takes his side about something. This new awareness and the feelings that it arouses now allow the helper to press the client to abstract his view of the situation. He might be asked something as simple as: "What does what you have been telling me make you think or feel?"; or a more involved question such as: "Let's suppose that you were going to write a TV series about you and your family..." It is impossible to indicate the kind of allusions that might be evoked by such questions, but if this query meets with any kind of success we will have moved at least a step away from mindless description or blame and we might have a better idea of how this client sees himself within his family — as, perhaps, trapped, out of control, outraged, alienated, lost, or whatever. We can now begin to exploit what the young man has learnt thus far by searching for more concrete ways in which he can actually begin to cope with the problem. Taking the family script as it has evolved, we might employ the theatrical technique of "doctoring the script" — that is, to attempt to modify the major roles, switch the dialogue, or suggest other motivations. Among other approaches, this can be accomplished by various types of role play: for example, the client trying out each of the parent's roles to discover what may lie behind their outward attitude toward him while the worker plays the client according to the way the client describes himself.

Other less dramatic approaches may be used to direct the client's attention to concrete details of the scenario that have escaped him thus far. We can also heighten consciousness by taking the client's perceptions to their illogical or absurd conclusions. At one extreme, we can *magnify* the client's misconceptions by underscoring and overstating how he sees things (e.g. "If you're right about how absolutely miserable your family is, then maybe we ought to forget the whole thing and make some plans about keeping you in this place for the rest of eternity"). *Minification* or *reductio ad absurdum* is at the other extreme (e.g. "So you can't make it with your family. Big deal! There are lots worse things than staying here. I know some residents that have been here for most of their life. They get used to it"). Either approach evokes a state of cognitive dissonance which the client will need to resolve — it is hoped in the direction of working out the weekend problem.

In this regard, we could take a dialectic approach and focus on the contrary implications of the client's story — the other side of his explanatory coin. To the extent that the client says that he is troubled about how things seem to be, he is, at the same time, implying how he would like things to be better. Hence, in response to his complaint, we could point out that what he seems to be saying is that he wishes that he could have a more comfortable arrangement with his parents, or that maybe he would like his mother to respond to him differently. If this is the case, how, specifically, does he want his parents to treat him, and what can he do about this wish?

These approaches to consciousness-raising are merely suggestive; the attempt to broaden and deepen the client's perceptions of his or her problem are really dependent on the inventiveness of the helper, and the extent of sensitivity shown to the client's subjective reality. They are not gimmicky techniques to be used in a trial-and-error fashion; rather, they are direct responses to the client's tale, a careful reading of the "fiction" that he or she has created to conserve his or her reality. It is worth adding that the creative imagination that the helper employs in this process may in itself be an indirect impetus for change to the extent that it may offer clients a new model of thinking — one that they had never considered or attempted.

Redefining reality

This next level of creative problem-solving, also called concept-learning (Goldstein 1981: 286–377), aims for the reconceptualization or reframing of the way clients construct their reality: if they can think about their problem differently, then they will treat it differently — and vice versa.

As we have established already, deeper understanding is achieved when we are sensitive to the metaphors that clients depend on to explain their world. It is on this level that we might share some small part of their subjective world. We cannot underestimate the power of the kind of spontaneous understanding (*verstehen*) that arises when we can finally allow our intuitions to override our more practical and analytic intellects. In addition, there are other more direct ways to press the client to begin to reconsider firmly implanted and unquestioned premises. A rather simple yet persuasive means is ask the client to exchange nouns and adjectives for verbs. An example:

Client: I just know that I'll lose this job too because, well, let's face it...I'm just incompetent.
Couns: I don't know what you mean by "incompetent." What do you do or don't do that makes you incompetent?
Client: I don't know...well, for one thing, I'm never able to get to work on time...

or

Client: Everybody thinks that I should be a better mother.
Couns: What about you? How do you think a "better mother" ought to act?
Client: Well...let's see. For one thing, she never gets mad at her kids.

Not only do we get a clearer picture of the relationship between thought and action, but of greater consequence, the problem itself becomes unstuck just a bit when the client's thinking shifts from conclusion to cause — or from "what I *think* I am" to "what I *do* that lets me believe what I think I am."

It was noted earlier that any strong, affirmative statement may imply that its opposite has at least equal weight. The following is an example of how these powerful contradictions may be illuminated:

Client: When I know that I will have to meet strangers, I just have to have a couple of drinks.

57

Couns: What you're saying is that you can't stop yourself — like you have no control.
Client: No, not exactly...if I really wanted to...
Couns: Oh, I see. You do have control. But you just don't want to deprive yourself...
Client: Hey, wait...you're confusing me...

This focus on the antithesis of the client's premises leads to a shift from an unquestioned belief about what makes things happen (cause) to the client's role in how things happen (intention) — that is, from "what *makes me* drink," to "*I may have some choice* in whether or not I drink."

A third approach is to shift from our tendency to ask "Why?" questions when confronted with a perplexing belief or action to questions of the "What for?" variety. The former have the effect of generating a circular, self-validating explanation. Ask almost anyone "why" they think or act in particular ways and they will reach back in their mind, recall some incident of the past, or otherwise dredge up some explanation or justification for the rightness of their behavior. "What for?" questions, in contrast, are far more penetrating; they press the individual to declare motives and intentions and, in some ways, loosen fixed conclusions about why things are the way they are. In so doing, they open the way for the consideration of other alternatives. To make these points, the following excerpts will show, first, an outcome of a "Why?" question and then the results of the "What for?" type:

Couns: You say that you just can't stop yourself from slapping your son when he gets on your nerves. Why do you think this happens?
Client: I don't know. I've wondered myself. It must have something to do with the way my father used to beat on me. Maybe I'm just like him.
Couns: You really think you're like him?
Client: Yeah. Now that I think of it, I can see how I act just like him...

All that evolves out of this exchange is a simple-minded, self-justifying deduction that leaves both counselor and client in dead center. There is nowhere to go except to continue to pursue this shallow account with the vague hope that some revelation will burst forth. Now let us consider what happens when a "What for?" approach is used:

Couns: What does it do for you? Where does it get you when you slap John when he gets on your nerves?
Client: Do for me? What do you mean? It does nothing except make me feel worse.
Couns (puzzled): If you know that then how come you keep doing it?
Client (disdainfully): I guess you don't know what it's like to come home from a

lousy job and face a kid who is constantly nagging at me...
Couns: Maybe not...what's it really like for you? (Client narrates details.)
Couns: It's really rougher than I thought. But if you could have it your way, how would you like things to be...I mean besides Johnny turning into a saint?
Client (now she is puzzled): How I'd like things to be? I don't know. Never gave it much thought...
Couns: OK, then suppose you and I think about it. I don't know if there are simple answers, but it's sure worth a try since you come out such a loser the way things are.

The consequences here are self-evident. Now let us consider other possible approaches to helping clients reconceptualize their distress.

Linking thought, behavior, and experience

The "denial" label is often applied to clients who do not seem to see that what they are doing may be connected with why things turn out so badly for them. Although in some instances they may in fact be trying to avoid responsibility for their actions, we cannot overlook the possibility that, in other cases, a conceptual gap may impede them from seeing the connections that are so apparent to others. The approach here is quite straightforward (and it applies as well to actual instances of denial); simply, the intent is to move beyond clients' global explanations of their problem or their need to blame others and, in effect, "walk them through" the experiences that create so much misery — point by point and detail by detail. In this regard, the purpose here is quite similar to the previous consciousness-raising approaches.

Creative thinking

What we refer to as "creative thinking" is given other names in the growing body of literature that points to the ingenious and even fanciful ways by which the human mind can transcend its self-imposed inhibitions, can venture into unfamiliar realms of thought in order to redefine reality in a meaningful fashion. James Adams (1974) speaks of "conceptual blockbusting." He proposes that in the face of an unyielding problem, one should try to use all of one's senses (e.g. imagery, sound, vision) to understand it in a different way. Also, the individual could be urged to redefine the problem even in the most irrational ways, or to attempt to view it from any and all perspectives. Edward De Bono (1970) proposes the idea of "lateral thinking" which represents movement away from practical and logical modes of vertical thought toward more intuitive and creative approaches. Watzlawick and Fisch (1974: 10) differentiate between first-order and second-order change. The former refers to the habitual patterns people employ so as to keep their life system intact ("convergent" thinking). Second-order change, however, is the creative mode in which people risk stepping outside of their familiar conceptions and attempt to envision more radical goals and actions ("divergent thinking"). To lead the client out of the narrow boundaries of thought, the *worker* must be willing to wander the strange corridors of absurdity, to be able to use puns and word play to make a point, and to be curious about the world of analogy and metaphor. Good theater tells us that tragedy and comedy are not far removed from one another. Thus, even in the most lamentable circumstances, the client's discovery that one can laugh at one's own peculiar tactics may be a sure sign of the emergence of creative thought.

Reinterpreting the past

Little will change as long as the client's version of the past remains intact. Thus, there are points within the ongoing dialogue where special incidents need to be recalled in order to bring the present and the anticipated future into a clearer light. In speaking of these points, I am not referring to the gathering of a formal social history or any other such ritual. Rather, there are times when progress becomes obstructed by the client's rigid conclusions about some important issue; it is then that it becomes timely to look backward to reconsider the salient events that the client believes justify his or her current premises. To put it simply, it is the nature of the immediate dilemma that dictates the timing of this historical review, and not some protocol or routine.

We can distill more precise meanings out of the client's global or diffuse recollections by searching for the pieces and details that are omitted or overgeneralized. For instance, when clients speak of people who, in the past, affected their life in some ways, some enlightenment may be gained by asking them to speculate about the needs and intentions of these people (e.g. "What do you think your brother had in mind when he...?") Or we might ask the client to recall forgotten successes to counter any fears about attempting other alternatives. In any case, the intent is to help clients re-examine their autobiography in order to free themselves from the control they believe it imposes on them.

Social/environmental deficits

Thus far, we have considered practice with clients who may appear to have some say about alternatives and choices for living. What about other clients who endure the kind of social, economic, or discriminatory conditions that reduce existence to a stark level of survival? The intimation that they have the option to consider other alternatives or that they might think about a better life-style is likely to strike these clients as absurd — given their absorption with the struggle to get through each day.

The helper should see to it that the client receives the commodities and services that are needed to ease suffering and deprivation. But the calculated intent and role of the helper obviously should go further than the fulfilment of material needs, however important a consideration this might be. If clients are to take the first small steps toward finding their way out of a demeaning existence, then helpers will need to exploit every opportunity to press them to find a fragment of dignity and strength in themselves and in their relations with others to help them discover some incentive for change.

I do not wish to create the illusion that this intent can be easily accomplished or to understate the dreadful plight of people trapped by poverty or discrimination. Clearly, any small choice that may be ventured may also be quickly obscured by the wave of futility that is so much a part of just trying to get by; for example, the single parent who now finds the strength to get her child off to school on time may again experience defeat when she is faced with yet another catastrophe — the car breaks down, electricity has been cut off, she will have to spend all day at the clinic with another sick child, or some other disaster that is so much a part of a marginal existence.

If there is to be any sort of meaningful change in the client's quality of life, the most cogent influence will be the worker's attitude, commitment, and role in helping the client find his or her rightful measure of integrity and power. It seems to me that the helper must first make some personal choices in confronting the enormity of the client's many personal, social, and environmental liabilities. The easy way out, of course, is to assume the role of the bureaucratic functionary and do the job precisely in accord with what the bureaucratic manual dictates. One can also detach oneself from the anguish of the client's suffering by taking a clinical stance and treating the "psychological problem." Or the helper may join with the client in succumbing to the wave of futility and hopelessness and either do nothing or assume a parental role by taking over full responsibility for the client's welfare. One might even choose to blame the client for making one's job so difficult and unrewarding.

The proper and helpful choice is the humanistic choice that is committed to the willingness to understand how things really are from the client's subjective outlook. If the helper can get hold of some small sense of what survival is like for the client and can in some way share the distress, the helping role will become at least a bit clearer. By no means is this an easy or straightforward task. As Rainwater (1970) says, the ordinary person experiences a disturbing sense of perplexity and anxiety when observing other people living under conditions which, to him or her, seem unlivable: "Since I cannot live that way, how do *they* live that way?" The human need to explain and make sense out of confusion poses the risk that further suffering will be heaped on these people should the question of "How do *they* live that way?" be solved by branding them with a seemingly benign, but exclusive label such as "the disadvantaged," "LSE," or "multi-problem" — never mind the other more pernicious labels of "pathological," "immoral," or "victim."

Yet if I, as the helper, can grasp why you, the client, feel hopeless, I will have a better idea of the goals and aspirations that we might explore. If I know how you have come to see yourself as powerless, I may be more astute about the aspects of your life where you might again discover your strength. If I can understand your reasons for your apathy and fear of asserting yourself, I might locate circumstances in which you can begin to declare your intentions and find some increased confidence. If I can identify with your anger, I might be able to help you find ways to express it so as to better help your cause. Basic to this willingness to understand is the unrelenting commitment to the individual's right to a sense of dignity — perhaps evident in the worker's own sense of outrage about the degradation that the client suffers. Even more important is the secure belief that clients must assume the obligation to seek and preserve a trace of dignity if they wish their life to be something more than defeat, drift, or emptiness. This humanistic choice and attitude is a prerequisite to anything useful the worker might do with or for the client.

Having presented some examples of approaches designed to enable clients to begin to reflect on and redefine their conceptions of reality, it must be noted that these approaches are not part of some larger inventory of techniques or methods. This is not said apologetically since such an inventory would presuppose that there exist a limited number of combinations and permutations of the way people construct their outlooks on the world; if this were the case, all one would need to do is find the technique that fits the set. Commonsense tells us that the opposite is the case: although as ordinary human beings we are able to share and participate in a common reality and are therefore able to get along on common grounds, we are also reminded that no two lives are the same. The inexhaustible variety of personal experiences, combined with our myriad ways of thinking about them, promises that each of us will remain unique in significant ways.

However, although the actual nature of human constructs cannot be catalogued in any final way, there is a commonly-shared intention which, if understood, will increase the likelihood that the helper will grasp the meanings underlying the client's outlook. I am speaking of the influence of *purpose* — the idea that we see things in the way we do for some particular reason. Preservation of one's sanity is perhaps the universal human purpose: as already noted, I am my reality; without that reality the "I" may cease to exist. Other purposes may be more adaptive — to save face, for example, to fulfill a particular passion, to control a relationship, to avoid danger, to prove one's rightness, and so on. Only as the helper recognizes the "for the sake of" qualities in the client's conceptions and actions, will his or her own role and purpose take form.

Risking the creative solution

In one respect, the client's risk-taking might be seen as the final phase in this episode of creative problem-solving. As it is really experienced, it is a phase that recurs in a spiral fashion throughout the helping process each time the client ventures to take a small but novel step forward.

What we call the creative solution does not burst forth as a sudden revelation; rather, it emerges as a natural consequence of fresh perceptions that now lead to new ways of thinking and/or to revisions of prior misconceptions of self and others. In fact, this sort of "knowing" may seem so natural, so totally owned by the client, as to be taken as given. The hapless mother, who now understands that her infant's unruly and negative behavior represents a developmental stage and not an assault on her self-concept, will more freely and naturally care for and love her child. The spouse of the alcoholic who now defines his or her personal boundaries more assertively, and who can see where responsibility for drinking really lies, will act accordingly. And the second-rate citizen, who succeeds in redefining and casting off the former role of victim, should now feel more secure about seizing a measure of power and control over his or her own existence.

63

In the dialectics of everyday living, however, finding a better solution does not mean that the solution is final, the problem is solved, and life goes on as before. Depending on the salience of the accomplishment, the solution can well have far-reaching consequences. The client, having risked new approaches to living, discovers new strengths and capabilities from within which serve to heighten self-esteem and the confidence to attempt other ventures: the unruly infant's mother may now see herself as a more worthwhile person and woman as well as a better mother; the reward that assertiveness brings might have all sorts of nurturing effects on the deprived or oppressed client.

The changes that are worked out oftentimes put little strain on the client's system. The mother who gets along better with her child or the person who successfully works out a career problem is not likely to incur much opposition from others. But there are other instances where the client's solution will have a direct impact on others of importance, thereby creating consequences which can lead to controversy or strife — this despite our attempts to anticipate such effects. The very fact that the solution is in some ways novel and creative can place a burden on others who must now cope with patterns of behavior that no longer conform to the rules of the system. The alcoholic husband, for example, may not eagerly welcome the responsibility that his wife now returns to him; and the community, however it is defined, might be somewhat reluctant to hear the strident voices of those who, at one time, quietly "knew their place." Again, the helper must be alert to the possibilities of tension that may be stirred by the creative solution.

There is one final consideration that needs to be addressed relative to the consequences of change. It is an issue that is somewhat harder to define than the previous ones since it involves the far less discernible questions of ethics, morals, and values.

Let me put it this way: some problems and solutions are fairly pragmatic, whereas others have more profound and lasting existential meanings. The need for employment, locating proper medical care, or getting out of debt are relatively clear-cut problems that require matter-of-fact solutions. What is "good" or "proper" in these instances is not particularly controversial. In other situations, however, the solution that one chooses may have some bearing on what can be called a principled way of living, a way of life that conforms to one's basic values, morals, and spiritual beliefs. Recalling the case in point that introduced the first chapter (the plight of Bob, Jean, and their parents), we saw that pragmatic solutions are not necessarily existential solutions; practical ends do not always take account of the burden of one's core beliefs and values. The option of an abortion, for example, may appear to be a practical and efficient way out of a grievous dilemma. But choices of this magnitude are scarcely pragmatic since they cannot be consigned to clear-cut categories of "good" and "proper." In these cases, what is "good" is not an absolute or conventional value, but an inner conviction, a set of moral and spiritual principles that serve as one's fundamental guides to living. Such choices then — whether they involve divorce, adoption, mid-life career changes, or whatever — cannot be measured by consensual or practical standards; ultimately, they will have to be balanced against the deeply-held principles and the sense of personal responsibility for those choices that are critical to the client's ongoing existence and relations with others.

All this says in closing is a reiteration of the assumption made at the outset of this book: the skills and knowledge derived from the fields of psychology and sociology may be necessary but are not sufficient in working with human problems of living. Without regard for the ethical, moral, and spiritual forces that infuse our clients' lives with vitality and meaning, helping — whether it is called counseling, psychotherapy, treatment, or whatever — is likely to be mechanistic and geared to some form of "adjustment" rather than to growth. We propose that constant regard for the client's subjective world and the cognitive processes that shape and give meaning to this reality permit us to understand how the social, the psychic, the moral, and the spiritual dimensions of existence shape the greater whole of the client's being. More important, this regard grants the client the dignity that is his or her due.

REFERENCES

Adams, J. L. (1974) *Conceptual Blockbusting*. San Francisco: Freeman.
Birch, D. and Veroff, J. (1966) *Motivation: A Study of Action*. Monterey, Cal.: Brooks/Cole.
Chomsky, N. (1976) *Reflections on Language*. New York: Pantheon.
Csikszentmihalyi, M. and Beattie, O. (1979) Life Themes: A Theoretical and Empirical Exploration of Their Origins and Effects. *Journal of Humanistic Psychology* 19 (Winter): 45–63.
De Bono, E. (1970) *Lateral Thinking*. New York: Harper & Row.
Goldstein, H. (1981) *Social Learning and Change: A Cognitive Approach to Human Services*. Columbia: University of South Carolina Press; pbk edn 1984, New York and London: Tavistock.

Hunt, M. (1982) *The Universe Within*. New York: Simon & Schuster.

Perkins, D. N. (1981) *The Mind's Best Work*. Cambridge: Harvard University Press.

Polanyi, M. (1966) *The Tacit Dimension*. New York: Doubleday & Co.

Rainwater, L. (1970) Neutralizing the Disinherited: Some Psychological Aspects of Understanding the Poor. In V. L. Allen (ed.) *Psychological Factors in Poverty*. Chicago: Markham Publishing Co.

Saposnek, D. D. (1980) Aikido: A Model for Brief Strategic Therapy. *Family Process* 19: 227–37.

Sartre, J. P. (1965) *Being and Nothingness*. New York: Citadel Press.

Taylor, G. R. (1979) *The Natural History of the Mind*. New York: E. P. Dutton.

Watzlawick, P. and Fisch, R. (1974) *Change: Principles of Problem Formulation and Problem Resolution*. New York: W. W. Norton.

Weiner, M. (1975) *The Cognitive Unconscious: A Piagetian Approach to Psychotherapy*. New York: International Psychological Press.

Whan, M. (1979) Accounts, Narrative, and Case History. *British Journal of Social Work* 9 (4): 489–99.

Wheelis, A. (1969) How People Change. *Commentary* 47 (5): 56–66.

PART II

Applications

Chapter 3

Adolescent Abusing Families:
A Cognitive-Family Approach to Practice

KINLY STURKIE

THE PROBLEMS

▶Shortly after he turned twenty-two, Sarah Boykin's father lost two fingers
and both of his feet in a farming mishap. His teeth, Sarah decided, he
must have lost one at a time, though she could never remember seeing
him any way but hollow-cheeked and drawn. Despite his problems, he
was the supreme tyrant, however, cruising the house in his wheelchair
alternately thrashing at his daughters with a sawed-off broom handle and
grabbing at their breasts.

Sarah and her sisters often whispered about rolling their father out the
door and off the porch, but they never did. Somehow, that bitter little
man controlled his daughters as much with his vulnerability as with his
broom; he dominated them in such a way that they were never sure
exactly how to fight back. Then one Christmas, Sarah established the
tradition. Each year, she and her sisters bought, fastidiously wrapped,
and gave their father two gifts: a pair of socks and a toothbrush.

The first time I met Sarah her father had already been dead for fifteen
years. But he had died nonetoosoon for her. To be sure, her second
biggest fear in the world was that he would not stay dead.

What led us together to that place was Sarah's older boy, Junior. At
fourteen, he had crowned a parade of petty skirmishes with the law by
charging four-hundred-dollars-worth of long distance phone calls to
no one in particular. At the juvenile court hearing, the phoning soon
became secondary, however. What captured the judge's attention was
Junior's older sister, Ginny, who had a black and lavender eye which

Junior had bestowed upon her during a dispute over a can of tomato soup. Ginny's eye, it was soon learned, was only the most recent in a long series of indignities which she had endured that included physical abuse by her father, two sorties into the foster-care system, and a half-dozen runaways. James Boykin had also abused Junior, and Junior had run away too, between arrests, but he had always managed to stay home. An unequivocal decision had never been made regarding whether he was a delinquent who should be incarcerated or a victim who should be placed in a "therapeutic foster home," a determination tempered by the fact that there seemed to be no foster home which could contain him. This latter realization inspired caution in the professionals with whom Junior came into contact and, for better or worse, he stayed with James and Sarah.

The judge was also struck by James Boykin's lack of attendance at the proceedings. Sarah noted, without elaboration or adornment, that James was at work. "And where was he when Junior was hitting his sister in the face?" the judge asked. But Sarah didn't know what a rhetorical question was, and didn't understand why the judge didn't listen while she gave her answer.

Unlike Sarah Boykin, whose entire life had been a meandering preparation for that day in court, Roy and Margie Jackson joined the child protective services system in a very straightforward way through a process that, from start to finish, took just four days. On Wednesday, their fourteen-year-old, Lacy, was asked for a date by a young man five years older than she. By Wednesday night, Margie had given an unnegotiable "No." All day Thursday Lacy threatened and whined, but her mother remained unmoved. On Friday, Lacy left for school at the usual 7.30 a.m., returning home exactly twenty-five hours later. Margie had called the police the night before and Roy had waited up with her until dawn. No word ever came but Lacy eventually did.

Margie saw the event less as an act of misbehavior than as an act of personal betrayal. For her, the fact that fourteen-year-olds should not stay out all night was more or less irrelevant. What enraged her and deflated her was that Lacy had done this to her. She had spent virtually every waking hour for the last decade and a half loving, feeding, pushing, caressing, teaching, and directing this kid and this is what it had all come to.

As Margie got out the belt, she observed to Lacy that she was too old to be spanked but would be spanked anyway. This was to be punishment, not discipline, though nothing was really to be hurt but Lacy's seemingly unblemished pride.

Margie had no intention of fracturing three of Lacy's fingers. But a fracas ensued and by 9.00 a.m., Lacy was at the emergency room being splinted and demanding that her mother be manacled, then arrested. Margie should have been so lucky, as she later observed. Instead she had to attempt to explain all this to a medical social worker.

I, for one, would have never expected to find these very different families anxiously loitering next to one another in a courthouse foyer, their lives becoming linked by a problem for which they didn't even have the same name yet. But they were there and I would be arriving soon. ◀

INTRODUCTION

The purpose of this chapter is to describe an approach to practice with adolescent abusing families which is jointly grounded in the premises of cognitive theory and family therapy. More specifically, the intent of the chapter is to make explicit the philosophical, theoretical, and practical nexuses between these two bodies of literature and to demonstrate how, together, they are applicable to the vagaries and dilemmas inherent in work with violent families.

The components of the approach are to be presented in conjunction with two case presentations rather than in the form of an abstract "treatment model." This format is being employed because it allows the existential and pragmatic demands of the helping process — for both the client families and the practitioner — to be more fully explored and clearly portrayed. At the same time, however, these components do constitute a coherent whole which is intended to offer the worker a longitudinal view of the "creative problem-solving process" with this client group.

AN ORIENTATION TO "TREATMENT"

The complexities and vagaries of human existence, which are intensified in the seeming disarray of the lives of violent families like the Boykins, demand cautious scrutiny. On the one hand, multiproblem families (as they are commonly termed) easily elude intervention based on highly schematized or doctrinaire formulations. At the same time, however, practitioners approaching such a family without a clear sense of direction — some explicit personal and ethical principles, some anchoring conceptual premises, and a practical plan for intervention — will soon find themselves dismally lost. One of the fluid balances which the worker must constantly seek to attain in working with violent families, then, is the development of a philosophy and a method of intervention which are

71

robust enough to provide guidance through the tumultuous, panic-inspiring periods of practice which will inevitably come, but which are not so rigid as to force the family to accommodate to the procrustean bed of the worker's own theoretical dogma and subjective reality. This balance can never be fully attained, of course, and, even then, its proximate achievement is more a product of judgment and sensitivity than calculation. In an attempt to clarify some of the basic issues which influence the pursuit of this balance, however, the approach to practice which is offered here includes three major components: a general framework for understanding the overall flow of the problem-solving process with adolescent abusing families; a body of constructs and concepts which have been drawn from the family literature and which highlight certain themes and life issues which are commonly being confronted by these families; and some methods of intervention which are both consonant with the cognitive-humanistic orientation and have been demonstrated to be useful in work with these families.

AN OVERVIEW OF THE PROBLEM-SOLVING PROCESS

The dilemma of the professional relationship

▶ It is the younger Boykin girl, whose name I do not know, that answers the door when I arrive at the house. She looks to be bright and sturdy — an "invulnerable child" as Lourie and Stefano (1977) have termed them — one who transcends the theories and the odds with her ability to thrive regardless of the circumstances. She tells me her name is Raylene.

Sarah emerges from the back of the house and, instead of inviting me in, joins me on the stoop. I remind her who I am and of my appointment with the family. I also apologize for being late. She says she remembered I was coming but remains uncomfortable and preoccupied. James is around back working on the vehicles, she tells me, and he probably isn't going to want to stop to talk. "Well, I'd like to meet him anyway," I say, and not anticipating an invitation, head around back on my own.

I wander through a maze of tractors and cars and find James working on an old Ford pick-up that he couldn't move out of the middle even if he got it running. He is not terrifying-looking like I have somehow expected; he is just very grimy and unresponsive beyond my wildest fears.

Popular wisdom holds that three of the world's greatest lies are readily transparent. The first one is: "The check is in the mail." The second is: "I will respect you in the morning." John has a look on his face like he is about to hear the third one. It goes like this: "I am from the government and I am here to help you." ◀

Goldstein has described the concept of *verstehen*, a phenomenological understanding of the client's reality which emerges only after the worker puts aside his or her own biases and preconceptions. The achievement of *verstehen* is, indeed, crucial to the collaborative, educational, problem-solving process freqently called "psychotherapy." In the context of therapy involving families which have been involuntarily drawn into the service delivery system due to behavior which has been deemed illegal, however, this concept has special significance. In this context, two contradictory demands are leveled at the worker simultaneously. As the "therapist," the worker must endeavor to attain an existential-inductive understanding of and appreciation for the client family and the worldviews it embodies. As an agent of social control, however, he or she must also unequivocally present and interpret the collective morality — in this case, the value that children have a right to be physically protected even when this entails the usurping of parental prerogatives. Thus, a major dilemma emerges. A fundamental principle of the cognitive-humanistic philosophy is that the worker must hold his or her own mind-set or "truths" in abeyance during the early client contacts. But the nature of the problem demands that the "truths" of society be articulated, even though, from the outset, this may precipitate a struggle with family members.

Another element of work with adolescent abusing families which serves to accentuate the proclivity for the worker to impose his or her own worldview — particularly through the over-application of theoretical dogma — is the degree of activity, directivity, and emotional involvement required of the worker. Since the nature of the problem prohibits a passive, detached, professional stance, and since the worker must often deal with the family members on their emotional and geographical terrain, a highly structured, prefabricated approach to intervention may be one of the few immediately available comforts.

What generates creative problem-solving in the context of these dilemmas is the worker's recognition that though he or she may provide form and direction to the change process, personal responsibility can never be dictated or imposed. This recognition is subtly reflected in the worker's level of commitment, involvement, and emphasis on the family members' competencies. In the humanistic tradition, it is also manifested in the belief that clients have the ability to construct a new frame of reference for living — to translate society's requirement for change into a challenge for growth rather than as a threat to autonomy. It is not change per se, but the context for change which the practitioner seeks to create.

Phases in problem-solving with violent families

▶We are spread all over the Jacksons' expansive living-room like four separate camps. It is their living-room but, for the moment, it seems my meeting, so I ask that everyone move in somewhat closer. It is a gesture intended to communicate that we can do sensitive business without any bloodshed.

"I appreciate your having these meetings. It takes a great deal of courage to confront your problems head on and there were other, self-protective, but potentially less productive, ways you could have responded to this crisis. These are not simple problems, but they are resolvable, and your committing to have these meetings, as painful as some them will be, is an extremely positive, productive step.

"You probably all have lots of concerns about how things are going in your family and before we are done, I hope we can deal with most or all of these concerns. For the time being, though, I suggest we focus on the immediate issue of Lacy's broken fingers and what can be done to simultaneously ensure that she takes care of the things that kids her age need to be taking care of without the occurrence of any more abuse." ◀

Like all forms of practice with families who are experiencing life-threatening symptoms (Minuchin *et al.* 1978; Berenson 1976), intervention with violent families is necessarily organized in sequential, though overlapping, phases (Sturkie and Flanzer 1981). In the first phase, the principal focus is on the elimination of the life-threatening symptoms. In adolescent maltreating families, this specifically translates as diminishing and ending the abuse through circumscribed efforts to engage and stabilize the family — in part, by endeavoring to move beyond those externally-imposed sanctions for treatment to those motivations tied to the family's own purposes and concerns. It is only after engagement and stabilization are accomplished that intervention moves to the second phase. In this phase, the focus shifts to those themes and transactions, both within the family, and involving the family and its wider social context, which have helped create and perpetuate the precipitants for and occurrences of abuse. Inasmuch as each *phase* of treatment includes all of the *stages* of problem resolution as elaborated in Dewey's classic paradigm (exploration, assessment and problem formulation, implementation of a potential solution, and evaluation), each client family is essentially involved in two "courses of treatment," one problem-oriented and one growth-oriented (Goldstein 1973; Madanes and Haley 1977).

Though from the cognitive-humanistic perspective, the worker serves largely in a collaborative role with the family, he or she must be comfortable in the role of expert in the realm of violence. This includes restricting the focus of the earliest sessions to this subject even in those families who, due to anger or fear, overtly avoid the topic or, more subtly, attempt avoidance by playing down the severity, frequency, or implications of violent behavior. In work with violent families, "beginning where the client is" often entails recognizing and exploring where the client is not. The process of leading the family members to re-examine and even re-order their priorities so that the most fundamental issue — that of violence — can be attended to first is a critical one which is prototypical for the entire therapeutic enterprise. It represents a form of "discrimination learning" through which the whole process of adequately defining problems is both articulated and demonstrated.

The problem-oriented phase: themes in engagement and stabilization

▶The Jacksons remain anxiously silent, so I continue.

"As you know, I did not attend your court hearing — you were not referred to me until after it was over — but I have been to a number of such hearings and know you may have some questions. You've had to deal with lots of different people from a variety of agencies since Saturday, and it might be useful to talk about that very complex system and your relationship to it before we move to the issues in your family which led you into that system. We don't have to start there but that's sometimes useful. Let me say two things which may seem a little contradictory. First, if you ever have a question about what happens next, want to re-approach the court before the next scheduled hearing, or think various members of the system are making contradictory demands on you, let me know. Part of my job is to help you get to the particular person you need to talk to. At the same time, it is important that you know clearly that everything that we say to each other cannot be held in confidence in the same way as it might be in another counseling situation. When Lacy's fingers were broken, your private struggles became a public matter. And the child-maltreatment law states that nothing which you say about that incident or any other incident of abuse — past, present, or future — may be held in confidence. I pledge to you not to disclose any information

75

about your family unnecessarily and I hope we can develop mutual trust. But that includes your trusting me not to get involved in keeping secrets in which the well-being of a kid is involved. Am I saying this clearly? Do you have any questions…?"

"Yes." For the first time Margie speaks. "Do you have to keep referring to this as *abuse*?" ◀

Families in which adolescents have been abused must contend with a variety of differing crises. First, they must confront the developmental "crises" — the normally-occurring requirements for shifts in the perceptions and mechanics of parent-child relationships — which often serve as precipitants for abuse. Second, they must contend with the crisis associated with their introduction into the service-delivery system. The experiences of being investigated, subpoenaed, labeled "unfit," and sometimes having a child or children removed from a family's custody are usually horrifying for the parents, the victims, and "non-involved siblings" alike — regardless of the fact of parental culpability. These feelings can also be intensified if the service-delivery system is poorly organized, lacking in direction, or is experiencing philosophic or procedural conflicts which exacerbate the family's feelings of helplessness and confusion.

A first step in helping a family resolve the crisis of being drawn into the service-delivery system is to provide information about the organization and workings of that system. To be able to make informed decisions, at some juncture the family will need this information.

Providing information about the service-delivery system may include describing the relationships between and responsibilities of the different agencies, reviewing a typical course of treatment including establishing time-lines, and clarifying behavioral expectations for change, particularly if children have been removed and family reconstitution has been specified as a goal. It is also important for workers to make explicit exactly what their role is and what the family can expect from them, including noting any legal constraints on their relationship. The practitioner may also inform or reiterate to those parents who have been involved in judicial proceedings that it is their right and prerogative to obtain legal counsel in either the public or private sector (Flanzer and Sturkie 1983).

▶ "Court was awful," Roy says, "and if we have any questions, we will check with you. We'll see how this counseling business goes for a while and then decide whether or not to get an attorney. We just want to get this all behind us. We just want to forget about it and move on…"

What he says is both a statement and a plea, the last few sentences directed to Margie who sits, unspeaking, with her head bowed. I have a sense she is on the shame-and-anger/shame-and-anger carousel but decide to let her join us on her own terms. Lacy sits erect, seemingly strong and composed, but she cups her crushed fingers and little girl vulnerability in her good hand like she is holding a sparrow.

"It was you," Margie finally says. "It was you who caused all this. You act like a whore and they threaten to put me in jail. The nerve of you sitting there like some pious little cherub." Margie stands unexpectedly, menacingly, then quickly leaves the room. She returns twice to momentarily scream invectives through the door jamb then disappears down the hall.

Roy is bewildered. It is painfully clear that "we" haven't forgotten yet.

"Please go get your wife," I say to him. "Tell her I would like her here but we go on whether she is here or not." Lacy doesn't even twitch — she doesn't even seem to breathe — through the lull though it is all I can do to quit pulling at my socks. Finally Roy appears again, followed by Margie who begins to weep as she sits down.

"Margie, I'd like you to tell me what you were thinking right before you got angry and left. I'd like you to tell me focusing on yourself, not your daughter or your husband; for example, start the first sentences with 'I.' Please tell me exactly what you were thinking about..." ◀

In addition to those crises already elaborated, families in which an adolescent has been abused must also confront the crisis associated with both the internal and external requirements for change which are crystallized by the presence of the worker. Some family members actively disclose their "toxic issues" through the expression of anger or by attempting to "defend" themselves; in other families these issues are brought to the surface by the worker's comments and questioning.

At this point in intervention, several techniques which have been developed by Bowen (1978), Stuart (1981), and others are useful. First, from the outset, family members are urged to make only "I" statements. It is common for family members, despite the nature of their presenting problem, to "punctuate" behavioral sequences in such a way as to suggest that their behavior was "caused" by the behavior of the other (Watzlawick, Beavin, and Jackson 1967). This punctuation is usually very evident in families who have utilized physical violence to resolve a problem ("I struck you because you..."; "If you didn't do that, I would never hit you..."; "Yes, but, you did..."). Requiring family members to use "I" statements serves both as a request that each take responsibility for his or her own behavior and as a way of ending the self-perpetuating cycle of mutual recrimination. This technique is particularly useful in families in which a parent is either situationally or perpetually hypersensitive to an adolescent's behavior and has not yet learned adequately to scrutinize his or her own.

Family members may also be asked to channel all communications through the worker during the early meetings. Later in treatment, members are encouraged to engage in productive dialogue. At the outset, however, suggesting that each member talk directly to the worker diminishes the opportunity for useless bickering and recriminations.

Stated in more abstract terms, the worker attempts to manage the mood of the sessions, particularly attempting to disrupt the tendency for family members to attack one another. Philosophically, this strategy is consonant with the approach of Haley (1972) who has suggested that there is little to be gained by family members expressing all their unsavory feelings about one another. Pragmatically, this approach is also in agreement with Stuart (1979) who notes that "therapy" is largely an educational process and that education better takes place in an emotionally neutral environment. This approach is also supported by the work of Straus (1974) who has determined that families in which the members verbally attack one another are also significantly more likely to attack one another physically.

The stability of the meeting is also influenced by the context in which the counseling takes place. For example, violent families may be seen in their own homes for a variety of reasons. "Home visits," which are as old as the social work profession itself, may be used to help engage a family by making the members feel less stigmatized and threatened, to resolve transportation problems, to emphasize the worker's commitment, and so on. When families are extremely volatile, however, the worker should unself-consciously impose the requirement that sessions be held in an office setting (with another worker close by). In addition to providing more security for everyone, this principle is grounded in the premise that the authority of the worker may facilitate the management of conflict and the use of the office tends to enhance this authority (Napier and Whitaker 1979).

Maintaining the focus in phase 1

▶Margie stays on the carousel for the remainder of the first meeting and most of the next two. She bumps up and down on, then slowly captures the rhythm of her rage and disappointment. Of course, there is the fury with Lacy. Margie intermittently storms around and makes veiled threats but she is also struggling with how unproductive this behavior is and she has begun ending it herself.

Margie also gets furious with me. She has caught on to the fact that as we discuss the myriad of issues of school performance, getting the table set, and when there will be another date, I will not join her in her efforts to overpower and subdue this cast-iron little bitch of a kid. I also refuse to become a convenient target for her anger by getting into a cross-generational coalition with Lacy. Her expectation is that I must support one side or the other and my electing a third position somehow violates the rules of the game as she sees them.

Margie's anger with Lacy and me, we talk about. Her resentment for Roy, we leave be. He, too, has remained essentially neutral — actually, aloof — which Margie seems to view as a monumental act of pusillanimous disloyalty. I am up to my ankles in the quintessential, interpersonal triangle, the cues and family theories tell me, but it is imperative that neither the family nor I become distracted. A little voice keeps telling me that behind all this momma-daughter noise is a couple's problem — a wife who does too much and a husband who reciprocates by doing too little — but it is still the issues of parents and child and discipline upon which we need to focus. ◀

More problematic than a family's attempts to circumnavigate the issue of violence is the worker's attempts to do so. A worker may wish to avoid the topic for all the same emotional reasons as the family members do (e.g. fear of conflict, fear of looking incompetent, and so on). Additionally, however, he or she may unwittingly create or collude in avoidance through the desire to apply a theory or ferret out an important family theme. Such themes may eventually prove to be extremely relevant. At the same time, they should not be broached until the physical well-being of all the family members, especially the adolescent, is reasonably assured.

The duration of the focus in the first phase is also clearly shaped by the chronicity of the problem. Several contributors to the child-maltreatment literature, including Lourie (1977, 1979) and Gabriano (1978), have described different patterns of adolescent abuse. In some families, for example, adolescents are first abused as very small children and continue to be abused until they leave home. Such seemed to be the case with Junior and Ginny Boykin. In other families, children are abused when they assert autonomy as two-, three-, and four-year-olds; the abuse abates through middle childhood, and then re-emerges as the issues of autonomy and control are crystallized again with the passage into adolescence. In still other families, physical punishment, mostly in the form of spanking, has always been utilized but does not escalate to abusive levels until the onset of adolescence. Such seemed to be the case with Lacy Jackson. Finally, some children are described as having required virtually no discipline until the onset of adolescence, at which time abuse rather unexpectedly explodes upon the scene. In the family therapy literature, Minuchin (1974) has made a similar though less-detailed observation by differentiating families whose symptoms are situational from those whose symptoms are chronic.

This aspect of problem formulation is important because differing forms of abuse usually impose different kinds of demands for change. Furthermore, this assessment helps the worker gauge how long a particular family will remain in the first phase of treatment. Situationally abusive families like the Jacksons tend to move more rapidly, occasionally progressing to the second phase of treatment in only two to three interviews. In chronically abusive families (in which abuse has become the preferred means for conflict reduction), the total reduction of violent behavior, if achievable, may take months. Of course, there is no way to accurately "predict" the length of time a particular family will remain in the first phase. Exploring the chronicity of the problem does serve to help the worker achieve the balance between over-focusing and under-focusing on the issue of abuse, however.

It equally should be emphasized that the "pace of change" is also greatly influenced by factors *external* to the client families. For example, also bearing on the intervention process and a family's participation in it, is the way that adolescents and their discipline are viewed in our society. Confounding the family members' perceptions of specific incidents is the fact that the standards for discipline in our society are quite different for adolescents as compared with children. Stated simply, the older a child becomes, the more liberal become the community standards defining the parameters of acceptable parenting (Fischer and Birdie 1978). Because of his or her presumed level of cognitive and emotional development, an adolescent might be viewed as willfully provocative, which may bear on the parents' perceptions of their responsibility in a way that might not be the case with a younger child (Flanzer and Sturkie 1983). Furthermore, as with the case of Junior Boykin, abused adolescents are frequently brought to society's attention only after having engaged in some antisocial behavior. Just to redefine such adolescents as victims may be a revolutionary act which greatly slows the pace of "treatment."

▶The next two visits to the Boykins are relatively uneventful except that I meet the other Boykin child, Richy, and finally get invited inside. The two meetings include Junior and Ginny and their mother, but James stays away.

We discuss in detail the "soup can" incident and the kids' earlier experiences with violence. Ginny responds flatly and cautiously; Junior, with anxious amusement. The trio quickly volunteers that there will be no more arguments, no more fights, however. They have established a pact of "pseudo-mutuality" which leaves me feeling shakier than the sum total of Margie Jackson's threatening and ranting and pacing.

On one occasion I take the meeting to James in the back. I deliver what is intended to be a bold, soul-stirring appraisal of what is happening with his older son. He just brushes it — and me — aside with amazing facility. The boy has required more discipline than some children, he says, but for the most part, he's no worse. There is a contradiction here so fundamental that it is unignorable, but I also find myself as strait-jacketed by James' thinking as he is. Somehow, in a way that speciously hangs together, he manages to justify harsh punishment for his son while, at the same time, dismissing him as an innocuous prankster.

We are a month-and-a-half into this and I have been unable to engage James in any "therapeutic" manner; to be sure, I have been unable to engage him in any authentic way at all. Finally, almost impulsively, I ask James to describe where he sees the boy in five years.

"I don't know what you mean," he says.

"I'd just like you to picture where you see him physically when he's nineteen. Do you see him sitting in the living-room, still with you and Sarah, do you picture him away in his own apartment somewhere, living alone or married and out working, or do you see him pulling time in some six-by-eight cage at Central Corrections? Where is your son going to be?"

James is visibly provoked by the unforeseen twist to this little exercise but he continues working. He thinks for a minute.

"I'm no crystal-ball reader," he finally says, and then goes silent again. ◀

It can not be overemphasized that a *sine qua non* of treating abusive families is the worker's managing his or her own feelings of panic, fear, apprehension, and responsibility during those times when anxiety and conflict are high and violence seems imminent. As the Jackson family illustrates, instability is not inherently problematic; it is a double-edged sword. Though it may serve as a precursor for abusive behavior, it may also precipitate the demand for positive movement, what Hoffman (1980) has termed "discontinuous change." To be sure, as the Boykins demonstrate, it is often "stability" — the facade of harmony — which works to a family's disadvantage. During these "stable" times, the worker may find him- or herself struggling with feelings of incompetence, impatience, or adolescent unruliness which, again, must be managed if the worker is to contribute meaningfully to the problem resolution process.

Meeting basic needs

▶When I am not meeting with Sarah and the older kids or stupidly scolding James, I also spend some time with Richy Boykin. He is a curious-looking little boy with a very odd gait, rather unintelligible speech, and incessant movement. Like most little kids, he thrives on attention. At the same time, he is so "driven," he can manage to assimilate only so much at one sitting.

Just when I least expect it, Sarah calls me at the office one morning. She is worried about Richy who has been saying that the front yard is full of snakes. Junior scoured the entire area and hadn't turned up so much as a worm. Richy has had his spells before, she says, but not like this. I tell her that I know a physician — a child psychiatrist — that is very good with these kinds of problems. She recoils at the word "psychiatrist" but is feeling desperate and will try anything. She pledges to call for an appointment immediately. I also call to clear the way and to be sure Richy can be seen immediately.

The arranging of the consultation goes extremely smoothly. That is good. And that Sarah would call also seems to signal some progress. If I could just come up with some way to get James into the living-room…. ◀

Though this chapter is concerned primarily with the provision of direct counseling services, it must also be emphasized that, in the social work tradition, the delivery of brokerage, advocacy, and concrete services is also essential with violent and multiproblem families. The idea that child and adolescent maltreatment occur at proportionate rates at all socio-economic levels has been discarded as a myth (Pelton 1979, 1981; *National Incident Report* 1981). Multiproblem families are significantly more likely to be poor, extremely unsophisticated, or both, and the providing of additional services, particularly concrete services, serves as an important tool for achieving both engagement and stability. Flanzer (1978) has even suggested that an unwillingness to address basic human needs has led many practitioners who regard themselves as "therapists" to avoid poor, multiproblem families. Thus, any approach to treatment with multiproblem families must emphasize and legitimize the practitioner's engaging in these less glamorous activities in preparation for and in conjunction with the implementation of psychotherapy (Flanzer 1978).

▶ James Boykin decided to take a run at getting into the poultry business. He bought a dozen hens and a rooster and banged together a coop to go out back beyond the cars. The rooster, which Richy named Edgar, was roughly the size of a condor and was brutally candid with his feelings. He reacted to my presence in a way that James had only approached.

"Why is he looking at me like that?" I ask Junior. "Do they have something about territory like dogs do?" Edgar is standing in Richy's lap, staring through me like I have just fried his mother for lunch.

"They can be mean," he says, enjoying my discomfort. "Them big ones will go for your eyes."

Sarah and the kids begin moving into the living-room. The kids are getting caught up in this little drama but they are unsure how to react. Sarah is not unsure, however, and she begins to giggle — respectfully — behind her hand. Buttressed by their mother's permission, the kids also begin to grimace and snicker.

"Richy, that's a wonderful pet," I say, "but I'd feel a lot more comfortable if you would take him outside." I find myself anxiously laughing, too, though Edgar doesn't seem the least bit amused. "My grandmama once told me she kept roosters but they don't like to be in the house."

This standoff between Edgar and I, which I am losing, has revealed a side of Sarah that I have never seen before. She has ceased her cautious giggling and has begun to laugh out loud. She is unguarded and alive — totally absorbed in the moment — attempting to regain control only long enough to look at Edgar and me, to look back to her children, and then to resume her unself-conscious howling. Richy's laughter, which is primarily in response to that of his mother and the other kids, is jostling Edgar who rotates his head to eye me from different angles. Despite my obsequious pleas, Richy stays seated looking to everyone but me for the next clue regarding what is transpiring and what he should do.

The exuberance of the squall reaches such proportions that it draws James inside to see what is happening. He pauses in the door to survey us.

He is unsure what is transpiring, his face says, though his gaze settles on Richy, the only other person as confused as he.

"Richy," he says almost automatically, "get that damn rooster out of the house." He is characteristically abrupt and autocratic but his anger and demand only increase the screaming and pandemonium. While Richy dutifully and shamefacedly complies, and with everyone else still roaring, I stand and extend my hand to him.

"Thank you; thank you," I say, and then sit back down. Unbelievably, after shaking my hand, he sits down, too. ◄

THE SECOND OR "GROWTH-ORIENTED" PHASE

As has been noted, the purpose of the second phase of intervention is to identify and confront those issues, both within the family and involving the family and its wider social context, which are hypothesized to be related to the development and maintenance of the maltreatment. Though both *phases* of treatment contain all of the major *stages* of the problem-solving process, the issues of how one defines the problem and what one does in an attempt to facilitate change are far more ambiguous and fluid in this phase than they are in the first.

Identifying and assessing contributory problems

Because of the nature of intrafamilial violence, the task of assessing its "underlying" causes is an extremely difficult one. Both practice-experience and the relevant literature suggest that the physical abuse of children and adolescents is, at the very least, the product of the complex interplay of systems at the individual, interpersonal, community, and societal levels.

The assessment process also includes identifying which system the worker believes he or she can generate the most influence upon. In a collaborative relationship, the family members will more or less directly define these areas. With involuntary families, the worker must simply exercise judgment based on his or her understanding of the precipitants of abuse in general and "hypotheses" about the functions of violence within the specific family.

As has been noted, the hypotheses one develops regarding the functioning of a client family may have as much to do with the worker's theoretical biases as with the behaviors and worldviews of the family members. These hypotheses are usually derived from a system of interrelated constructs, which in turn, derive from a more or less explicit system of norms — a presumption of how things ought to be.

Constructs are important in that they help give form to the process of problem definition. At the same time, however, their use inevitably confounds this process since they are intrinsically reductionistic. The sole function of constructs is to distill the complexities of reality into a conceptually manageable form. As a result, they do violence to the reality which they attempt to catch (a phenomenon commonly known as the "Heisenberg Uncertainty Principle"). Furthermore, since from a pheno-menological perspective, there is no single "reality" anyway, a construct is, in actuality, a general distillation of reality which is based on an idiosyncratic one.

Despite these problems, the real danger in utilizing constructs lies less in their reductionism than in their reification. The critical problem is not the avoidance of constructs; it is being able not to confuse the metaphor with what it refers to. As Madanes (1980) has suggested, when the Oedipal conflict was an idea, it was extremely useful; after it became a *thing*, however, it became a tyrant. In short, constructs are important heuristic devices if, to paraphrase Gregory Bateson, one does not confuse the menu with the meal (Watzlawick, Beavin, and Jackson 1967).

Another premise of this approach is that any conceptual scheme which elucidates the problem for the worker and the family is acceptable. Despite all the ideological range-wars between and among the various individual and systems camps, the potency of any particular theory of behavior probably lies less in the theory itself than in the practitioner's belief in its truth and utility (Frank 1967). As is implied in the chapter's title, those constructs which have the greatest utility for me are those drawn from the family therapy literature. Several of these are noted below. These are clearly not exhaustive. Rather the purpose is to illustrate a particular way of thinking.

Family organization and the construct of cohesion

▶Lacy Jackson is looking for some more "space" in her life, though if she were to say it that way, it would sound even more jejune and clichéd than when I do. She and her mother are in the "sweatbox," as Hoffman (1980) has called it, tussling through the complicated business of discovering where one person — a parent — ends and the other person — an adolescent — begins. As Goldstein noted in Chapter 1, viewed dispassionately this is a commonplace struggle, essentially devoid of heroics. But for those persons directly involved in the struggle, these issues are at the center point of existence.

"She had a great week, both here and at school," Margie beams. "She hasn't been a minute late for class and she has gotten all her work in on time." This is a compliment though it will not be taken that way.

"She knows this because she's been phoning school three times a day. God, I can't breathe..." Lacy simulates gagging while she rocks in her seat and rolls her eyes.

Margie remains unself-consciously in personal control. "Lacy does feel I'm crowding her," she says, "but as you know, it's the only way to get the trust back."

It is Lacy, who has stood firm under direct fire, who is now provoked. She breaks in, getting louder as if this were merely an issue of volume adjustment.

"No, it's not, Momma. I can't live the rest of my life with you breathing all my air..."

So, the conflicting realities for these two are that, from Margie's perspective, Lacy will die with less supervision, and from Lacy's perspective, that she will die from more. ◀

Perhaps the most ubiquitous concepts in the family literature are those which deal with family cohesion. Family cohesion has been defined as the amount of "emotional bonding members have with one another and the degree of individual autonomy a person experiences in the family system" (Olson, Sprenkle, and Russell 1979: 5). Families which are extremely high in cohesion, that is in which closeness and nurturance are highly valued while individual autonomy is valued much less, are generally termed "enmeshed" (Minuchin 1974). In contrast, families in which closeness is undervalued and the members operate functionally independent of each other are termed "disengaged." The concepts of "overinvolvement" and "peripherality" (Haley 1976) which essentially parallel the "enmeshment" and "disengagement" concepts, respectively, have also been developed to characterize the relationships between particular individuals rather than to characterize entire family systems.

The cohesion construct and its related concepts are noted because an exploration of this dimension of family functioning can be useful in providing a starting place for examining the possible functions and meanings of an abuse incident. This is in keeping with the general systems premise that a "symptom" in a family represents an attempt by the family members to solve a problem (Haley 1976). In some families, for example, one or both parents may have the perception that their adolescent cannot function without their "hovering." This is not to suggest that enmeshment "causes" abuse or vice versa; the two emerge in a recursive spiral though one may be more clearly manifested earlier than the other. But whether the parents' overinvolvement with an adolescent is most clearly manifested prior to or following an incident of abuse, the worker's focusing the family on these perceptions and their behavioral transactions represents one opening — one entree — to problem resolution.

It also should be noted that incidents of abuse may be associated with disengagement or peripherality. While working with the Boykins, for example, I surmised that James often abrogated a number of his parental responsibilities for his children, though he also occasionally attempted to re-establish authoritarian control through acts of violence. If the problem is formulated in this way, it would therefore follow that if he and Junior could become appropriately engaged, then the violent behavior in this particular dyad might be stripped of its purpose.

Family interaction and the construct of adaptability

That our perceptions, both individual and shared, become "reality" is of paramount importance to the problem-solving process. The problem definition imposed on a set of circumstances by a family and the family's primary style of problem resolution greatly influence the speed with which the problem will be solved.

It has been noted in the family literature that families can be distinguished according to the relative structure of their attempts to solve the problem (Olson, Sprenkle, and Russell 1979). At one extreme are those families who tend to employ the same method of problem resolution even though it has never worked. Margie's increasing vigilance with her daughter, for example, represents the use of a problem-solving approach which may, in fact, serve to perpetuate rather than resolve a problem. In systems terms, Margie was endeavoring to promote "first order change" ("more of the same") in circumstances in which "second order change" was indicated (Watzlawick, Weakland, and Fisch 1974). Or, to use Goldstein's terms (1981), this family needed to engage in "divergent" rather than "convergent" thinking; they needed to expand rather than focus their problem-solving repertoire.

Multiproblem families such as the Boykins, in contrast, tend to employ a more "chaotic" approach to problem-solving (Olson, Sprenkle, and

Russell 1979). In this family, which is more heavily characterized by "divergent" than "convergent" thinking, the understructured approach to problem-solving, as exemplified in James' unpredictable responses to Junior's aggression and delinquency, serves only to perpetuate these problems. Thus, if one formulates the problem in this way, the goal of intervention becomes helping to focus, rather than expand, the family's problem-solving repertoire (Sturkie and Flanzer 1981).

The constructs of personal and developmental time

▶Out of the blue one morning, after I'd called Sarah to check on Richy, she began talking about her father. It was a long, fragmented discourse, a search through opaque half-memories which were linked only by an amorphous ache. Though she never established a discernible connection to the present, to Richy or James or Junior, it was clear she somehow suspected one. There was a special quality in the way she spoke; in some way she was struggling with the hazy idea that her past and her present were converging — not in a straight line but from different directions. Then this confluence of "times" would slip away, and I was left talking with a little girl who wanted no explanation, just verification, that a set of circumstances, not its inhabitants, had been crazy.

The calls went on for months — sometimes regularly, usually not — and she never once mentioned them during the meetings at the house. I thought about mentioning them a time or two, but, being unclear of how appropriate this would be, I did the easy thing, which was to stay quiet. ◀

Though the nature of interpersonal violence imposes a "present orientation" in counseling, personal, historical time is important to explore when the themes of "then" are seemingly being duplicated by the themes of "now." This exploration is not begun with the expectation that "insight" or "cartharsis" will resolve the thorny concerns of the moment. Appropriately timed, however, this examination is one method of achieving self-validation and a sense of meaning and purpose.

As has been emphasized, the concept of developmental time is also important in work with families in which an adolescent has been abused. Several writers in the adolescent maltreatment literature (Lourie 1977, 1979; Libbey and Bybee 1979) have noted that the family reorganization ("second order change") prompted by a child's movement into adolescence can precipitate abuse. Abusive acts, in this formulation, may signal, for example, that a family has been unable to make the discontinuous shift in the perception of relationships naturally prompted by the maturation process. Furthermore, this already complex shift in the family is even more difficult if it, too, duplicates a parental experience.

Techniques of intervention in physically abusive families

▶About four months out, life got very settled at the Boykins. This quiet period, which marked the transition from the first to the second phase of treatment, is so common in work with violent families, that my colleagues and I used to spend hours during staffings speculating about its meaning. The "lull" was variously seen as a product of the tactical wizardry of the problem-specific, Phase I interventions, a resistance maneuver cooked up by the family to lull the caseworker into complacency, and, simply, as a result of the length of time that the case had been open. (The latter supposition was based on the idea that if the worker is patient enough, every family will settle down, at least temporarily, sooner or later.)

Regardless of its cause, this tranquil period usually proves to be critical. The family members often seek to leave treatment at this juncture — especially when there is no judicial mandate to continue — and the worker, wanting to leave well enough alone, is often anxious to accommodate them. (You know you are at this point when you begin saying to your supervisor: "I think this family and I have gone about as far as we are going to go.") Of course, termination is appropriate in some cases. On the other hand, to agree with a chronically abusive family that a few months of tranquility means that all of their problems have been resolved is an act both of self-deception and collusion.

In any event, at about the time the Boykins were moving into their tranquil period, I began toying with the idea that James could help resolve most of his son's problems in six or seven months or so if he just got committed to the idea. If they could spend time with one another around anything that didn't have a conflict at its core, their relationship might take off.

One week, I casually asked each to prepare a list of some things they might do together; the next week, based on their lists, I would give them a directive to actually try the chosen activity. As it happened, James didn't make his list, though in the meeting he rattled off a litany of jobs that required some kind of heavy lifting or parallel work. I refused to let the issue die, however, and eventually he also mentioned shooting pool, an idea which conspicuously aroused Junior's interest. Pool, then, they decided, it would be.

Sarah was apprehensive, to say the least. I think she wanted these men to get along but feared some kind of real bond — a dangerous coalition — might develop. But James was outwardly pleased at the prospect of taking his boy out and Junior was simply delirious.

The weight I was gaining at the meetings at the Jackson's, and Margie's profound calm, suggested that things were getting too tranquil. If I did not take the initiative to stir things up again in a controlled way then Lacy might, and the family would be back to square two.

"Margie, I really admire your spunk and commitment but I am also concerned you're going to get an ulcer. As you've mentioned, you've been slaving away tirelessly for fifteen years now. It's just time for a vacation. For the next week, I want Roy to do the calling to the school. Five times a day, if you think it's necessary, Roy, but at least twice through the week."

"I may complain," Margie says, "but I've never said I am a 'slave.'"

"That's true; that's my word. But anyway, instead of calling the school, I'd like you to call me at least twice. We'll have this check-in in lieu of our regular meeting next week."

Lacy is rolling her eyes at me now.

"How come we can't do this so nobody calls the school? Why can't those two call each other?"

I pause and mull the idea over with a readily observable intensity. That her idea would be worthy of such consideration magnifies Lacy's involvement, which further engages Margie and Roy.

I let the time drag even more before finally responding to her.

"Listen. You go along with what I've proposed and we'll discuss your idea again."

Lacy agreed, which meant Roy and Margie had to. ◀

During any problem-solving effort, a number of "choice points" are encountered at which one course of action is selected to the exclusion of its alternatives. As London (1964) and Goldstein (1981) have noted, the choices one makes during "therapeutic" problem-solving are principally determined by three considerations: (1) one's philosophical and episte-mological assumptions about the nature of humankind; (2) the theories of personality and human behavior one embraces; and (3) the arsenal of techniques one employs to catalyze "change."

Of course different schemes for conceptualizing the problem can result in divergent forms of intervention. For example, one practitioner may believe the client is best served by helping him or her to behave into a new way of thinking. A behaviorally-oriented therapist may believe, for example, that if the helper provides a father with the new experience of appropriately controlling his unruly child through the implementation of a contingency management program, this experience will subsequently alter the father's perceptions of the child and of his relationship with the child. In contrast, another therapist may posit just the opposite. He or she may believe that it is best to attempt to help the client think into a new way of behaving. For example, a therapist might work with a father to change his perceptions of his child by helping him re-examine his self-defeating measures to control the child, by providing information on normal development in children, or by exploring feelings of helplessness left over from the father's own deprived childhood which lead him to attempt to over-control in the here and now. This therapist's intervention would be based on the belief that the father's altered perceptions of himself and/or the child will lead to new parenting behaviors. A "psychodynamically-oriented" therapist, for example, might be expected to embrace this "theory of change."

Still another therapist may posit that both ways of "punctuating" the change process can be correct, though depending on the personal style and worldview of both the client and the worker, one approach to change may work better in one context than in another.

Even the most cursory review of the "psychotherapy" literature, particularly in the burgeoning family-therapy field, reveals an extensive array of techniques which are presumed to facilitate change. There are so many different techniques, in fact, that one may wonder how this body of techniques may be organized so that it constitutes a coherent, comprehensible whole. For the purposes of this chapter, two corollary questions can also be raised. Which, if any, of these techniques are consonant with the principles of "cognitive-humanism," and which, if any, of these techniques are useful in work with families in which an adolescent has been or is being abused?

Based on data derived from 210 social workers who suggested that they specialized in family treatment (Sturkie 1979), a paradigm has been developed which provides a framework for inquiry into these questions. In this framework, change techniques are distinguished according to two major dimensions. The first relates to the primary *goal* of intervention — specifically, whether the worker endeavors to enhance and expand awareness or whether he or she purports only to attempt to bring about "systems change" (Madanes and Haley 1977). The second dimension relates to the basic *mode* of intervention: specifically, whether the worker

Creative Change

TABLE 1   *Paradigm of therapy techniques*

	mode of intervention	
goal of intervention	*reflection*	*action*

expanded awareness	clarification
	explanation
	interpretation
	confrontation
	"I" — positioning
	exploration
		contingency programs
		family sculpting,
		   choreography, and spa-
		   tialization
		role playing, role reversals
		charting procedures
		maintaining a journal
		letter writing, visitations
		gestalt techniques

"systems" change	reframing, positive in-
	   terpretation
	ascription of noble in-
	   tention
	Stuart's "as if" tech-
	   nique
	positive connotation
		directives
		metaphoric directives
		prescribed ordeal
		paradoxical directives,
		   symptom prescription

attempts to accomplish his or her goal through reflection and introspection or through the use of some activity.

If these two dimensions are presented in juxtaposition, a two-by-two contingency table is created which can serve as a paradigm for comparing intervention techniques (see *Table 1*). It is emphasized that though the paradigm has been filled in with a group of common and representative techniques, the listing is intended to be illustrative rather than exhaustive.

A number of the techniques presented in the first quadrant — particularly explanation, interpretation, reflection, and confrontation — though still widely used, have been at the heart of the traditional, psychosocial approaches to social casework, group work, and dynamic psychiatry for decades. In more recent years, these techniques have been augmented by interventions developed by the cognitive therapists, members of certain of the major "schools" of family therapy (such as Bowen 1978), and others. Despite differences in these techniques, they are all based on the premise that a change in subjective experience, especially if awareness is expanded and the skills of purposeful decision-making are enhanced, will subsequently lead to a change in individual behavior and interpersonal transactions.

The interventions in the second quadrant are also employed to expand awareness. However, the proponents of these techniques believe that a learning experience is more valuable if it is intensified and actualized through the provision of a behavioral assignment or experience. Having a depressed person keep a log of pleasurable events (Beck *et al.* 1979), suggesting that a client maintain a journal (Goldstein 1981), or recommending that a person who is cutoff from his or her extended family write or visit them (Bowen 1978) all exemplify forms of intervention deriving from this "change theory."

Techniques from this quadrant may also be used with abusive families. For example, instead of having an abusive parent reflect upon and describe a child's behavior, a worker who shares the premises underlying the techniques in this quadrant might have the parent chart all his or her children's behaviors, distinguishing among appropriate behaviors, inappropriate behaviors which can be ignored, and totally unacceptable behaviors which cannot be ignored. Through this exercise, the parent may discover that a targeted child's behavior is no worse than that of his siblings (Flanzer and Sturkie 1983). In another case, a mother who attempts to control her daughter physically because she fears she is losing emotional contact with her, might be asked to dramatize physically her feelings and beliefs rather than simply expressing them verbally. Or, in still another case, a parent who is simultaneously overinvolved and exasperated with an adolescent may be asked to clarify and express these conflicting feelings openly, taking one position while sitting in one chair, and the other position while in another chair.

Most of the techniques in this second quadrant involve the client's following a directive from the worker. As is evident from *Table 1*, however, the fourth quadrant also contains a variety of forms of "directives." Again, the principal difference is that the purpose of the second quadrant's directives is always to expand awareness, as well as to change and structure behavior. With the directives in the fourth quadrant, though a change in subjective experience *may* occur concurrent with or subsequent to a change in behavior, learning is *not* an intended outcome.

The interventions listed in the third and fourth quadrants emerged in response to and out of dissatisfaction with the more traditional interventions of the first two quadrants. Beginning in the late 1960s a trend developed in the family therapy field in which techniques intended to augment awareness and purposive decision-making were rejected and vilified. Haley (1976) has suggested, for example, that to do well in the therapy business, one needs to get rid of the idea that people have rational control over their behavior. Whitaker and Keith (1981), in a similar vein, have recently suggested that it is self-deceptive to think that family members are "able to take intellectual input and convert it to a family change process." An account has also been presented of Minuchin (1979) refusing to discuss even the possibility that "learning" takes place in therapy as he practices it. Over and over again, many of the pundits in the field have suggested that providing family members with information about their functioning not only fails to contribute to problem resolution, but may actually confound the process by precipitating "resistance."

In the interventions listed in the third quadrant, for example, the family members may be asked to think about their problem in a different way through the use of "reframing." For example, Virginia Satir is purported to have told a woman who had been chased by her husband with an axe that this was the way he showed affection (Beels and Ferber 1969). Such an observation is not intended to "explain" the nature of a relationship as much as it is intended to provoke the family members to behave differently. Congratulating a symptomatic child for sacrificing herself for her family or having a child "pretend" that he has a "symptom" which he already has (Madanes 1980) are other examples of this form of intervention.

In the interventions in the fourth quadrant, family members are explicitly asked to interact differently by requiring changes in their behavioral sequences or by changing the physical or temporal context in which a symptom occurs. The mechanism by which the intervention is supposed to work is not clarified for the family members, however; to be sure, the rationale for the worker's action may be muddied or obscured.

For example, Haley (1976), who maintains that what symptomatic families need is not self-understanding but a new set of behavioral sequences, often employs directives to "precipitate a crisis" in families which habitually, unsuccessfully attempt to solve a problem in the same way. The directive, in effect, "requires" the members to use an alternative solution though their achieving heightened awareness is regarded as superfluous. For example, creating a homework task in which an overinvolved, abusive parent is "required" to allow a peripheral, non-abusive parent to take over disciplinary responsibilities within the family may result in the diminution of abusive behavior, though the mechanism of the intended change is never discussed.

Though it may be necessary to destabilize some rigid, situationally abusive families with the interventions of the fourth quadrant after the abuse has abated, for the most part it is best to avoid these interventions in work with chronically abusive families. Obviously, one cannot ever prescribe the symptom or attempt to move it in space or time; the use of paradoxical directives would be absurd. With these families, however, simply issuing a "blind" directive—i.e. one for which the rationale has not been made clear—is also problematic. When a worker presents a "blind" directive, he or she takes on the principal responsibility for "creating" change (Madanes and Haley 1977). But the theme of personal responsibility is so critical in these families that by employing such a technique, the worker would essentially create a process issue which runs counter to a central content issue.

▶ Junior got drunk when he went out with James to shoot pool. Ten days after, Junior decided he would go out on his own for a few more beers. He would not say where he went or how many he had had, but it was enough to make him sick. He stayed up most of the night oscilating between being independent and argumentative and needing to be helped and comforted. James was very unhappy about the incident which led me to think he had gotten himself into an ideological bind. There was simply no contradiction, no lesson, for him, however. That he could subsidize the drinking one week and condemn it the next simply did not pose a problem. It came down in the end, he said, to letting the boy suffer the consequences for his actions. It was all so neat and uncomplicated for him that I even began thinking the problem was that I am just narrow-minded.

The punishment was an appropriate one, even if the language in which it was couched was a bit extreme.

"I'm going to bust his ass. I've got a buyer for one of the wrecks and Junior's going to give me an hour's worth of work for every beer that he drank. As tore-up as he was, I figure about a week's worth of work, four hours a day, should just about do it. Sarah has also called his probation officer to let him know what's happening. We've taken care of this."

There was an unquestionable finality to James' position. Junior hadn't drunk a case of beer, of course, but I decided that this was not an issue to quibble about. I just kept thinking about a paper I had read which said every family contains forces which promote change ("morphogenesis") and forces which keep things the same ("morphostasis"). But with this crowd, I can't tell one from the other.

Margie called religiously. I had no agenda other than to keep her busy through her restless time but she was sensitive and a pleasure to talk with. The parameters were unstated but she must have inferred them – she could talk about anything but Lacy. Roy, the husband, she could talk about; Roy, the father, she could not.

When she called the third time, there was a resolve in her voice.

"Roy called the school and they said Lacy missed two classes Wednesday and he wants me to help him work out a consequence. I understand I agreed to this vacation business but I also think I have a right to participate in handling this. Roy and I agree that it is something we should do together."

It was a two-hour call. There was a lot to talk and think about, a lot at stake. But when it was all over I said, "OK, Margie, if you and Roy insist."

Over the next three to four weeks, Junior and James disassembled and sold parts from five wrecks. It was a strange alliance — productive, but with that unmeasured quality which worried Sarah. There had been another drinking episode also; the two of them had gone out on a $20 cut from Junior's end of the salvage business.

After Junior's fourth drinking incident, James began coming to the meetings less regularly. When he did, he usually didn't say much. Occasionally he would impart some truism about parenting, but for the most part, he was petulant and sullen. It began to dawn on me that I was more than a weekly annoyance, more than a crimp in the way James wanted to run his petty empire. What was happening between us was having less and less to do with Junior or any of the other children. It began to dawn on me that my mere presence symbolized for him all the things in life that had somehow not worked for him.

Junior was slipping away, too. He began missing meetings and Ginny began showing up more bedraggled and bruised. I raised the issue with the whole family, and then asked the kids to leave. This was a parents' issue and I had also not discarded the idea that Junior, too, was wearing bruises and James was behind them all. He denied it unequivocally, condescendingly.

"Well, I have no illusions that Ginny will file assault and battery charges if Junior attacks her again, though I'd report the incident to his probation officer; the judge might revoke his probation on general principles. But Junior's not going to be intimidated by any police-talk from me. There are no guarantees, but he may respond to your demand that he quit it. If you two can agree it must be stopped and tell him that, he may. There are some kinds of control kids fight; other kinds they sometimes respond to."

"I don't much care for the hitting," James says, "but they are getting to the age when they will have to decide for themselves. Ginny's basically full-grown and will probably be married in a few years. Its time she learned to defend herself."

James stands up. "I've had enough of this shit," he says. "I'm a working man." He then heads out back.

For all practical purposes the meeting was over but I just could not let it be.

"Sarah," I ask. "What are you planning to do when Ginny does leave and Junior starts up on Raylene?" It was such a natural question, I thought, but it caught her completely by surprise. It was written all over her face that, incredibly, she had never thought about it.

"Really, Sarah. What's your plan? What are you going to do?"

It was peculiar. It was Junior, both powerful and vulnerable, who was hatching the unhealable rift between Sarah and Ginny. But from the way Sarah was looking, I could tell it was me, not Junior, that she wanted to roll out of the door and off the front porch.

When Ginny did leave, it was without fanfare. She simply packed her stuff and moved in with a schoolmate. There was no attack, no emotional scene. Ginny just found her limit and moved.

Sarah refused to fall apart about it though the pain showed even when she talked about the most innocuous topic. She was really hurting, as were Raylene and Richy, but then Sarah was also sure that there was absolutely nothing that she could do about it.

Ginny left home the week I saw the Jacksons for the last time. Lacy found a boyfriend her own age who was both a prima donna and a junior scientist which helped settle things down. During the last month I met with the family, Margie also decided that Lacy wasn't going to be around forever and that she should begin going back to work. This generated considerable conflict between her and Roy but, in their own words, it wasn't anything they could not handle. They believed, and I agreed, it was time to stop. We settled out of court with a letter and a pledge to call if things heated up.

97

As Ginny's departure illustrated, the issue of family dissolution is a critical one in abusive families. Of course, the bottom line in work with violent families is the protection of the victim particularly when the victims are children. This is the case even in "family-oriented agencies" and communities which set family reconstitution as a major goal of treatment.

In the adolescent-maltreatment literature, it has been noted that physically-abused adolescents are both removed from their parents' custody and remove themselves through running away. That this physical separation occurs at a time when the adolescent is psychologically differentiating from his or her parents anyway inexorably leads one to the question of how appropriate physical reconstitution ever is in such cases.

Obviously, in families in which the adolescent victims are younger, a family wish for reconstitution is usually present. Though the differentiation process may have begun, the adolescent may be too young to "launch." In cases of extreme abuse or when the adolescents are older, however, problem-solving may focus on separation.

It is useful to examine the separation-differentiation issue along two different axes: (1) whether the separation occurs in a planned, orderly, or disorderly manner; and (2) whether it results in an experience which is basically positive or negative for the child.

A positive, orderly separation is exemplified by those adolescents who are removed or leave home of their own volition, state their intention not to return home, and receive the blessing of their parents. This includes young people who work out their own alternative living arrangements including enlisting in the military, the Job Corps, or a similar organization. The worker's role in such cases is to serve as a broker and information resource as these plans are being negotiated.

Some adolescents are removed from their homes in an orderly manner but with a negative outcome. This category includes young people who are ultimately removed by the courts, and are placed in a juvenile correctional facility, for delinquent behaviors which occurred before, after, or concurrently with their abuse. Had Junior been removed from James and Sarah, obviously this is the category into which he would have fallen.

Some kids leave home under very disorderly circumstances but with positive results. They remove themselves through running away during a crisis and may even stay on the streets for a while. At the same time, however, they have demonstrated the resolve to protect themselves, and one hopes they can learn from their parents' mistakes. In such cases the worker may serve as a broker between the typically angry adolescent and his or her angry parents while the family attends to the issue of emotional separation. Such work is very important for those siblings who have been left behind. It is into this category that I would place Ginny's departure, inasmuch as her leaving was neither negotiated with nor blessed by her parents.

Unfortunately, there are also numerous negative and disorderly separations. In these cases, young people sometimes take an impulsive leap into a bad marriage in which the conflicts of the family of origin are only duplicated. In my experience, these kids frequently attempt to come home again — if not in a literal, in a symbolic sense. The worker may contribute here by noting this possibility and helping the family prepare for this return.

After Ginny left, the whole tone of our meetings changed again. Sarah's attendence became perfunctory and obligatory, though seemingly she didn't trust me to see Raylene and Richy by myself. I was determined to see them, however — my impasse with the adults had not lessened my responsibility to them — and Sarah knew that. Just as importantly, her calling about her father ceased.

At nine months, we hit the time for Junior's second follow-up hearing. With Ginny gone and Junior having become disinterested in the telephone, it was decided that the family did not have to remain in counseling unless they so chose. Not surprisingly, they didn't. As abruptly as we had started, we stopped.

EPILOGUE

One afternoon, four months after Junior's second hearing, the director of the local Women's Shelter called.

"We have a woman here with two kids," she says. "She was not attacked personally but her daughter, Raylene, was beat up by her husband. She wanted the child to stay with her instead of going into foster care so we agreed to take them in temporarily. I was asking her if anything like this had ever happened before and she said that it had and you had seen the family for a while. I was wondering if there is anything you could tell me about her situation since we are attempting to do some long-range planning."

"I'm not sure I know anything Sarah can't tell you herself, but if she signs a release, I'll be glad to talk or drop by. In the meantime, please tell her I hope Raylene and Richy are alright."

Sarah did have a plan, though it was hard for me to tell at the time just how many people she was leaving behind. ◀

REFERENCES

Beck, A. (1979) *Cognitive Therapy of Depression*. New York: Guilford.
Beels, E. and Ferber, A. (1969) Family Therapy: A View. *Family Process* 8: 280–332.
Berenson, D. (1976) Alcohol and the Family System. In Phil Guerin (ed.) *Family Therapy: Theory and Practice*. New York: Gardner Press.
Bowen, M. (1978) *Family Therapy in Clinical Practice*. New York: Jason Aronson.
Fischer, B. and Berdie, J. (1978) Adolescent Abuse and Neglect. *Child Abuse and Neglect* 2: 173–92.
Flanzer, J. (1978) Family Focused Management: Treatment of Choice for Deviant and Dependent Families. *International Journal of Family Therapy* 6(1): 25–31.
Flanzer, J. and Sturkie, K. (1983) *Final Report: The Arkansas Alcohol and Child Abuse Demonstration Project*. Little Rock, Ark. (unpublished manuscript).
Frank, J. (1972) *Persuasion and Healing*. Baltimore: Johns Hopkins University Press.
Gabriano, J. (1980) Meeting the Needs of Mistreated Youth. *Social Work* 24: 122–26.
Goldstein, H. (1973) *Social Work Practice: A Unitary Approach*. Columbia: University of South Carolina Press.
—— (1981) *Social Learning and Change*. Columbia: University of South Carolina Press; pbk edn 1984, New York and London: Tavistock.
—— (1982) Cognitive Approaches to Direct Practice. *Social Service Review* 56 (4): 539–55.
Haley, J. (1972) Approaches to Family Therapy. In J. Haley (ed.) *Changing Families*. New York: Grune & Stratton.
—— (1976) *Probem-Solving Therapy*. San Francisco: Jossey-Bass.
Hoffman, L. (1980) The Family Life Cycle and Discontinuous Change. In E. Carter and M. McGoldrick (eds) *The Family Life Cycle: A Framework for Family Therapy*. New York: Gardner Press.
Libbey, P. and Bybee, R. (1979) The Physical Abuse of Adolescents. *Journal of Social Issues* 35 (2): 101–26.
London, P. (1964) *The Modes and Morals of Psychotherapy*. New York: Holt, Rinehart & Co.
Lourie, I. (1977) The Phenomenon of the Abused Adolescent. *Victimology* 2: 268–76.
—— (1979) Family Dynamics and the Abuse of Adolescents. *Child Abuse and Neglect* 3: 967–74.

Lourie, I. and Stefano, L. (1977) On Defining Emotional Abuse. In M. Lauderdale (ed.) *Child Abuse and Neglect: Issues in Innovation and Implementation*. Washington, D.C.: DHEW.

Madanes, C. (1980) *Strategic Family Therapy*. San Francisco: Jossey-Bass.

Madanes, C. and Haley, J. (1977) Dimensions of Family Therapy. *Journal of Nervous and Mental Disorders* 165: 88–98.

Minuchin, S. (1974) *Families and Family Therapy*. Cambridge: Harvard University Press.

Napier, A. and Whitaker, C. (1978) *The Family Crucible*. New York: Harper & Row.

National Study of the Incidence of Child Abuse and Neglect (1981) Washington, DC: NCCAN, Dept. Health and Human Services.

Olson, D., Sprenkle, D., and Russell, C. (1979) Circumplex Model of Marital and Family Systems. *Family Process* 18 (1): 3–23.

Pelton, L. (1978) Child Abuse and Neglect: The Myth of Classlessness. *American Journal of Orthopsychiatry* 48: 608–17.

Straus, M. (1974) Leveling, Civility, and Violence in the Family. *Journal of Marriage and the Family* 36: 13–79.

Stuart, R. (1979) *Helping Couples Change*. New York: Guilford.

Sturkie, K. (1979) A Survey of Family Treatment Orientations Employed by Social Work Practitioners. University of Southern California (unpublished dissertation).

Sturkie, K. and Flanzer, J. (1981) An Examination of Two Social Work Treatment Models with Abusive Families. *Social Work Papers* 16: 53–62.

Watzlawick, P., Beavin, J., and Jackson, D. (1967) *The Pragmatics of Human Communication*. New York: Norton.

Watzlawick, P., Weakland, J., and Fisch, R. (1974) *Change*. New York: Norton.

Whitaker, C. A. and Keith, D. V. (1981) Symbolic–experiential Family Therapy. In A. Gurman and D. Kniskern (eds) *Handbook of Family Therapy*. New York: Brunner/Mazel.

Chapter 4

The Chronically Ill Patient:
A Cognitive-Existential Approach to
Medical Social Work

AUDREY BOHNENGEL-LEE

The types of patients seeking medical treatment have changed drastically over the last three decades. With improvements in civil engineering and public health, as well as the advent of antibiotics and vaccinations, diseases due to infection no longer account for the majority of hospitalized patients. In former times, treatment of these acute conditions was characterized by a specific outcome; patients were either cured or they died. Now that there are more effective remedies to these acute illnesses, it is the person with a chronic ailment that has become the typical patient. But the treatment of chronic conditions does not produce clear and immediate results. Instead, these patients live, in some cases for years, in the shadows of the medical-delivery system. These are the patients who frequent doctors' offices and occupy hospital beds during their many re-admissions to acute-care settings. These are the people whose care poses unique problems to our health-care system. It is the provision of medical care for this population that now challenges the entire medical-care system.

In response to the unique needs of these patients, the medical profession has developed a wider range and more sophisticated levels of specialization. The organizational structure of institutions has changed. It is no longer unusual for hospitals to have a variety of specialty units, e.g. the oncology ward, the cardiac monitoring unit, and the surgical and medical intensive care units. Likewise, doctors are pursuing careers in subspecialties. This degree of refinement clearly reflects the medical profession's recognition that the medical needs of these patients require the particular knowledge of the various specializations.

High technology and specialization are not without considerable expense, however. For example, the annual bill sent to the government to maintain about 60,000 dialysis patients is now estimated at $1.4 billion. When it was believed that resources were limitless, these expenses went unnoticed in the name of humanitarianism. But now, as the government's Medicare and Medicaid programs pay a substantial part of the bill and society is becoming more sensitive to the cost, legislators are questioning the benefits derived from these health-care programs.

The capability to extend life seemingly indefinitely with the assistance of medical-support systems gives rise to many difficult ethical issues. In a system with limited resources, how does one determine an equitable and just plan for distribution? (Who should receive which resources and for how long?) One approach has been to consider who would benefit the most from receiving medical care and delineating when the benefit is outweighed by the liability. For example, how does one reconcile the worth of life with the cost of medical treatment? "Benefit" remains a difficult concept to define but is generally related to whether the patient is rehabilitated in accord with his or her own definition. Thus, attention is now shifting to factors affecting quality of life. Are people with chronic illnesses able to maintain a meaningful, purposeful, and productive life? What are the problems imposed by a chronic disease which may interfere with a person's ability to achieve a satisfying life and how are they overcome?

Chronically ill patients are faced with many losses and the need to learn to live the lives of "marginal people." Neither healthy nor ill, they are left to create a lifestyle which accommodates both states. They are frequently expected to live "as though they are 'healthy' and will live indefinitely." For example, just ten years ago young men with testicular cancer faced a 90 per cent probability of dying within a year of the diagnosis. Now they have a 90 per cent chance of being "cured" (i.e. five years with no signs of recurrence), which means living with uncertainty and less assurance of a predictable future. For some, chronic illness means a constant vigilance for signs of a recurrence, while for others such as arthritis patients, it's a fight to manage pain, as during the periodic attacks of inflamed joints. For still other patients, chronic disease means loss of function and the loss of the ability to perform accustomed social roles. The chronically ill face uncertainty not only about their longevity, but also their day-to-day well-being. The patient with sickle-cell anemia can feel fine but, with the sudden onset of a sickle crisis, will be reduced to intractable, debilitating pain with little to no warning. The future is not only uncertain, it is also unpredictable and frequently beyond the patient's control. As the trajectory or course of illness varies from disease to disease, the feared element of the disease which is hidden in the uncertain future also varies from person to person. For some it is pain, for others loss of function and physical control, and for others it is the loss of life itself.

The chronically ill patient must also contend with a medical treatment which may be almost as debilitating as the disease. It is not unusual to hear hemodialysis patients complain that they feel far worse after their treatments than before. Other treatments, like radiation and chemotherapy, can be disfiguring with the loss of hair or the development of a cushnoid appearance after a regimen of steroids. Some diseases are managed in part through special dietary restrictions which require self-discipline and the avoidance or limitation of particular types of foods. The diabetic must limit sugars, the heart patient salt and cholesterol and the renal patient must limit protein, sodium, potassium, and fluids, just to mention a few.

As the physical needs of the chronically ill patient are different from those of the acutely ill, so also are their psychological and social needs. The impact of an illness is not limited to its effects on the body but also has far-reaching ramifications for the realms of the social and psychological reactions to disease. The family unit also undergoes many changes in adjusting to the altered state of one of its members. Responsibilities are frequently shifted to other, healthy family members. Although they do not adjust directly in reaction to the disease, they too must adapt to change. Not only are they expected to accept some responsibility for the care of their family member, but they must alter their plans for the future. Because of additional obligations they may not be as free to travel or as available to career opportunities. In the midst of major life-changes, the chronically ill frequently meet the world and their families with anger, hostility, depression and embitterment as though the world was responsible, with the patient feeling somewhat cheated.

Multiple approaches have been used to understand powerful emotions. Kübler-Ross's work in the 1960s represents the advent of a new understanding of the dying and grieving process. Her work is as relevant to those adjusting to the loss of function due to a chronic illness as it is to the terminally ill. In her original book, *On Death and Dying* (1969), she not only explored how patients adjust to a terminal disease but also scrutinized what influence the medical professionals had on this process as well as their reactions to the dying process. Her work cast light on the medical staff's difficulty in accepting a patient's death and the staff's tendency to avoid or dismiss conversation with patients regarding their mortality. These findings provoked many questions with respect to how our society in general regards the issues pertaining to death. On closer observation, what becomes apparent is that in our fear of death we deny its implications and finality. To further protect ourselves from these existential anxieties, we send the chronically and terminally ill away. In the 1960s, people did not remain at home in their familiar surroundings with the loved ones attending to their needs as was the custom in Europe. Instead, they went to the hospital to die.

During the late 1960s and early 1970s our social standards on how to die were adjusted, seemingly in response to our fear of facing death. Rather than denying the eventuality of death, we now began to romanticize it. Films such as Segal's *Love Story* was the first of a series as Hollywood draped the sad and tragic lives of those who were young and dying or permanently disabled with artificial trappings that reduced the anxiety and fear associated with these conditions.

Unlike Hollywood's portrayal, people who are dying are not always likeable, or even reasonable. To the contrary, many patients facing chronic or terminal disease exhibit a full range of emotions, many of which are quite unpleasant and include denial, anxiety, anger, and depression. Some mental health care givers, particularly those who follow a psychiatric model, identify these emotions as psychopathological, overlooking the possibility that they may be a necessary part of a natural reaction in the dying or grieving process. Consequently, these disquieting emotions are labeled as deviant or abnormal, and as such become the focus of psychiatric intervention. However, as a result of continuing research, expectations regarding the psychological aspects of normal human behavior have changed. Today many are questioning the appropriateness of imposing a psychiatric model on chronically or terminally ill populations. A psychopathological approach assumes that neurotic anxiety or anger associated with chronic illness is generated by unrealistic fears spawned during childhood. To expect people to face a life-threatening or chronic illness with confidence and with freedom from anxiety, depression, fear or anger is unrealistic. Such adaptation frequently requires a compromise of physical capabilities or resignation to the loss of physical function and freedom to perform typical tasks. Risk-taking, in an attempt to establish new limits and to minimize the effect of that loss, frequently culminates in a series of failures leading to discouragement and frustration until the new boundaries are tested and proven. The anxieties and fears associated with adaptation are a natural part of the process. In fact, one noted psychiatrist who spent much of his professional career studying the adaptive process of renal-failure patients, reported on his own personal struggle with heart disease:

> [Psycho]analysis did little to help me accept my illness or come to grips with many of my obsessional fears about it. I have concluded that my heart disease is a part of me and that my anxieties about it will always be with me. They are never out of my mind.... I know nowhere to go with my anxiety but to live with it.
> (Abram 1977: 226)

An alternative to the psychopathological approach to understanding the chronically ill patient can be found in crisis theory (Hill 1958). Many clinicians have found this to be a useful model; perhaps its greatest contribution is its introduction of the idea that adaptation involves a dynamic process which normally encompasses a wide range of emotional reactions. From this perspective, the individual is conceived of as an open system in transaction with the environment — constantly influencing and being influenced by that environment. With the onset of the crisis, the individual, stunned, disorganized and overwhelmed by the new situation, finds him- or herself unable to integrate and comprehend the elements of the crisis. With time, the situation takes on better definition and one begins to understand one's state. As more information about the nature of the crisis is incorporated, coping strategies are adjusted until a new steady state is established. The shortcoming of this theory, however is that it fails to provide us with any explanation of the cognitive process used to interpret environmental information, how understanding is formulated, which aspects of the self are protected, and how the desired end or new steady state is established. Goldstein's paradigm of the self and cognitions fills this void.

Changes in the Self with Chronic Disease

With the onset of a chronic disease, the sense of future necessarily takes on a new meaning. Those who become ill face the sudden loss of future goals and aspirations: projected hopes, plans or dreams to partake of, watch, do and even be, begin to dissolve. Their ability to deal with their immediate environment to prove their mastery and secure a future goal is compromised. When one's future is uncertain, ordinary goal-directed behaviors lose their meanings and frequently are seen as useless. Careers may suddenly be lost after many years of hard work and the satisfaction of success that comes with achievement is denied. Child-rearing may be radically changed for the person who no longer has the strength to lift the toddler; one may be deprived of the pride and joy of seeing children graduate from school as well as other rewards of parenthood. Plans to travel after retirement may be impossible and other fruits of one's labor may remain untasted. As ability is lost and life goals are dashed, the intentional, motivational inclinations of the individual are compromised.

With the onset of a physical disease and the loss of these future goals, the self-concept is brought into conflict. Some patients must confront the physical effects and palpable signs of treatment or the symptoms of their disease. Others must contend with the loss of strength which has been sapped by some invisible, insidious process invading their bodies. Both the disease processes as well as the treatment can alter physical attractiveness, replacing vitality and health with the ashen tones of sickness. The identity of the self also may be altered as one's membership in various social or reference groups is challenged by the loss of physical strength and energy. Mr B., a twenty-five-year-old dialysis patient who had recently received a kidney transplant, illustrates this point in the following comments regarding his relationship with his girlfriend:

The change that happened was funny. I used to think that she was wonderful and enjoyed her being outspoken. After I got sick, things changed. She still wanted to do the things that I had liked when I was healthy, like hanging out at bars. But after I got sick I couldn't do that anymore and she started lying to me. I think what happened was I got sick and went through all those silly stages. You know, blaming everyone else for what had happened, being hard to get along with and short tempered with everyone. I think that that was the problem. Now I am different and I don't care about hanging out at bars and drinking all the time so we don't have much in common anymore.

After receiving a kidney transplant, Mr B. compares his new state of well-being with that during his time on dialysis:

With dialysis I never felt good; I didn't want to be around no people and I was grouchy. If people came by, I'd just go sit by myself. Now it is different, I enjoy being with people. First of all, I just feel good and I don't feel tired. Before people would talk about what they did during the day. What was I gonna say? "Well, I spent three-and-a-half hours on dialysis and the next eight in the bed." I had nothing to say and really didn't care about what they did 'cause it only made me miss what I couldn't do.

Gender identity may also suffer when a disease affects primary or secondary sexual organs or sexual characteristics. Women on dialysis rarely have regular menstrual periods and men are often sterile and impotent. Much has already been written about women who have mastectomies or hysterectomies and the impact of these losses on their self-esteem. When people define themselves according to the functions they serve or the titles they hold and lose the capacity to fulfill these obligations, what happens to their personal definitions of self-worth? Mr G., a dialysis patient, describes the impact of his inability to maintain premorbid functioning:

> I didn't want them [friends] to know what was happening because I didn't want them to feel sorry for me. I hate that. I don't want anyone's sympathy and for them to say "poor Joe" or "his poor wife," I guess it makes me feel like less of a man. Before I got sick I used to do a lot of things around the house like take care of bills and stuff but now my wife does all of that. I want to do as much as I can for myself. I don't like being taken care of. You wonder what good you are.

We can appreciate the impact of an illness on the self-concept only through an understanding of how one builds a reality that connects one's inner self with the outer reality of one's life's state. This process of reality building is blocked by dissonance in the case of chronic illness particularly when one's physical limitations are inconsistent with one's self-definition. From a cognitive perspective, the task is to reconcile the schism between the individual's premorbid expectations of self and his or her current level of functioning, meanwhile preserving or developing a new sense of self-worth. Each disease will have a unique effect on each person and that person's definition of the self. One's mode of adapting to an illness will be unique and dependent upon one's conceptions of one's own life and the meaning which the loss imposes on future goals and self-concept.

Chronic illness and consciousness

The first task in comprehending how patients understand their disease and what meaning it has for them and their family is to enter their reality. This reality is a composite of the shared symbols which we utilize in social interactions as well as the subjective awarenesses which are unique to each one of us.

Patients might build their reality by the use of a number of cognitive functions. One is the intellect which collects and integrates information to formulate a more or less objective understanding of their illness. Medical staff, doctors, nurses and dieticians as well as various technicians will offer "factual" information about the disease, its cause (if known), treatment, the disease process or trajectory (static or progressive), and the prognosis. Rarely, however is a patient's understanding of the disease limited to these factors. Patients may also draw from their previous life experiences which brought them into contact with others who had had similar conditions. Or they might seek out other patients to inquire about how their experiences were for them. Patients may also request reading material to broaden their knowledge of their disease.

However, it is not safe to assume that because the information — written or verbal — has been given that it has also been received or, if it has been received, that it is understood in the way it was given. Instead, there are many points at which an obvious fact may be given an altered interpretation. For example, patients selectively attend to the myriad of stimuli in- and outside themselves and may often deny knowledge of their condition even immediately following a seemingly intelligent and open conversation with their physician. At times this ignorance may result from the fact that the information is given in technical terms that are incomprehensible. However, at other times this apparent denial may reflect information overload — a state when the patient is no longer able to contend with an excess of disturbing information. Other patients may acknowledge hearing certain devastating information but then dismiss its importance by adding: "But the doctor didn't seem worried so I don't think that it is too bad." When affect and content are incongruent, confusion is created. In an attempt to resolve this dissonance some patients may attend only to the less disturbing information while others may lean toward attending to one form of communication over the other. For example, one patient reported the following:

When he [the doctor] came in [to the hospital room] he was smiling and seemed happy. When he said that I couldn't donate the kidney to my dad — that the transplant was off — I couldn't believe it. I though he was just joking and I kept telling him that I didn't believe what he was saying. I finally realized that he wasn't joking and after he left, I got mad. Seemed like he was making fun of me — that that was why he was smiling.

In this case, is the patient's confusion a matter of selective attention, information distortion, denial, or was the physician inadvertently

communicating a mixed message? For the doctor, the verbal message was
the more significant while for the patient, it was the emotion (smiles and
happiness) that initially caught her attention.

At the intellectual level, data about one's condition, capabilities and
losses are also collected through physical activity and observation, as well
as somatic awareness of more subtle changes that may be preclinical and
undetected by laboratory tests. By successive trials, while risking failure
and hoping for success, new limits of activity are tested to discriminate
between those which are still possible and those which are lost.
Consciousness of one's body image and functional capabilities is
developed and tested in this manner. At times this awareness will conflict
with what others say and predict; patients may find that they are able to
achieve more or less than what their doctors had indicated. Where the
over-achiever may experience great pride, the under-achiever has an
additional problem to resolve: one must struggle with the question of
whether the physician is incorrect, or whether one is a failure or too lazy
to achieve potential. Typically, an easy way of resolving this conflict is by
discrediting the physician's credibility.

A second factor affecting consciousness is the kind of subjective
"knowing" that appears in the sudden flash of awareness — often in the
form of personal images. These images may not, at the moment, be
translated into communicable concepts; rather, they are retained in this
state until some future time when, in response to a critical event, they are
expressed as beliefs or opinions. For example, every hospital has its story
of the patient who did not want to go to a nursing home but had no other
alternative. Knowing the patient's troubled feelings about the discharge
arrangements, plans were made by the staff and the discharge date set up
without informing the patient. On the designated day, shortly before
being informed of the pending arrangements, the patient dies. Did this
patient "know" about the plans which were so unacceptable? Another
example of this type of awareness is found in dreams. At times events
may be extremely frightening and create so much dissonance that the
patient is prevented from processing data at the factual, analytic level. At
these times, dreams may be the patient's only means of expression. For
example, a renal transplant patient reported the following experience:

After the doctor told me that I had started rejection, I was so upset I didn't know
what to do. I went and sat in the bathroom and held my head. Then when you
came by later, there were so many things going on inside my head but I couldn't
find the words to tell you about them. That night I had a dream. I dreamed that my

body was covered with antibodies and no matter how hard I tried I couldn't brush them off. I guess that it was from all that talk about rejection.

These cognitions, the literal and imagined pieces of data which are products of both the intellect and the subjective "knowing," are organized into patterns of thought which represent individual, stylistic variations. One factor affecting how these thoughts are organized is the individual's belief system which includes assumptions about oneself, one's health, the contingencies that link one's behavior with the occurrence of specific events, and above all, the order or purpose of life events. The literature on the problems of adaptation for the chronically ill is replete with references to the patient's question, "Why me?", or "How did this happen?" and "For what purpose?" These questions reveal the human need for order, the belief that events do not occur serendipitously but for some specified outcome which has meaning and significance. The types of answers which patients give to these questions reveal much regarding how they order their reality, what contingencies, if any, they perceive in relating events to each other, and how they understand what their lives are all about. These answers include: (1) shifting responsibility for and control over their condition to other, more powerful people; (2) perceiving the course of events to be under their own control; (3) a belief that fate causes things to happen; or (4) a belief in a specific divine purpose — simply, an act orchestrated by God.

Those who search for an external cause place much negative or positive weight on their physicians: "If my doctor had taken better care of me, this wouldn't have happened" or "I don't worry about anything — I know my doctor will take care of it." By shifting control to others, the world appears to remain predictable and orderly even though it is managed by others.

In contrast, other people construct their reality on the assumption that they are able to control or at least have some influence over their life's events. These are the people who take charge of their life situation. Bulman and Wortman (1977) in their study of paralyzed accident-victims found that those patients who coped effectively tended to perceive themselves as being responsible for their accident even when, from an objective point of view, they could not be held accountable. For example, some said that if they had not decided to accept a ride with a friend they would not have been involved in the ensuing accident; therefore, only they are responsible. The researchers interpreted these reactions as revealing the need to perceive events as following some understandable order which was under the individual's control.

111

The third method of understanding contingencies between events is through belief in a cosmic order or fate. Occasionally, when patients have been asked if they had been able to discover an answer to the question "Why me?", they have responded "Why not me?" What usually follows then are comments such as "Things are always hard for me" or "No matter what I do things always turn out wrong — like there is a curse on my life." This position seems to reflect a belief in fate and the acceptance of a destiny which one cannot alter. Their illness, probably seen as similar to other life events, happened as a part of a general life-pattern which continues to evolve through its own energy. From this perspective, events are beyond human control but follow some preordained order. Although events are not occurring haphazardly, and life is orderly and predictable, it is also not under human control.

The last approach to understanding the order of events is through a spiritual faith in a divine being who structures life in accord with a preconceived purpose. For those who are chronically ill and are trying to respond to a situation which is truly beyond human control, great comfort is derived from such a faith. These people search for the lesson to be learned from adversity and pain. They struggle to understand God's purpose and the reason they are being tested through a disease. For these people, pain takes on a new meaning and purpose, distinct from all the others. These are the people who attempt to rise to the challenge and learn about life, the way of life, and themselves.

As perceptions of life situations vary, so also does the meaning, significance or importance attributed to the event. For some, attention is riveted on the disease and the negative impact it has on their lifestyles. In contrast, other patients who reflect on the totality of their life situations will step back and attempt to integrate rather than analyze the impact of their illness. They look for the larger order of life, for its purpose and value rather than ask the question of culpability. In these patients' perceptions, disease is understood as only one part of a larger, multifaceted existence. In other words, the total impact and overall importance of the disease is given new meaning as it is defined in relationship to other more highly valued factors in life. Rather than its becoming the primary focus of attention and concern, one seeks a purpose which transcends the pain. Often, family and friends and rewarding employment are the typical, overriding considerations which give life purpose and meaning. For example, the following comments are quite common: "I don't think that I could have gone through this if I hadn't had my family for support"; or "It would be different if I didn't have my wife and child who need me to take care of them. I can't give in or give up."

As can be seen, these cognitive patterns express the patient's "schema"; how one understands oneself in relationship to one's world and what gives life events meaning and purpose. The disease is given meaning in relationship to the self and the self is redefined relative to the disease. Patients differentially select and attend to different types of information. Some will rely primarily on the factual data, interpreted intellectually, to formulate an understanding of reality — i.e. what, physiologically, is happening within their bodies. In contrast, others construct a more encompassing spiritual interpretation so as to comprehend the significance of these disturbing events while placing less importance on objective information. Perceived contingencies and causality also vary. In some situations the perceptions of these conditions may strengthen one's worldview while in others, one's basic assumptions about life are threatened, producing a degree of dissonance which forces one to reconsider old belief systems. Elements which had never been questioned, aspects of life which had been ignored or taken for granted, now take on a new importance. Even awarenesses of basic bodily functions, such as urination in the case of renal failure, or breathing in the case of asthma or emphysema, now take on an inordinate importance.

The point to be made thus far is that it would be erroneous to assume that a patient's concern and understanding of the disease is limited to the factual information he or she receives regarding its process, treatment and prognosis. These facts are also contemplated in relation to their impact on other aspects of the patient's life which he or she defines as important: implications for one's family, the need for assistance from others, loss of control, and forced dependency are but a few considerations. For others, it is the fear of the unknown that lies on the other side of death, the leaving of unfinished business, or the loss of family.

Among the chronically ill, those who have lost some capability or function have to confront the loss of future potential to enjoy rewarding experiences. The loss of a leg is the loss of being able to walk, as well as the future dreams or aspirations which are dependent upon that ability to walk; for the terminally ill, it is the loss of a future. Recalling the dimensions of the self, one's loss of future dreams and goals or aspirations results in the loss of an essential aspect of the self, that of motive and intention. Thus the process of adapting to a chronic illness cuts deeply into the very essence of the person. Adaptation constitutes the process by which patients develop and construct a new way of defining themselves in some ways consistent with the limitations of the disease. This is the process which most clinicians refer to as "acceptance." More precisely, we underscore the acceptance of self despite the loss rather than acceptance of the disease per se.

The adaptive process as described by Kübler-Ross (1969) entails the resolution of questions on several levels, including the essential and the existential. This process of adapting to a chronic disease is frequently defined in the literature in terms of adjusting to a "loss," but little mention is made about what is actually lost. By implication, it is loss of function. But much more is at stake in this catastrophe; there is also the loss of hopes, dreams, and the "perfect" future.

Adaptation

Because the significance of these losses or fears can be overwhelming and immobilizing, particularly as the patient and family are initially struck by a new diagnosis, multiple techniques can be used to help cushion the shock. Adaptation to a major life-change follows a process, the elements of which are as varied as the number of people who are adjusting to a chronic disease. However, there are some general similarities which have been recognized to repeat themselves with some regularity across a large population. At first, when the medical information is too overwhelming to be incorporated into one's life images, information is selectively filtered — a process which some call "denial." This state should not be confused with ignorance or lack of information. Most clinicians have come to realize that this stage of adaptation to a loss constitutes an extremely important coping strategy. Inattention and the inability to process threatening information allows time to mobilize energy for confronting the meaning of the loss. Later, new dreams and directions in life that might be compatible with the disease will be developed. This hiatus in time provides a sanctuary of sorts during which the patient has the option of formulating a new self-definition.

Denial, or the failure to integrate data, is manifest in any of several different forms: denial of fact, denial of consequence, denial of implication, or denial of feeling. The *denial of fact* is evident when the essential symptoms of the disease are refuted and is illustrated by such comments as : "What disease? I'm not sick." When facts relative to one's health are denied, imprudent or self-destructive behavior may follow. If the patient has no apparent reason to comply with medical advice, the disease process can be hastened.

The second form, *denial of consequence*, is suggested by such comments as: "This is temporary, it will go away." If people believe that their condition is only transient, they can avoid facing the implications of the loss. Although the realization of the permanence of a condition may eventually evolve, the difficulty here is that the patient's natural support system which might rally at the critical onset of a problem may erode before the patient begins the adaptive process.

The third type is *denial of implication*. Here patients acknowledge that they have a disease which is not likely to be cured, but deny that it will necessitate a change in their life. The disease is stripped of its import, and patients believe that they will not need to adjust their basic assumptions about themselves. This state is revealed in comments such as: "So what if I am sick, it really won't change anything — it's not a big deal unless you make one out of it." This form of denial is difficult for family members who actually observe changes which the patient continues to avoid or fails to acknowledge.

The last form is *denial of feelings*. Here the patient intellectually acknowledges the permanence of the disease and the implications for change but disallows that he or she is upset: "I'm not going to let it get me down." With this form of denial it is always difficult to ascertain if the patient's verbal comments indeed reflect denial or possibly other factors. For example, in the case of denial of fact or consequence it is always possible that the patient has not been fully informed or has not been informed in a way which he or she can comprehend and integrate. When feelings are denied, patients simply may be protecting their "public" self while struggling privately with their pain as well as with a self-definition that precludes the sharing of their feelings with others.

These four types of denial constitute the essential factors to be resolved: the integration of the facts, consequences, implications, and feelings jointly constitute the meaning of the disease through multiple layers of cognitions. Most people striving to adapt to a disease experience some or all of these levels of denial. This process is quite normal. A problem develops only when the patient becomes "stuck" at one stage — particularly when this interferes with the patient's compliance with the medical regimen. Obviously if patients do not believe that they have a chronic, life-threatening disease they will be less likely to follow medical recommendations, particularly if these include some noxious process such as self-deprivation through diet restrictions. If the patient believes that the condition is time-limited or will have only a limited effect upon lifestyle, the implications of that disease process and the necessity for adjustment will be minimal. Finally, if feelings are denied, if patients avoid or suppress all emotional reactions to their disease, adaptation is limited to the narrow intellectual realm of awareness.

Adaptation then refers to integrating new information, the intellectual and subjective awarenesses about one's life, into one's orientation about the world. It is the process of redefining one's conception of self, reconsidering some basic assumptions about the order of the universe and resolving any disparity in the relationship between the two. The process is slow, particularly when the repercussions of the disease are extreme, cutting through to even the most fundamental expectations of life. Needless to say, this is a painful process, a venture which most people do not undertake without some purpose. Under consideration is not only a way of life, but also a belief about life itself: the things we value and hold as being of import and worth in our lives are now at risk and the turmoil which ensues can reach into the bare essence of one's very understanding of life. Many patients report a reassessment of the things in their lives which have significant meaning for them. These major life-changes produce a sense of disorientation, of being "out of touch," which sometimes raises questions of one's basic ability to "test reality." At this point some patients question whether they are "going crazy." If this disorganization leads to reorganization the patient is likely to see and interpret his or her life in very different ways. For example, altruistic goals and spiritual endeavors may replace a former interest in the acquisition of material goods or power as the primary motivators in establishing a meaningful direction in life. Not all patients complete this transformation. Some are too fearful even to begin, to take the leap of faith and risk which entails giving up the security of the "known." To do so leaves one with the uneasy experience of being out of control and helpless. These patients struggle and refuse to relinquish their premorbid lifestyle and remain stagnant — caught in one of the stages of denial. These are the patients who develop problems in the future: the dissonance between their expectations for life and their ability to function and achieve these goals becomes too great to suppress or ignore. Others are willing to enter the turmoil of adaptation but become frightened and resist the flow of change as they struggle to recapture or regain what has already been lost. They are the ones who are hospitalized in acute panic — suspended between the identities they have abdicated to the disease and a new level of self-awareness that is not yet formulated. This state may produce such acute distress that some consider suicide or with-drawal from treatment as their only options to escape from the emotional pain. These are the patients who experience a profound sense of hopelessness through loss of meaning in life and identity.

A third group may retreat from the adaptive process for still very different reasons, particularly when the physical pain and limitations necessitated by the treatment are worse than the consequences of the disease — when the quality of life has ebbed and the misery inflicted by the treatment is no longer justified. Although most people continue to re-evaluate their lives in such a way that they are able to find value and worth despite their limitations and avoid such decisions, a few request to withdraw from treatment. Most professionals who have worked with chronically and terminally ill patients have faced this dilemma at least once. The difficulty is determining how to discriminate between those patients who are caught in the panic between identities and those who have rationally chosen to live without the assistance of a life-sustaining treatment. Is the patient truly choosing his or her destiny, or is the decision made in the midst of a transitory depression which will pass as the patient changes the outlook on the quality of his or her life? Differentiating between the two states is never easy.

Schreiner and Tartaglia (1978) reported on two such cases with dialysis patients. Both patients stated that they wanted to withdraw from dialysis — a decision which would result in certain death. The medical staff assumed that these requests were made while the patients were depressed and uremic, a metabolic condition which can produce mental-status changes. As a result, the staff suggested several weeks of more rigorous dialysis treatments before complying with the patients' requests. Following this plan, both patients returned to their doctors. One patient commented: "I'm glad that you didn't listen to me when I was wanting to be withdrawn from treatment." In contrast, the second patient continued to insist upon being free from dialysis. For him a truncated life without restrictions was more satisfying than the pro-longed existence with dialysis. Clearly, life for the chronically ill is so different from that of a healthy person that we can hardly apply our standards or values to the lives of the ill and make judgments regarding what their future decisions ought to be. Our only recourse is to allow, if not encourage, our patients to bring forth what is real and meaningful for them and to help them make their own decisions based on what they value and hold to be of worth and meaning.

Moral and ethical issues obviously come into question any time a patient requests to have life-sustaining treatments terminated. Although these issues, which theologians and moral philosophers are still debating, are beyond the scope of this essay, we do need to know something about each patient's definition of his or her *own* moral and ethical beliefs. They too must be explored in gaining an understanding of what the patient deems of value in life and how various options may be in fundamental conflict with choices offered by others.

Unlike other more changeable situations in life, living with a chronic disease demands awareness that there is virtually nothing that can be done to change the condition or remove the noxious cause. Adaptation means learning how to live not only with one's disability but also with the constraints imposed by a disease and its treatment. By definition, a chronic condition is not curable. The patient may hope for remission or envision escape through death but unlike, say, the alcoholic who can alter the problem by choosing not to drink, the chronically ill patient cannot actively do anything to escape suffering. In contrast to others in conflict who have some options, the person who is chronically ill cannot implore others to change their behavior, negotiate a new relationship to improve the situation, nor escape from his or her predicament since the conflict remains within the body.

The options typically offered in a problem-solving approach are simply not available to these patients. Their condition is not a state over which they have control. Hence, their only option is somehow to learn how to live with their physical state. Adjustment must be made as the individual tests the new limitations, risks failure, and contemplates how these changes will alter his or her lifestyle. It is important to note that although the disease has a primary victim, the illness also affects the entire family unit. As the patient is no longer able to maintain previous responsibilities, others must adjust by assuming new tasks and at the same time, share the loss of hopes and dreams.

Some professionals have written that the preferred outcome of the adaptive process is the patient's "acceptance" of the new, limited lifestyle. This over-romanticized goal is not only unrealistic, it is also repugnant to most who work with the chronically ill. It is absurd to expect a young mother to "accept" cancer and the implications of an early death, meanwhile wondering whether her children will even have a memory of her when they are adults. It is unrealistic to expect the executive who has

118

spent a lifetime working toward some end to accept never seeing the fruits of that labor.

The goal of therapy must be threefold. First, patients must construct a new sense of self in terms of who and what they are as well as a redefinition of their bodily image and a sense of self-worth. Secondly, they need to formulate a new understanding of the world about them and how they relate to this world, one which has perhaps violated a trust upon which their life assumptions had been based. Finally, these changes must be considered as they bear on the patient's future, taking account of lost dreams and aspirations. To be of any help in achieving these goals, we must appreciate, even humbly, how the impact of a chronic disease can be so devastating that it forces the individual to lose faith in the most basic and elemental assumptions about life and self. As one faces one's physical vulnerability, all other aspects of the self are also challenged.

ROLE OF PRACTITIONER

Meeting the patient: beginnings

To many people who are ill, the role of the medical social worker or liaison psychiatrist may be obscure. When introducing myself to a patient, I frequently have been greeted with comments such as: "I have a physical disease. I am sick but I am not crazy too." There are good reasons for this kind of response. First, the patient usually did not ask to be seen by a social worker; as far as he knows, he is being treated for a physical condition, not some emotional problem. Second, this comment probably reflects a lack of knowledge about the professional role and its relation to the type of emotional strain which so frequently accompanies a chronic disease — and even more important, what professionals might be able to do to help relieve the strain. Also, if patients are newly diagnosed, they may still be so overwhelmed by the magnitude of what they see happening to them that their emotions are nebulous, without definition and form. We must consider, however, that this comment may reflect a larger, more pervasive pattern in the patient's life — namely the inability to identify, acknowledge, and therefore express his or her deeper emotions.

To begin to appreciate the subjective meaning of the patient's doubtful reaction, a careful explanation of the helper's role in relation to the typical problems faced by many people in similar situations may suffice for some people, along with the reassurance that some kind of emotional reaction is very normal and to be anticipated. In other cases, it may be necessary to wait until the passage of time and familiarity with the medical system and disease allow the patient to feel secure enough to begin to confront the reality of his or her situation and to articulate thoughts and feelings about this sudden change in his or her life. It must also be noted that not everyone with a chronic disease needs or will benefit from the services of a hospital social worker. Families, friends, or clergy often provide the needed support and the opportunity to contemplate the meaning and impact of the disease; the power of a long and loving relationship itself may be what is necessary to help the patient adapt to illness. However, at other times when family members attempt to protect each other from pain or fears associated with the disease, the use of a professional "outsider" may be indicated.

As the helper approaches the patient and begins to create the climate in which communication can develop, the emerging relationship has characteristics which distinguish it from most other social contacts. If helpers have not experienced a life-threatening illness themselves, they cannot know, in subjective terms, the threat that it poses. And if they are tempted to pose a solution for a patient, the response is likely to be: "You don't know what it is like, how it feels to live like this." The gap between the helper and patient may widen further as the patient's life-story and the pain or fear of death associated with the illness awaken, and bring the helper face to face with, his or her own existential fears of mortality. The natural temptation at this point might be to withdraw or to distance oneself from the patient's world by objectifying the patient's state and labeling him or her or the particular condition. This process of separating from the patient gives the helper protection from the emotional threat. Such an escape into "professionalism" must be resisted.

The role of the humanistic helper is extremely demanding at best, for as we attempt to help patients confront their own morbidity (and possibly mortality), our own vulnerability challenges us. If we are honest, we have very little to offer these patients save ourselves and our willingness to be with them as they grapple with the difficult questions which pertain to and penetrate the enigmas of life and death. As patients begin to probe their formerly unquestioned assumptions about the meaning of life, ours also are subject to challenge. We cannot be so arrogant as to suggest that we have useful answers for others; rather, we must be humbled by the dreadfully few choices which these people face. We can share "truths" which we or others have found to be meaningful, but we cannot assume that they are universally relevant. We can walk with or perhaps follow, but we can never lead as the other confronts his or her frailty. We can offer some objective data regarding the usual trajectory of a disease and its probable problems; however, as patients venture to search the recesses of their minds to determine what or who they are or have become, they must make this painful journey alone. Each explorer necessarily blazes a unique trail shaped by one's own meaning, and the nature of one's relationship to these elements. For example, Mrs M., a thirty-year-old woman, wrote the following poem describing her struggle with life and its slowly ebbing process which was taking her away from her son, Shon and husband, Larry:

> I try to be brave for you Larry
> but it's a mask I hide behind
> because I'm dying inside.
> Other people are healthy
> why not me?
> Who can I talk to?
> For Shon, I move around playfully
> what a torment
> to love him, to want to live for him
> and watch the pieces of my body,
> like a scrambled puzzle
> falling apart.

This very personal statement shows that as images are concretized in words, and free-floating amorphous fears take the form of ideas, what seemed at one time to be overwhelming may now become manageable — or at least comprehensible. In the end, the patient may discover that life still has some meaning and value; or, by the same token, that it now is devoid of purpose. In the latter instance, the patient may elect to withdraw from treatment or to refuse any additional procedures. Only the patient bears the consequence of such a decision; only he or she can make it. Therefore, no matter how the social worker and other professionals may try to dissuade the patient from this choice, in the final analysis, only the patient can determine his or her future.

It is obviously disruptive for a medical team to be as open as possible to the patient's deepest fears; thus there is the persisting tendency to shut off any attempts on the patient's part to disclose feelings of anguish. The glib comment, "Don't worry, it will be OK," in response to questions about the state of his or her health or future possibilities insulates the team from these disquieting fears and communicates to the patient that such worries are not acceptable. And, since many people try to be the "good patient," they will not insist on being heard. The result may be that such behavior on the part of the medical team will encourage patients to further deny the meaning and importance of their disease and its consequence. Ironically, the same patients may later be criticized by the staff for not facing their medical state in more "realistic" ways.

As already noted, the goal of helping is to support the patient to achieve a greater degree of personal integration — the evolvement of a conception of self that retains a strong sense of personal worth while acknowledging the limitation of the disease.

There is no one way to begin to achieve this goal, given the complex diversity and interrelationship of factors that characterize each patient's circumstances. Among these many conditions there is, first of all, the level of self-esteem and the general conditions of living that pre-exist the onset of the illness; very simply, how clients think about themselves and the kind of life with which they have been trying to cope sets the starting point of their venture into a redefinition of self, relationships, and the world in general. Second, there are the actual losses and limitations that are peculiar to the patient's particular condition: clearly, it makes considerable difference if these limitations bear on diet, mobility, typical activities, or other restrictions. Third, there is the question of opportunity. Are there sufficient outlets in the client's environment and relationships that will allow him or her to pursue some sort of productivity and reward? And finally, we must consider that these and other factors are contingent on the trajectory of the disease and the course of treatment. The interdependence of these conditions can be illustrated in the following example.

Mrs G. is a thirty-year-old diabetic patient with recent onset of blindness and renal failure. She has been married for ten years to a man who is now thirty-three. Mr G. had been laid off from his job which culminated in an exacerbation of his former drinking problem. With the onset of his wife's blindness, he no longer beat her but instead resorted to verbal abuse. As she described her situation during her initial adjustment period to dialysis, Mrs G. stated that life would have meaning as long as she could still walk outside, feel the sun on her face, hear the birds, and play her music. However, as her diabetes progressed, her neuropathy became worse and she became wheelchair-bound. Likewise, she began to notice some hearing loss. At the same time, her husband was diagnosed as having cancer of the pancreas and was given a prognosis of one to three years to live. At this point both partners were included in therapy sessions. As Mr G. was helped to face his own mortality, he became much more understanding of his wife's situation. Responsively, she began to appreciate his fears and apprehensions. A few weeks later, when both were unexpectedly hospitalized, they were evicted from their apartment and lost most of their possessions. Mrs G.'s mother and sister arrived from outoftown to help re-establish the couple. This gesture enabled Mrs G. to see her family and their support as something that provided her with the reason to continue living. As Mrs G. experiences additional physical losses which preclude her enjoyment of music, she now states that family love and support are the most critical factors in her life.

The crucial element of this case was Mrs G.'s sense of worth that allowed her to redefine the things in her life which would provide pleasure and meaning despite some incredible losses. Clearly not all chronically ill patients are so determined. Many give up much earlier by withdrawing from an active and meaningful life to settle for a state of low-level and chronic depression. This is the group that confronts most medical social workers.

At times the trajectory of a disease is such that dissonance between the four essential items cannot be reconciled. When pain or loss of function from the disease becomes intolerable some people choose to live without life-sustaining treatments, which will produce certain death, while others will take active measures to shorten their own lives. One cancer patient's goal may be to live a satisfying life as long as possible despite painful treatments. The incentive for this goal could be a loving family. In contrast, another patient may choose to endure because of unfinished business which, once reconciled, will remove any purpose in prolonging a painful existence. To be sure, assisting the patients by allowing them to discuss and weigh the consequences of various treatment choices is, at the very outset, a crucial part of the social worker's role.

The helping process

The helping process begins when the chronically ill patient is first referred for service. Frequently the identified need is something as practical as assisting the patient in applying for proper disability and medical insurance, making transportation arrangements for regular treatment appointments, or providing for the needs of dependent others.

Attending to these concrete needs at the very outset is essential. First, it allows for the formation of a working relationship and the development of a degree of trust. Second, patients are unable to focus their attention on the more esoteric aspects of their adjustment to their disease until their primary needs are met. As noted, newly-diagnosed patients may be too overwhelmed by the implications of their disease to begin to think how they might cope with it. Thus, to reflect on the meaning of their disease would be premature. Although each patient has his or her own unique reaction at this point, some have commented that this period is like "having a dark cloud hanging over your head. You know that something is wrong, something has changed or is going to, you don't known what or how, but from the way others are acting and what you know about the disease, it is going to be awful."

As medical treatment is instituted and patients begin to resume routine responsibilities for their personal care as well as activities of daily living, they may be ready to explore the limits imposed by their disease, particularly as their knowledge about and meaning of their illness grows out of medical as well as experiential information. For example, patients cannot know what chemotherapy entails until after they have received the treatment; however, there is no assurance that one's reaction to any two treatments will be the same. Some hemodialysis patients have noticed that if they are emotionally upset when they present for their treatments, they are more likely to have difficulty or complications than if they are calm and relaxed.

As the disease changes, so does the patient's perceptions. During an acute period one rarely finds a patient in the same state from one day to the next. Pain levels change, signs of relapses or remissions and transitory effects from medication all affect the patient's understanding of the illness and his or her state of being. Hopes for remission may be dashed with a sudden fever spike, or the despair of constant pain may be alleviated with a new drug which reduces it to tolerable levels. Such fluctuations are frequently predictive of the instability of a future state — that is, what patients can expect for the rest of their lives. Thus one essential intent of the helping relationship is to enable the patient to learn to live with the lack of predictability and to deal with one day at a time. Consider that the client confronts perhaps the most formidable loss — the relinquishment of one's claim on a hopeful future.

Once the actuality of having to live with a chronic illness comes to consciousness, the first attempts at adaptation involve some testing and risk-taking to determine one's new limits. To some extent, this venture will result in the painful experience of failure and the acknowledgement of loss — loss of the ability to function and perform, loss of future hopes and dreams, and quite possibly, the loss of self-esteem that was carefully nurtured over a lifetime. As patients begin to tell their story of who and what they once were, who they are now, and what they once hoped to be, the listener becomes acutely aware of the meaning and impact of the various levels of loss for them; what emerges are the aspects of their life in which they have most heavily invested, and which are the most painful to relinquish.

Metaphorically, what we term the adaptive process can be likened to a series of deaths and rebirths. If patients are to do more than just survive, they must lay to rest some venerable truths about themselves and their former capabilities and strengths. The demise of these personal conceptions is surely accompanied by many expressions of grief including outrage, frustration, and a deep sadness. Consider, for example, the person who had comfortably assumed the role and definition of self as a provider and protector of his or her family. Constantly fatigued, weakened, or in other ways debilitated by the physical condition, the patient now asks: "What am I good for?" Since there is little of meaning to replace this cherished image of self at this point, patients will naturally cling to their ideas about their past life which once gave them a sense of security and stability. They may repeatedly tell their stories about how things once were — and who they once were. This repetition can be annoying unless its function is appreciated. Frequently, in this narrative, patients are able to discover certain strengths which persist despite their disease and on which they can rely as they begin to reconstruct their present and future. They can appreciate that although the truths of their healthy past may no longer be pertinent to their present life, the essence of their personage transcends the loss.

This process of bereavement inevitably alters one's established principles and values of living, the preferences, priorities, and ideals that once gave life its meaning and purpose. A dialysis patient, although referring to her own value orientation, speaks for many patients when she says:

I used to think that going out all the time, having a lot of clothes and things like that were important. Now I realize that what really counts is your health and really caring about people — not just running with them. I have learned a lot of things — people who I used to think were my friends didn't really care about me.

When I needed them, they weren't there. The only thing that I regret is that it took something like dialysis to make me stop and re-evaluate my life. I like myself a lot more now.

The role of the social worker in this process is emotionally difficult — but at the same time extremely rewarding. In one sense, the helpers are asked to willingly allow themselves to enter into the immediate reality of the patient; if this is their intent and commitment what they need to ask is some form of the question: "What is it like for you?" Indeed, it is an intent to share sadness and despair but this concern also represents a willingness to move with the fluctuations and convolutions that are part of the patient's struggle to make some sense and meaning out of a condition that was never anticipated. In another sense, helpers are more than caring listeners particularly as they are sensitive to the distortions, denials, or diversions that prohibit the patient from moving forward. With awareness of the subjective meanings of these evasions, workers carefully bring these tendencies to the patient's awareness. What is intended is not to confront patients with their errors, but to urge them to reconceptualize what they fear or what they have at stake in redefining their life.

Although the goal at every stage is to enable the patient to define an emerging image of a competent self within a particular set of limitations, this endeavor is inextricably dependent on the course and trajectory of the disease itself — each having its own unique profile and characteristics. In the case of rheumatoid arthritis, for example, the patient must cope with the diminution of function that is accompanied by an intensification of pain. Some diseases are marked by alternating stages of remission and relapse while others follow a gradual deterioration of the body (Strauss 1975). In still other cases, the patient must endure severe iatrogenic complications. Although many of the same emotional issues may be brought to bear at each new incident, the patient will resolve them anew each time. With each new episode, one will grapple with issues of self-concept as one's body changes over time. With each new limitation the environment will again be reassessed. With each successive episode, the process of adaptation is a little quicker as the patient has acquired the skill of re-establishing new steady states.

Simply put, the crisis of self-redefinition is painfully complicated by other medical and physical crises. With each succeeding amputation, diabetics find it necessary to reconstruct their body image and their ideas about their capabilities. The sickle-cell patient facing possible loss of organ function with each successive crisis is left with the question of when the sickling process finally will destroy vital tissue and so result in death. In this case, each crisis constitutes a new threat of death. Sickle-cell patients must prepare for possible separation, but not so completely that they cannot re-engage with life if their body is able to tolerate the additional assault. These crises, it must be added, are exhausting not only for the patient but also for the family — and frequently for the social worker who has something invested in the client's dignity and well-being.

One man who illustrates this process is Mr S., a thirty-seven-year-old man who endured six severe and numerous minor sickle-cell crises over a two-year period prior to his death. Those sickle-cell crises, necessitating hospitalizations, produced pancreatitis, cellulitis, and cirrhosis of the liver in addition to damaging both his heart and gall bladder. As the physicians became more guarded about his prognosis with each succeeding crisis, Mr S. began the long slow process of re-evaluating his life, and adapting to this chronic debilitating illness while his body deteriorated. Mr S. based much of his self-worth on his community involvement, dedicated to improving the life situation of the poor. This commitment at times demanded an inordinate physical exertion. Paradoxically, physical exertion is thought to precipitate the sickle crisis which in turn threatened Mr S.'s life. With each crisis and each of the last three re-admissions, Mr S. had to come to terms with the knowledge that death may be the outcome and to learn how to live with his tenuous hold on life. Each time, following doctors' orders to limit activity, he vowed to withdraw from his community activities, saying that other people could take over. He withdrew from his family and was far less verbal in general with all visitors.

With each hospitalization our discussions repeatedly focused on the meaning which Mr S. found in life consonant with his self-worth. Each time, after the resolution of the crisis and discharge from the hospital, Mr S. would find himself impelled to resume some, if not all, of his previous activities. He finally concluded that regardless of its effect on his health, life without involvement and commitment was devoid of meaning. Regardless of multiple efforts to be satisfied with a sedentary lifestyle, he never succeeded in finding meaning. Although the life pattern which Mr S. selected hastened his death, it was a life that provided a richness in purpose which Mr S. would not sacrifice.

My role in this process was rather simple, albeit painful. I had known Mr S. for approximately three months prior to the onset of this series of sickle crises. The foundation of our relationship had been my desire to appreciate the social problems faced by the black community. With the development of his medical crises, the topic of our conversation changed to "What is it like to face a life threatening condition at the age of thirty-seven?" As Mr S. attempted to describe his situation to me, he also raised issues which he had never before articulated. I had no answers, only questions — questions about the things in his life which were important.

My final responsibility was to be available and present myself without an agenda or preconceived plan. At times Mr S. was not interested in talking and my visits were brief. On other occasions when he was caught in his struggle, he would talk at length, disavowing any attachment or commitment to his life's activities. At still other times he questioned how one can walk away from a "job" without having completed it. Clearly these issues take on their relevance and meaning from Mr S.'s perspective. As we explored and articulated some of these elements, specifically the definition of life's work and when it would be completed, Mr S.'s fear of failing lessened. The reframing process then shifted the focus from what had not yet been done to all that had been completed. Mr S. was encouraged to reminisce about his life, particularly emphasizing the many achievements over the past twenty years — the time period which he found to be the most relevant. He recounted the many successes — recalling how his life had changed dramatically with age and the maturation necessitated by a chronic disease. This process extended over many visits with multiple recappings and repetitions. It is a process which cannot be hurried — when the patient sets his or her own pace. This type of refocusing broadens one's perspective through highlighting achievement. The outcome is very powerful as patients come to their own realization about their worth based on self-report.

The conflict about his definition of quality of life culminated shortly before his death when Mr S. spoke of being "tired" and wanting "to be called to rest," while family and friends encouraged him to "continue to fight." During this period Mr S. wanted to talk about his need for peace, to rest and relinquish his body which now produced constant pain. He needed permission to die. Mr S. struggled with the dilemma of wanting to appease the need of others for him to live while he longed for freedom from pain. He shared what dying meant to him and his hope of being met by his mother and father who had died six years earlier. I responded to his inquiry by listening and separating out his desires from those of others around him. He was able to speak of his longing to die without being chastized or cut off. We were able to arrange for him to finish his life — to say goodbye to family and friends and to see his children for one final visit. When he had come to closure with life, when nothing else was to be done, my visits were characterized by periods of sitting together in silence.

In the final analysis, it is the shared conviction that something more than mere survival is possible that enables the patient to manage the crises, the progression of the disease and the final choice for death: the realization that one can — or for that matter, must — set forth on a journey that seeks out new definitions of self and life, which arms the patient with new strengths that can be brought to bear on each new crisis or setback. As each crisis is endured in something other than a passive or victimized fashion, self-esteem grows which magnifies one's belief in an ability to cope with the next crisis.

To summarize, the chronically ill patient poses a special challenge to the social worker. Unlike the situations encountered with other clients where there may be potential options for an active problem-solving approach, these patients are unable to directly affect the course of their discomfort. Hence, treatment is aimed at helping people live with their disability in as creative and rewarding a way as possible. Yet, this goal is obviously dependent upon how patients define their condition. This definition, in turn, takes on meaning which influences their self-concept and affects how they function in and relate to their social and physical environment. This cycle is further affected by the trajectory of the disease. As it progresses and continues to alter physical function and capabilities, the ability to relate to the environment and definition of self-concept are in turn adjusted. The process ends only with death.

As such, adaptation is a normal, ongoing process through which people begin to integrate the impact of their disease and its implications for their lives. This adaptive process unfolds quite naturally for most as they begin to explore how their futures will be changed. Occasionally these people may request the attention of an interested person with whom they can share their fears or anger when family members are unavailable or too tired and frightened themselves. These patients are searching for confirmation of their new understanding of themselves and the meaning of their lives. Sharing these awarenesses and having them accepted by another person affirms their reality.

Others may become caught and immobilized in the midst of the adaptive process. These are the patients who need special attention as they grapple with issues relative to their self-concepts and how they now will relate to their environment. It is with these issues that the cognitive-humanistic approach is also effective in deciphering elements which had been pertinent to a healthy lifestyle but which are no longer possible. A more active role is required with these patients to sort out the distortions and address the uncertainty of the new life. The therapeutic process of relinquishing old truths and beliefs about self and life develops as patients are allowed to recall their history, experientially recounting their past losses and successes as well as beginning to let go of dreams for the future. Through a trial and error process new limits are painfully learned.

As information relative to their medical condition becomes available, patients use multiple techniques to cope with the impact of their disease. These techniques include: (1) withdrawal; (2) redefining the meaning of the situation to diminish its importance; (3) intellectually appraising the facts and interpreting their meaning; (4) projecting control responsibility onto a powerful other; (5) belief in fate; (6) a reliance on the benevolence of a supreme being and some divine purpose to be found in the situation. Eventually the various shields from the reality of the situation give way to patients' new awareness of themselves which now includes their illness. Sometimes this new definition provides a richness and depth in appreciation for life which is beyond that of most healthy people. At other times life fails to provide the rewards to justify the pain of the disease and the patient may decide to withdraw from treatment and allow the disease process to run its course uninterrupted. Only the patient can make the decision as to how long and how much he or she can endure. Those of us who are only onlookers must respect this judgment.

It is recognized that these patients are a particularly difficult group with which to work as they threaten the essence of our own existential fear of mortality. Their behavior is at times difficult to tolerate particularly when their angers and frustrations with their lives are directed toward us as well as others in their environment. Although the process takes a unique course for each person, it is normal and predictable. The cognitive-humanistic approach considers each individual's problems as he or she so perceives them. As such, it recognizes the uniqueness and autonomy of each person and is instrumental in dealing with the complex task of adapting to major life changes.

REFERENCES

Abram, H. (1977–78) Emotional Aspects of Heart Disease: A Personal Narrative. *International Journal of Psychiatry in Medicine* 8(3): 225–53.

Bohnengel-Lee, A. (1982) An Analysis of Coping Behaviors in Renal Transplant Patients. Case Western Reserve University (unpublished dissertation).

Bulman, R. and Wortman, C. (1977) Attribution of Blame and Coping in the 'Real World'. *Journal of Personality and Social Psychology* 35: 351–63.

Hill, R. (1958) Generic Features of Families Under Stress. *Social Casework* 39: 139–50.

Kübler-Ross, E. (1969) *On Death and Dying*. New York: Macmillan.

Schreiner, G. and Tartaglia, C. (1978) Uremia: Soma or Psyche? *Kidney International* 13(8): 2S–4S.

Strauss, A. (1975) *Chronic Illness and the Quality of Life*. St. Louis: C. V. Mosby.

Chapter 5

The Alcoholic Client:
A Cognitive-Physiological Approach to
Dependency

WILLIAM F. VANEK

> "I can't tell you...just how wonderful she is. I don't want you to know. I don't want anyone to know...She's life and hope and happiness, my whole world now." He felt the quiver of a tear on his eyelid.
>
> (Amory Blane, in *This Side of Paradise*, F. Scott Fitzgerald)

Those of us who have come in contact with the alcoholic (or chemically dependent) client may describe him or her as "hard to reach," "difficult," or "unmotivated." We may try to impose solutions so as to overpower the chemical dependency, to negate or deride the alcoholic's beliefs, or to get at the underlying psychodynamics. Without some understanding of the intense nature of the alcoholic experience as it is lived by our client, we will find ourselves a poor match for the chemical. Our own despair and feelings of failure can lead us to invoke the old, somewhat exaggerated stereotype: "Alcoholics are a tough lot to work with, best left to find their own help after they have 'hit bottom.'" Although there is an element of truth in this, as there is in most stereotypes, we believe that it is possible to help alcoholics and those close to them take responsibility for the direction of their lives. But we can do this only if we are willing to enter their lives and world in the attempt to understand the process and meaning of alcoholism in their terms, through which we can help them to look honestly at themselves. It needs to be said clearly at the outset that working with alcoholics will be demanding and difficult. As our clients come to face the reality of their circumstances, their emotional pain and need to escape will be disheartening; as we challenge their personal beliefs our own are challenged as well; as we are tested by our clients, we test ourselves as well. We are in it together — each facing the opportunity to reaffirm ourselves in our respective ways. How do we begin to make sense of the client's chaotic world? What knowledge can we draw on to explain the alcoholic? Two major perspectives are available: one is an objective view, most notably the illness concept that provides a framework that defines cause, course, and recovery; the other is subjective, an existential concept that is concerned with the deeply-held meanings and strivings of the person. The first takes account of the psychological, biological, genetic, and environmental conditions that appear to be related to the progression of alcoholism. The second represents the persons of principle and faith. These views cannot be described in isolation — they are necessarily intertwined in any effective description and understanding of the alcoholic experience.

OBJECTIVE VIEW: THE ILLNESS CONCEPT

Many socio-cultural, biological, and psychological explanations of alcoholism appear to contribute to the whole; it would be foolish to imply here that any one factor could be completely isolated or singled out. Schuckit and Haglund (1977), in their review of the etiological theories of alcoholism, admit that the "arbitrary division" of theories does not obscure the interrelatedness of factors that make it obvious that there is no single cause for alcoholism. In fact, it is often difficult to distinguish between cause and effect when we study cases of alcoholics. What we find is more of a self-perpetuating, confused cycle of low self-esteem, alienation, and powerlessness. Zimberg's research (1978) on oral fixation indicated that early deprivation and dependency needs may underlie the person's search for a sense of omnipotence through the alcohol effect. However, this intent ultimately fails, leading to further despair; an internal conflict is created which, as Zimberg noted, will lead to alcoholism particularly when it is coupled with a genetic predisposition. (We can see the high risk in children of alcoholics since both components — early deprivation and predisposition — are likely to exist. In that case, the "cause" traces further back to the "effect" of the pre-existing family alcoholism.) Zimberg added that though strong feelings of dependency, low self-worth, and a need for nurturance may pre-exist, such character-istics are often repressed in favor of others such as perfectionism. He concluded, then, that it is inappropriate to look for an "alcoholic personality" although certain common characteristics exist. Alcoholics are as diverse a group as people in general (Wallace 1977). While we can identify some major common characteristics, we find also that no two alcoholics experience their drinking in an identical way. Neither do they share the same life story.

In our attempt to understand the alcoholic phenomenon in descriptive terms, we can turn to E. M. Jellinek (1960), a pioneer in research into alcohol use and addiction, who provides a way of understanding the varying types and processes of alcoholism. He introduced five types (Alpha, Beta, Gamma, Delta, and Epsilon) (Wallace 1977) in order to study such concepts as psychological *vs* physiological dependence, inability to abstain *vs* loss of control over drinking, daily *vs* episodic drinking, physical health *vs* disease, and the area of nutritional deficiency disease.

Jellinek expanded his theory through the addition of a framework depicting four phases of alcoholism (1952): pre-alcoholic, early alcoholic, crucial, and final (chronic). These phases pointed to alcoholism as being primary, progressive, chronic, and terminal, if not arrested.

In the pre-alcoholic phase, the person initially drinks to cope with everyday tensions; alcohol is used here as a "release," a problem solver. As he or she continues to drink to seek intentionally the effect of alcohol, toleration of the chemical increases and more is needed. Some say that early on the alcoholic experiences a "heightened reaction" to the chemical that the social drinker does not. (This may be due in part to a "need" for the high.) Later the alcoholic, in retrospect, may recall his or her alcoholic experience as pleasurable to avoid the emotional pain that has been experienced.

The second phase, the early alcoholic phase, is apparent in the experience of a blackout, a temporary period of amnesia in which, to the observer, the person actually may appear to function normally. As tolerance and need increase, alcoholics become preoccupied with the use of alcohol and begin to employ devious methods to allow them to drink greater amounts more often. If they feel some guilt for their behavior, they seek to excuse it both to themselves and to others through denial or otherwise becoming defensive.

The third phase is the crucial one when actual addiction is said to occur. Signs of physiological dependence become evident. Social consequences, such as loss of a marriage, broken friendships, and job difficulties are likely while aggressive, withdrawn, or otherwise harmful behavior continues. Drinking is placed before any other activity, responsibility, or relationship in life even though tremendous losses and problems begin to accumulate.

The fourth phase is the final, chronic phase of alcoholism, perhaps the most commonly stereotyped. By this time serious physiological damage has occurred. Cessation of drinking may bring on hallucinations, extreme agitation, "shakes," and a host of other symptoms of withdrawal. A pervasive but vague type of apprehension and paranoia along with other signs of severe disturbances of the thought processes are experienced. Anxiety leading to panic and loss of hope are coupled with the pain of self-hatred. The intoxicated isolation and futile view of the future often lead to suicidal thoughts or impulses and other self-destructive, reckless acts.

Whether or not Jellinek's phase model is representative of *all* alcoholics, it does identify the general progression of isolation, self-destruction, and anguish in the alcoholic experience. It can help us appreciate how the progression influences each aspect of the person's life and how the alcoholic experience blunts individuality and renders a sorrowful, painful identity in the later phases.

Johnson (1980) described this progression of alcoholism in his "feeling chart," that shows how emotions, thoughts, and behaviors increasingly become entwined in the pattern of the alcoholic experience. Within a continuum of "pain" on one extreme and "euphoria" on the other, Johnson's four phases portray a learning process that ultimately skews the alcoholic's living experience toward the painful extreme. The first phase is that of "learning the mood swing." The individual finds that he or she can use the chemical to obtain a temporary swing toward euphoria that can be regulated by the amount used; the chemical can at this point be trusted to provide the effect reliably. Most casual drinkers also experience this phase.

The second phase sees the person "seeking the mood swing." Alcoholics may be considered social drinkers in that social contact is most important to them; the controlled use of the chemical itself can enhance the pleasure of the social experience. The "five o'clock rule" is an example of setting a socially acceptable standard for use. On occasion, this user may abuse the chemical and suffer the physical pain of a hangover without much emotional pain. The use is still secondary to one's friendships, obligations and responsibilities.

Those who move into the third phase, "harmful dependency" (or harmful abuse), find a major change in the chemical experience. Alcoholics now begin to experience a "loss of control" over the chemical; they can no longer be certain as to what the outcome will be. Their

135

intoxicated behavior assaults their sober value system repeatedly and, as Wallace (1977) states, this "Jekyll and Hyde" experience severely confuses and shakes their belief in their own integrity and self-worth. We might say that the result of this is two selves: the sober self-concept that sees itself assaulted by the out-of-control intoxicated self.

As a result of this pain, spontaneous defensiveness and rationalization lead alcoholics either to retain their negative thoughts and feelings about themselves or to project them onto others. As inner distress and isolation grow, preoccupation with the chemical use increases. A higher tolerance is developed as is the need to find ways to continually obtain, protect, and assure the supply. One's lifestyle changes, particularly as friendships and responsibilities become secondary to the chemical. The observed rules are broken and are displaced by rigid patterns in the form of "times I *will* drink" rather than "times I will not." The progression continues at the expense of the person's total well-being — physical, emotional, social, and spiritual.

The fourth and final phase involves "using to feel normal." No longer is the person seeking the euphoric mood swing; now he or she is using the chemical only in the effort to find balance and to deal with pain. Physical addiction is likely and blackouts occur more often; paranoia, suspicion, and other thinking disorders block attempts at logic. Tolerance now decreases as the body's ability to process the chemical breaks down. The user may unrealistically dream of escape — say to another geographic area — in the hope of eluding the suffering. This hope, unlike productive creative thought, is built on a foundation of hopelessness and avoidance as the person increasingly loses any spiritual meanings and desire to live.

The violation of one's personal values and the attempts to avoid dealing with the subsequent pain contribute to and perpetuate the alcoholic process. Tiebout (1954) describes the presence of an extremely narcissistic "ego" central to the personality of an alcoholic. This "egotism," compensating for the pain of violated values and feelings of low self-worth, often brings on a "reactive grandiosity" (Zimberg 1978) or a facade of extreme well-being and power. We may also sense the aspiration to be known as a sort of tragic hero, smiling in the face of doom, rather than someone suffering from loss of control.

Wallace (1977) shares the view of the alcoholic as one who clings to the destructive hypothesis that, given enough time, perhaps even the "next time," he or she will be able to control the chemical. This cannot be disproved, because there always is the possibility of a next time — until, of course, death occurs.

Those involved with alcoholics may actually "enable" them to continue their behavior out of a need to maintain some stability and restore control. They may accept the blame and take the responsibility to cover up or try to control the drinking. Their adaptive roles become as central to their lives as the chemical is to the user and in stages which tend to parallel the alcoholic progression.

Children of alcoholics also attempt to "balance," take responsibility, or otherwise defend the family out of a need for attention or control, or to express their own strong, often fearful and angry feelings. Some may adapt by rebelliousness, withdrawal, trying to be "perfect," or through other means that seek to unify, control, or protect not only the family's survival but their own as well. The family, in turn, may play up to this performance and present the "problem child" rather than the secret of alcoholism as their concern. These roles express the voice and plea of the child and family — only dimly heard through the silence. Thus, members of the family, out of their preoccupation with his or her chemical use, find and cling to their adaptive roles as rigidly as the drinker holds to the drink. They experiment and develop a dependency on their "survival" roles just as the alcoholic progresses in his or her chemical dependency. The blame and role assumption become predictive and self-perpetuating. This misdirection may extend to co-workers and employers alike when they, too, attempt to "help" alcoholics by covering up for their poor work and absence, and otherwise excuse or ignore their behavior.

Implications

These conceptions of alcoholism as an illness have both negative and positive implications for helping the alcoholic, depending upon how they are interpreted and used. The idea of alcoholism as illness diminishes myth and moral stigma; yet it could also be misused by the alcoholic as an "out" insofar as he or she may reject personal responsibility by blaming the "sickness." The illness model can be distorted and misused as can any concept. It can be applied to include one and all if our need is to "prove" everyone alcoholic. Others can certainly find themselves an "exception." It can be misused to create a stereotyped "real alcoholic." Those who use it in its purely clinical application distance themselves from the personal, painful meanings that interweave the lives of those affected. We may, on the other hand, find ourselves in the dilemma of avoiding the medical model, not wishing to "diagnose" a patient; in this case we lose the invaluable understanding of the power of the alcoholic-addictive process

137

which can more clearly be brought to light if we seek to understand alcoholism as a progressive, primary illness.

The illness concept offers us a guide to understanding; it sensitizes us to and enables us to address the progression of physiological and life changes that have become the alcoholic process. The awareness of these stages of physiological, psychological, and social deterioration allows all concerned to appreciate what the individual has undergone and thereby, most critically, what may well yet lie ahead. This does not serve to excuse alcoholics from responsibility for their condition; rather it focuses on the choice of outcome as their responsibility. They can learn that they can come to understand, and in an ongoing way, master their condition much like other people who must live with other incurable diseases (e.g. diabetes, emphysema, heart disease) through acceptance and responsible living.

Finally, a brief review of what has been said thus far about the objective illness concept reveals that it is not "cold and objective" in the true sense, but rather is closely aligned to such subjective factors as need, cognition, self-concept, and choice of decision that represent not just the biological person but the persons of mind, community, principle, and faith that together support our need to believe.

SUBJECTIVE VIEW: THE NEED TO BELIEVE

The objective illness concept ostensibly requires that we stand back, observe and assess the phenomenon of alcoholism from a somewhat detached, theoretical perspective. A subjective or cognitive-humanistic viewpoint that searches for meaning demands we grasp the alcoholic experience from within the world of the client. The deeply-held meanings contribute and are dialectically related to the reasons we see, the defenses and isolation described in the illness framework. Thus, we meet Jay who, at thirty-three, now lives alone in his cramped apartment. Up to a year ago he was husband to Beth and father of two sons, aged nine and six, and a daughter, aged four. His loneliness is not something he lives and feels; rather his existence is mindless, part of a pattern, an assumption that life is basically worthless and that there is no reason to be hopeful.

There were times when Jay would display the grand gesture when he went out with his dwindling group of friends, but he usually knew that it was all put-on, part of his "routine." He scarcely concealed his resentment and sarcasm as he indicted his family, his job, politics, the world, and life in general when he talked about his values and the "idealistic bull" that led him to the painful "reality" he must now endure. That reality, according to Jay, is the reason he must drink to get by. At other times Jay can be quiet, very passive, and uncaring; he can play the "suave but secretly suffering noble role" to the hilt.

Although he did not drink continually, the idea of the next drink was ever-present in his plan, design, and mood. Increasingly, he spent time alone and had periods where he lost count of days. His work, the last thing to fail, began to suffer when his wife, his friends, and co-workers no longer felt responsible for covering up his lateness, absence, and poor quality of work. His "working lunches" were really "drinking lunches." Co-workers and customers alike eventually were estranged by Jay's mood swings.

Jay seemed oblivious to the disaster. If anything, he recalled his past drinking experiences with fondness — along with the "injustices" in his life that allowed him to seek solace in the glass. The burning glow gave him a familiar comfort and the mounting loss and futility gave more meaning (albeit painfully) to his life than he had ever known. This was Jay's life until he found himself in a dimly-lit bedroom, sitting upright and naked on the disheveled bed with the barrel of his old hunting shotgun in his mouth.

The sight that he beheld in the dressing mirror was so absurd that he fell into wild laughter. Though he was alone, he was deeply embarrassed. The rush of emotion burst forth as a desperate sob as he painfully faced the pathetic sight that was himself.

What kind of story leads to such a climax? As Jay later narrated his version of his life, he began, interestingly enough, with the fact that he grew up in a family with a harsh, "heavy drinking" father and a gentle, loving mother. Neither ever confronted the father. He had no brothers or sisters, and, except for the love of his mother, felt alone in the world.

Later, Jay responded to the caring attention of his teachers who encouraged him to pursue his talents in track and in creative writing. Jay loved to run. As his body built endurance under stress he felt relaxed, even experienced a "high." He was not only more in touch with himself but felt closer to God as his confidence and pride grew with each accomplishment.

Writing gave Jay the medium for expressing the emotions which were ordinarily withheld at home. His own metaphors expressed the exhilaration of running and touched on the inner struggle with which he had been enmeshed. He longed for contact with others and wanted to think of himself as worthwhile, but feared that others would see that he really was as "bad" as his coldly critical father had said he was. In time, Jay gradually overcame some of his fear as he gained success with the track team and recognition as a writer.

At college, Jay met Beth, an old high-school friend who was attending nursing school. Jay and Beth enjoyed a very carefree romance. They were moderate in their social behavior, especially in their use of alcohol. Jay recalled that they spent long hours talking about their dreams about making the world a better place. They completed college and soon were married. With an almost unbelievable sense of fulfillment, Jay returned to his high school to teach English and to coach the track team. Beth took a nursing position in a physician's office. The birth of the children followed. Beth continued to work as much as she was able, partly to stay with her career, mostly to add to family finances.

Somehow the dream began to tarnish for Jay. He and Beth were struggling just to "get by," Jay's efforts to guide and understand his students seemed to fail, and he often found himself at odds with the administration. He began to feel like a "burn-out" and found others who felt the same. They shared their sentiments over a drink after work.

The evening stops became an important part of the day for Jay. He was becoming more "nervous" at work, and, feeling somewhat ostracized, looked forward to his time at the familiar bar with his friends — a sort of cushion between work and the growing problems he had to face at home. Intimacy with Beth was rare, and usually perfunctory.

The problems at home most often seemed to be focused on sex, the children, or, particularly, money. For some reason there was much less to go on and Beth eventually lost her sympathy for Jay's small pay check. Jay would rage about how he was beset with problems, especially the nagging wife who pressed him to account for "every dime."

When his older son had been in several fights at school, Jay missed the school conference, just as he missed taking his daughter to the library — a promise he did not remember making. Beth's disapproval of Jay increased into resentment and distance.

Jay's stops after work became more frequent and continued until the end of the school year when he decided to find other work. Beth agreed that maybe that would "turn us around"; she did not know that he had been pressured by the administration not to renew his contract. He quickly took the best job he could find as a service representative for an office machine company. He liked the personal freedom and the feeling that he did not have to care or think about anything other than the machine that needed repair.

Always the life of the party, Jay became the unofficial chairman of the celebration department. Whether it was a birthday, a raise, or impending surgery, Jay was there to offer the standard liquid lunch. He also extended that role to his customers, and an occasional "lunch" would last the entire afternoon. Soon he gladly began to offer heart-wrenching accounts about how his wife had asked him to move out. Their friends had "deserted" him, and *she* was the one "tired of lying and living alone...." "She got the lying part right! The truth of it is she's tired of having to *work* a little bit! I'm not the big deal she thinks she needs, and her mother is right in there pitching! And then there's that 'marriage counselor' she's been seeing... that's where the lying really starts!" — a few mumbled words, a pat on the back, and his "friends" were gone. Except one.

Jay remained with this one true, magical friend and together they closed off his world to others. This was his world now, his "life and hope and happiness." He would either ignore the anguish he was creating, or resentfully take a sort of confused pride in closing out those whom he saw as having hurt him. When, on occasion, he faced his emotional pain, it was distorted; it became his justification, if not a purpose. However, Jay, like Amory Blane, felt a tear on his eyelid.

Jay's story differs in narrative detail, of course, from the stories of other alcoholics. However, the plot and the variations on its theme are fairly consistent with the personal memoirs of many alcoholics: Georgia who from the time she was raped by her father and was accused of being a "seductive whore" by her mother, accepted the belief that she was a "sinful woman" who only could know a life of immoral relationships. Her alcoholism was in part a sanctuary within which she was able to perpetuate this belief with some justification. Carol, the daughter of an alcoholic father, was surely convinced that her arrest for shoplifting was final "proof" that she was the problem child her father had long accused her of being. Jack, withdrawn, defensive, and illiterate, maintained his belief he had always been and would always be "kept away" by others, thereby justifying his disdain. In contrast with Jack, David is a corporation vice-president, an over-achiever most of his life in order to stabilize his alcoholic parents' home. He now feels disillusioned, unfulfilled, and unimpressed with the material success he has acquired. The older Kate, children grown, husband deceased, says she is "of no use to anyone" any longer.

What do these stories mean when the purposes of the narrator are considered? Why does the alcoholic choose to select these accounts and not others? Do these stories have any basis in fact or are they altered a bit for some self-serving reasons? Do they really explain *the cause* of alcoholism or are they a product of it and now an excuse? These and other puzzling questions cannot be answered by some abstract, objective assessment of these accounts; rather, we must know something about the subjective processes of thought and interpretation in the mind of the alcoholic before we can begin to make some modest speculations about the meaning of these autobiographies and what they intend to tell us. We may well find the addiction and the meanings come to serve one another.

Alcoholics will laugh off suggestions that they have a drinking problem, even to the point where they convince themselves. But as the alcoholic progression continues, the pain, for both alcoholic and family, increases unattended. As the addiction worsens, they struggle to find a trace of meaning and justification in their life, whilst protecting their drinking as their one salvation, their one justified "high." While they feel compelled to drink, they insist that it is their choice, that they are in control. Their confusion is now used as a reason for drinking rather than seen as the result. And so the vicious circle continues. Alcoholics strive for acceptance, but when this fails to materialize, this striving turns into scorn, self-pity, ambivalence, or apathy. Thus they may find meaning and purpose in suffering, in the idea of becoming a "noble failure" — a martyr to the gross insensitivity of the world.

Our client Jay has set the stage much like Fitzgerald's Amory, narrowing around his desperate belief until it was his whole world...a painful but unquestioned existence and a mindless pattern of life. His story tells us that he had once sought a vulnerable ideal but with fear and uncertainty. The perfection he demanded met with imperfect reality; but he found within that the meaning in being a noble failure, and sought solace in the alcoholic world he once feared but now embraced. He had conceded, become resigned, and the world that he pulled in close around him became his whole world though he would not see that that which he now loved was his deepest enemy.

Observing the family members engaged in their various roles, we see that they may actually enable the pattern of alcoholism to continue. They live in a fallacious world in which they place their focus *around* the alcoholism, hoping to take on an issue they can control and use for an explanation, rather than direct their attention *at* it. They, like the alcoholic, deceive themselves in believing they are in control of their lives. Rigidity and isolation are the essence of the alcoholic experience and of all concerned. Even if drinking ceases, part of continuing recovery is the need of both the alcoholic and his or her family to recognize and deal with harmful, ingrained thought patterns.

OBJECTIVE AND SUBJECTIVE: A DIALECTICAL INTERPLAY

As we seek to understand the alcoholic experience, we can see that it is difficult to separate the objective nature of the illness from the subjective experience itself, even for the sake of study. Efforts to trace "which came first" — the physical progression or the self-defeating beliefs — may end in impasse. We cannot get a view of the past which is not distilled and interpreted through present needs and meanings. Further, a focus on the past tends to avoid the present situation and excuses the alcoholism unless we see the past in reference to understanding the progression of the phases of alcoholism.

Similarly, a focus on the physiological causes without attention to the complementary self-defeating and harmful beliefs and feelings will not reach the alcoholic in any way that is personally meaningful. Such a view may likewise provide alcoholics with the excuse that they are victim to an overpowering illness that controls them and, at the same time, justifies their actions. Thus, in speaking about the objective nature of alcoholism seen as an illness and the subjective domain of cognition and meaning we confront the long-standing problem of mind and body — the artificial separation that, by theory alone, reduces that which is essentially irreducible (the whole person) to incompatible parts. Our endeavor, then, is to show how the biological and existential dimensions of the alcoholic experience are distinct only in theoretical and abstract terms; they are experienced, in dialectical or interactive terms, as complementary facets of the same experience.

Looking at the alcoholic progression, we see that there is a physical dependency which may take place as the body adapts to the chemical. (This may coincide with over-exposure to the chemical as a problem solver in times of crisis, though not everyone so exposed becomes addicted.) For some more than others, this adaptation may cause increasing discomfort during non-drinking times. Thus, conscious discomfort, added to the stresses of life from which one might wish relief, may be associated with the "need" for alcohol to ease it. Such physical adaptation and sensation may be different, due strictly to physical make-up, more for some than for others. Further discomfort may be felt as a physical craving; and since a cognitive connection has been made between such discomfort and alcohol as a relief, the person may begin to act more or less on impulse to satisfy it by drinking. Inasmuch as one may not consciously plan each amount that one drinks in this now-patterned response, one may be, in a matter of speaking, losing control to it. The discomfort and the response increase in a progressive way.

As the alcoholic process intensifies, the body's ability to adapt to and process the chemical becomes increasingly erratic, and the body is forced to manage greater quantities of alcohol over longer periods of time. Not only do side effects of physical deterioration begin to loom but the ability to deal with them, to explain them, or to preserve a dwindling self-concept is confounded by the accompanying erosion of the individual's cognitive functions of perception and judgment. For example, alcoholics may find themselves demoralized and trapped by the loss of sexual prowess. Without facing and changing their entrenched patterns, how will they explain this crushing failure to themselves or their partners? If alcohol impairs judgment and inhibition and acts as a depressant it may likewise stimulate the brain in ways that evoke all sorts of fantasy and fanciful thinking. While we may say that there is a physiological source, the net result is an experiential event of confusion, erratic and unpredictable moods, as well as thoughts and actions which might violate the person's sober ethics, principles, and values. Confusion is increased by blackouts which add to the individual's sense of loss of control and guilt. As in the case when we feel battered by forces we cannot understand, never mind manage, relief is sought by narrowing or closing out the world of threat and danger. This the alcoholic does in a gross and distorted fashion — but in doing so, creates an outer world that is even more distant and menacing. And so he or she turns further inward into the alcoholic depression.

Even to the interested and concerned observer, this tortuous pattern may be seen as absurd, self-destructive, and atrocious — given the misery the alcoholic heaps not only on his or her life but on others' lives as well. Above all, it may appear to be pointless. This is not the case at all; woven throughout the pattern of compulsive drinking is the compelling search for some semblance of meaning — a shred of reality that somehow saves face and makes sense of the horror that is endured. Now this existential pursuit that we call the search for meaning may seem to romanticize alcoholics or raise them to a more deserving plane. Although, as noted, their search marks them as being as human as any of the rest of us (and it is this fact that first enables us to meet them on a common humanistic ground), it is *how* they go about the search that stirs up so many distasteful feelings. For example, they are outrageously selective in what they attend to and perceive; it is indeed a remarkable feat that they are so able to ignore not only the weight of their habit but its onerous effects, on themselves and others whom they claim to care for. They are equally or even more selective about the facts they dredge up out of their past, for these, too, have to conform to their rather shriveled view of their world. How they think would drive the most saintly and patient helper to helpless frustration; the blending of the physical effects of alcohol on the brain with their convoluted, circular, and self-serving conceptions creates, to say the least, some curious versions of self and the world. And the interpretation that is ultimately attached to these cognitions — often the bitter-sweet "noble failure" denotation — not only increases their alienation but, in terms of its intent, justifies and in turn is confirmed by their drinking. But, as incongruous as the "noble failure" role (or the martyr, the unrequited lover, or the tormented clown) may seem when we see the alcoholic standing knee-deep in the self-made debris of his or her life, consider first that this interpretation or role is a metaphor — a symbol of something else in the mind of the alcoholic.

Such a metaphor may be said to allude to the notion of *virtue* — that even though one has failed or hurt others at least one did try to do good. It refers to *value* or the idea that personal standards and beliefs have not entirely vanished. It touches on *morality* insofar as the alcoholic wants to believe that, despite his or her debaucheries, some goodness and righteousness endures. It has to do with a distorted sense of *power* in that the alcoholic may picture him- or herself as the wounded but still upright warrior or as one who, with the help of a few drinks, can still be tough and aggressive. And in whatever way it is meaningful to the alcoholic, it concerns *spirituality* since this sort of nobility or martyrdom somehow connects one to the image of divinity or saintliness. In its overall intent, this metaphor attempts to create the illusion of worth and personal value. Although this illusion, like all others, is fabricated by excesses and distortions in perception and thought, it is after all, the only reality within which we can begin to help this client discover and realize the possibility of a more authentic existence.

But if the root source of the alcoholism lies somewhere in the person's past, is it not pointless to give all this attention to these matters of cognition, meaning, or the stages of the illness? Will it do any good to help alcoholics redefine their meanings and conceptions of self and world if they are still burdened by the permanent baggage of their early life or by some kind of allergy to alcohol itself? Indeed, if they are "allergic," do they really have no choice but to expose themselves to it? Must one live out one's addiction, the course that is plotted out? Is there no choice at any turn? Some of the stories narrated by alcoholic clients may seem to point in this direction. Jay's tale is an example. But then, how do we explain John, who did not become an alcoholic even though his parents were confirmed drinkers whose irresponsibilities ultimately led to John being forced to live in foster homes from the time he was thirteen? Why was John open and trusting with others in a way that encouraged those around him to respond with closeness and support? More important, why didn't he find solace in alcohol since he had all the "reinforcements" and if there is a genetic determinant, he was probably endowed with that as well? Perhaps Jay did have an "active ingredient" John did not have. Quite possibly, someone may advance the notion that John is no doubt a "latent alcoholic" which is, to all intents and purposes, a non-explanation. If we have enough difficulty understanding what someone is doing even when his or her attitudes and actions are patently apparent, how, then, can we make any sense of things people are *not* doing?

Whatever import the past may have as a cause for present behavior is necessarily obscured by the dulled, clogged filter of the mind of the alcoholic as we meet him or her in the midst of one or another of the stages. In one respect, the client's story would, to some extent, be fractured by the effects of prolonged consumption of alcohol on the mental processes of recollection and judgment. Of even greater consequence is the client's need to create meaning and sense out of his or her life. Hence, since the present is so tenuous and undependable and the future is so much in doubt, where else is there to turn for an explanation of "why it turned out this way" but the lush repository of all sorts of experiences (which don't need to, and cannot, be proved) of one's previous days? One can pick and choose, ignore that which may prove to be contradictory, rearrange sequences of events, call forth certain heroics or failures, lay blame anywhere, and otherwise create a tautological tale that comfortably proves whatever needs proving. And in the final analysis, this created meaning serves a purpose — absolution, preservation of dignity, helplessness, or some other intent that perpetuates the noble myth.

Borrowing from the field of genetics, let us invent our own metaphor — *the alcoholic double helix*. Visualize one strand that represents the objective progressive stages of addiction and physiological deterioration and the life patterns that become increasingly absorbed with alcohol. The second strand is pictured as the subjective search for meaning that grows more intense and frantic as it simultaneously becomes more confused and distorted. The progression of one helix is dialectically dependent on the progression of the other. As we have shown, the search for a "high" does not occur randomly but is accompanied by all the reasons the person uses to justify getting the "high." Likewise, the degeneration of personal and social skills, sexual ability, and other functions is rendered meaningful by any number of cognitive inventions. Although the linearity of our language suggests that these relationships are sequential — that one follows the other — this may not be the case as these progressions may well be simultaneous and interdependent.

The evertightening knot that this progression creates ultimately represents the driving force in the life of the alcoholic until life loses its meaning or death occurs. It is an addiction not just of body but of spirit as well; it is like a love that forsakes all others, leaving only itself. As it intensifies it turns inward, further increasing its power and its resistance to contrary information and facts from the outer world. Although each case is a variation on the theme, we can see how, like Amory, the alcoholic builds an entire world on the love of alcohol. The illness and the belief become one.

IN PRACTICE

The assumptions and philosophy covered thus far now need to be translated into some principles of practice that are pertinent to the alcoholic client and his family. We are not proposing a uniform scheme of practice or a therapeutic mold within which the client will need to be fitted. Nor do we intend to give much emphasis and speculation to the "whys" or causes of alcoholism. Following the attention we have given to the signal importance of the way people define personal and social reality (and in the case of alcoholics, the way they persist in behaving so as to perpetuate that necessary reality) we are particularly concerned with the alcoholic's life as it is lived, its meaning, and its purpose. We will see that this humanistic intent does not ignore the pressing need in some way to control the drinking and achieve abstinence. What we wish to stress is that abstinence is necessary but not sufficient to achieve not only lasting sobriety but also a way of life within which that sobriety has some value.

It bears noting at the outset that the helper who works with the alcoholic confronts some very confounding ethical questions — questions that will intrude into every aspect of practice. Although the tenet of self-determination can be grappled with in something of a consistent fashion with non-alcoholic clients, it does not resolve itself very comfortably with the compulsive drinker. The point of the matter is that alcoholics will not determine for themselves to give up their "love"; that is the pivot around which all else turns. Now the helper might assume the practical posture of the surgeon, dismiss the ethical question, and "for the client's own good" cut into the client's patterns and impose his or her will on the situation. This will perhaps do the job, but it will not do much to achieve what we are seeking — and that is a mutual relationship in which the client can begin to assume responsibility for his or her own life.

Goals

We must, for ourselves as well as our clients, begin with as a clear a picture of the problem as possible if we are to help. We need to have some initial grasp of how the client is living out his or her life, and of greater importance, how he or she sees it, explains and expresses it. Some may be abusing alcohol as a temporary reaction to a life crisis. (We need to be open to the possibility that we are *not* dealing with an alcoholic before we can realistically offer help to those who are.) Where it exists, we can usually see the alcohlic progression given enough information. Our goal then would be to help our client (alcoholic and family) to see that as well. This awareness and learning process may begin in treatment, but continues throughout life.

Paradoxically, although one aim is to help clients to make their own choices, we are forced to be somewhat directive in pressing them to abstain from the alcohol and chemical use. As noted, this creates an ethical dilemma for the helper that involves questions of self-determination; yet, clients must be removed from the active progression before they can begin to see their situation clearly. They have an alternative to the power struggle with alcohol: they can "opt out," concede and get support for it. The family likewise can detach from their adaptive roles and resume responsibility for themselves.

148

We do not see abstinence as the panacea nor do we believe it is a one-time decision. Rather, it is a daily choice that must be made within a new style of life that allows new growth to occur. We cannot pre-set *our* desired goals; rather, sincere movement out of the alcoholic progression begins when clients (a) realize that they have the freedom, ability, and desire to set their own goals, and (b) they choose to act on them. This choice may have a far-reaching positive effect for the recovering alcoholic and those around him or her, beyond issues directly discussed. A new priority on a productive family life and social worth can create a new spirit and belief in oneself in sobriety that can grow beyond the old limitations and doubt.

We hope to help those we see to be able to live not for the highs or lows, but for the overall goodness in life. Being well certainly means more than just "not being ill" (Pelletier 1977); we need to strive out of a *basic acceptance* of ourselves, life and an enthusiasm to learn. It is a basic appreciation of life for what it is, rather than resentment for what it is not, that allows for spiritual peace and true growth — ultimately the greatest high.

If we understand alcoholism as primary, progressive, chronic and terminal, we see abstinence as our goal, and the only means to arrest the deterioration. From that beginning, with support, motivation, and awareness, creative life problem-solving can grow into a new belief about oneself, life and sobriety made meaningful for all its joys and disappointments.

The tenets of Alcoholics Anonymous conform in important ways with cognitive-humanism. For many alcoholics, AA can provide the necessary first and lasting steps towards the redefinition of oneself, one's purposes, relationships, and reality.

The AA Twelve Steps (1976) emphasize personal responsibility and the seeking of spiritual growth in recovery. A new brotherhood is based on the once deeply-denied but shared illness of alcoholism. AA helps through "tough-love" to give structure, but also to encourage personal meanings. Alcoholics can focus on the manageable "here and now." They have successful models before them and they can be helped to see the effect of their actions upon others. In making their daily decision for sobriety, they also reaffirm their commitment to a new life and can appreciate that they do indeed have value.

This new belief must have honesty as a basis for an assertive, caring, and direct effort to understand self and others. The alcoholic (and family) frequently will tend to fall back on old patterns of thought; this, and the presence of a physical addiction, make for powerful reasons to look to sobriety as a way of living. False hopes that one might later learn to control drinking undermine the immediate commitment to recovery. The alcoholic again will likely be caught in trying to prove he or she can control the drinking and that there is "no problem."

Generally, the more severe and long-term the alcoholism, the more structured the setting needs to be since the alcoholic lives in a system of patterned behavior that in itself sustains his or her drinking. At least initially, the environmental change to a live-in atmosphere supportive of sobriety, education, and more open communication is preferable if not necessary. Also, the alcoholic may well need detoxification and medical supervision early on during abstinence.

Such an initial program should offer the control and structure the alcoholics need at the early stage of recovery. Here they can learn about alcoholism and be involved in group counseling as well as informal supportive time with their peers. They can apply this learning to their life, supported by individual counseling and family involvement in each step. There should be a collegial, democratic approach where the group members decide issues that bear on their daily lives. Alcoholics can both experience the effect of their actions upon others and help in setting positive plans for themselves and for the welfare of the group.

The alcoholic may be introduced to AA while in the program and begins work on the Twelve Steps. Upon discharge, he or she continues that work, and usually attends a weekly aftercare discussion group that lasts one year. Family, having been involved in the educational program as well as family sessions, are now encouraged to attend Alanon and may be involved in aftercare. Whether alcoholics return home or not, they will be in contact with their family, especially if children are involved. Even if not, the influence of the family roles will still be felt in old and new relationships. Alcoholic patterns tend to recur, especially within the first year, and each person involved needs help to see this. The formal program is only an intensive beginning to a new life-style. Some alcoholics may need further structure and be unable to return home after this formal treatment process. For them, longer-term residential programs or half-way houses may be needed to help them rebuild a solid foundation.

If we work with the alcoholic in an outpatient setting, this needs to be done within a very intensive schedule utilizing daily AA supports and

usually offer a choice of treatment or the loss of their relationship. What is conveyed is that this is done out of caring, usually desperately so, in a very direct way and seriously meant. With all present and with little room for denial, the alcoholic is "walked through" the consequences of his or her alcoholism. This involvement serves to heighten the awareness of all concerned, not solely that of the alcoholic. The awareness may begin at the "bottom," but it is an ongoing, fundamental process throughout treatment. One can hear a hopeful message in the stories of others and the new acceptance they feel as they work to recover. This awareness works reciprocally with sobriety to form both the means (incentive) and the end result (motivation) of a new belief.

Again, this heightening of concerns carries with it our responsibility as helpers to be as clear and honest with ourselves as possible as to whether we have evidence of alcoholism as we look at and experience our client's story. If we so suspect, we need to work further to clarify how it is showing up in our client's experience and to help him or her to see as clearly.

Jay "hit bottom" when the image in the mirror was painfully clear. He came to the alcoholism unit very confused, and under pressure from his wife and friends. He was looking for a label, thinking himself insane. That, at least, was some kind of answer. Beth was reluctant to enter the program, feeling that would imply that she would take Jay back. Eventually, she not only came to help Jay, but also to help herself. Gradually, through the education about alcoholism generally and the hours in which we applied this knowledge to their lives specifically, Jay and Beth set forth to learn how they lived this alcoholic progression to this point in their lives.

At first, both wanted to believe that "Now we're cured!" — as if knowing *about* alcoholism as an illness would itself resolve all the pain. Soon enough, their anger and suffering came to light. Beth recalled years of feeling alone and unwanted. She didn't know if she should blame Jay or herself for being weak, distant, too idealistic, or not hopeful enough. She had to take on home and family responsibility by herself and hated Jay for that, but now could not give up that control she had so relied upon.

Jay swung from feelings of hopefulness, to anger, extreme guilt, and depression. He felt torn and confused by his desire to gain a worthy place with his family, but he was undermined by the guilt that he lived as if he were immoral; he feared he had no value in which to believe. He blamed

Beth for not accepting him back, then would martyr himself and say "Why should she want a dumb fool like me?" We often engaged in a "parley," and I suggested his pain was proof of his value, so deeply violated by his alcoholism.

Gradually the story evolved of how the children coped with the family alcoholism. They showed the pain and disappointment of many broken promises and the fear of what might happen next. The oldest son talked of his role of "protecting mom." This was very difficult for Jay to hear; he felt a deep hurt.

Throughout our working together, Jay and I often "sparred." I was a constant nuisance to him in that I would throw out another view when he tried to make flat judgments about himself and the world. I reminded him of how he had hidden his hopes and feelings in his alcoholism and that he now had to work to accept the ambiguities of life; in many ways I expressed my expectations that he could realistically work to change what was in his power to change. He could start with admitting to his alcoholism and set about re-earning the trust of those close to him to rediscover faith in himself. I brought much of his "existential intellectualizing" down to his primary need to stop avoiding his fears and to accept the consequences of his own behavior: I adopted a somewhat hard line: i.e. "If you don't like it, work on it...," but also let him know he would have my support. Jay's response showed that we both had grown in our relationship.

Gradually, Jay was able to disclose his feelings and, as a result, his severe mood swings diminished. He began to see that reality does not need to be lived at such extremes, and that he was desperately searching for the *absolute* answer, much like one he sought in his earlier years. In first learning to live within the treatment group, Jay began to learn to live with others, to accept his own faults and frustrations, and to accept himself as someone of some worth. The only absolute answer he needed was sobriety. On occasion, he would become very angry at a newly admitted alcoholic and confront him mercilessly. We would ask Jay: "Who are you working on, him or yourself?" At the same time, Jay developed a deep sense of caring that brought others close to him. We reached a point where we could joke about the inconsistencies of life, saying: "Well...on the other hand, maybe it's not *so* bad."

Jay began to define himself as a person of worth and, with this recaptured self-image, began to earn back his self-respect and the trust of others. He spent his weekend passes with his children and began, though tentatively at first, to regenerate their trust in him that he would continue to be there for them as a father.

Upon his leaving the program, Jay continued in aftercare and with AA. He returned to work and found that being sober, he could be accepted and supported for being himself. He began to enjoy his job and found satisfaction in performing his work well and being of service to others. Eventually, he opened his own office-service business. Later he even took up part-time writing for a local sports page. Jay has since stated that, for all he lost, he feels he gained himself.

It needs to be said that we cannot guarantee nor can we seek any one preferred outcome for any one alcoholic and his or her family. Their roles fit together as a system, in a constant effort to achieve stability and control. These roles and beliefs intensify along with the alcoholic pattern; concurrently, they seek control by evasion and denial and by creating other diversions, which encourage the alcoholism to continue. Increasingly then, personal control is abdicated as it shifts to the dominant system. In a sense, the system itself becomes autonomous, out of the control of the members; hence it may well encourage the newly recovering alcoholic to return to the old behavior. "I almost wish he would drink again" is a statement often made by the skeptical wife of an irritable, recovering alcoholic. It is the system that must change in a way that enables each member to become more conscious of his or her part, and to look toward a new goal of self-awareness and growth.

Such growth is creative and continuing. For example, after years of silence, the beleaguered wife of an alcoholic who begins attending Alanon and tells her husband she is doing so, is taking a creative new step. Sally, the girl who stole from her employer, also begins to grow and re-create her life as she challenges her old beliefs that she *had to be* a failure. The couple in counseling who agree to a "mock divorce" creatively put some of their rigid values in a clearer light as they begin the courting process again, this time with a more realistic foundation for their spirited dreams.

Although the helper can count on the helping experience being chaotic, frustrating, and frequently disheartening, within it the alcoholic can be helped to find his or her way through the successive stages that can lead to a redefinition of self, one's relationships, and one's purposes in living. From a cognitive perspective, the process begins precisely where the alcoholic happens to be — usually a sodden debacle of some sort. Whatever new awareness can be mustered will depend on a day-by-day commitment to sobriety. As consciousness begins to displace mindless-ness, it becomes possible for alcoholics to redefine not only the self-serving reality they have created but also their role and responsibili-ties within it. From a humanistic standpoint, it is assumed that ethical, moral, value, and often spiritual issues and questions permeate the former reality and will need to be brought to light if they are to help shape and validate a new and more rewarding reality — "a new life and hope and happiness."

REFERENCES

Alcoholics Anonymous 3rd edition (1976). New York: Alcoholics Anonymous World Services.

Fitzgerald, F. S. (1920) *This Side of Paradise*. New York: Charles Scribners Sons.

Jellinek, E. M. (1952) The Phases of Alcohol Addiction. *Quarterly Journal of Studies on Alcoholism* 13: 673–84.

—— (1960) *The Disease Concept of Alcoholism*. Highland Park, NJ: Hillhouse.

Johnson, V. E. (1980) *I'll Quit Tomorrow*. San Francisco: Harper & Row.

Pelletier, K. (1977) *Mind as Healer, Mind as Slayer*. New York: Dell.

Schuckit, M. and Haglund, M. (1977) An Overview of the Etiological Theories on Alcoholism. In N. Estes and M. E. Heineman (eds) *Alcoholism: Development, Consequences, and Interventions*. St. Louis: C. V. Mosby.

Tiebout, H. (1954) The Ego Functions in Surrender in Alcoholism. *Quarterly Journal of Studies on Alcoholism* 15: 610–21.

Wallace, J. (1978) Working with the Preferred Defense Structure of the Recovering Alcoholic. In S. Zimberg, J. Wallace, and S. Blume (eds) *Practical Approaches to Alcoholism Psychotherapy*. New York: Plenum Press.

—— (1977) Alcoholism from the Inside Out: A Phenomenological Analysis. In N. Estes and M. E. Heineman (eds) *Alcoholism: Development, Consequences, and Interventions*. St. Louis: C. V. Mosby.

Wegscheider, S. (1976) *The Family Trap*. New York: Johnson Institute.

Zimberg, S. (1978) Principles of Alcoholism Psychotherapy. In S. Zimberg, J. Wallace, and S. Blume (eds) *Practical Approaches to Alcoholism Psychotherapy*. New York: Plenum Press.

Chapter 6

The Battered Woman: The Role of her Hope and Fear in Theory and Practice

JUDITH C. HILBERT

Those whose hope is weak settle down for comfort or for violence; those whose hope is strong see and cherish all signs of new life and are ready for every moment to help the birth of that which is ready to be born.   (Fromm 1968: 9)

Mary entered the office looking physically and emotionally downtrodden. Her swollen and blackened eye contrasted incongruously with her attractive glasses and neat clothing. She was one more battered woman requesting help with her violent relationship through the Victim Service Unit of the Justice Center.

Taking a seat in the waiting room among other women displaying varying severities of lacerations, bruises, fractures, and swelling, Mary blended into the atmosphere of resignation and defeat. Although these women shared the same visible and noxious problem, each waited silently, immersed in her own personal thoughts about her shattered dreams and doubtful futures. However, the fact that these women were actually present, reaching out for help (often for the first time in spite of a number of years of beating and abuse at the hands of their partners), symbolized a degree of hope. The nature of that hope, its intensity and direction, is yet to be determined. At this point all one can speculate about is that within each battered woman's despair is an element of desire for something better. We wonder what Mary wants, what she is willing to do, what she hopes for.

Within the past decade or so, spousal violence has become identified as a major problem in American homes (Straus, Gelles, and Steinmetz 1980). Extensive research has been conducted to determine the extent, breadth, and causal factors related to domestic abuse. Simultaneously, programs,

157

initially designed in a grass-roots fashion, have evolved wherein helping professionals now approach intervention with individuals in violent relationships from a number of positions. For example, some services support victims' advocacy for protection and/or prosecution within the criminal justice system. Others offer individual counseling either for the victim or the defendant in a case of domestic violence. Services designed by some traditional therapists, on the other hand, might offer conjoint therapy, discount the violence as a criminal act and consider it more as symptomatic of say, a sado-masochistic relationship. Finally, feminists may design services from the position of the need for separation and provide secret and safe housing for battered women and their children.

Such a range in service approaches underscores the diversity in philosophy, policy, emphasis, and effectiveness inherent in service designs that often represent particular ideological beliefs. For example, diversity exists even among the various shelters for battered women. The feminist shelters, with their "separate but equal" perspective of person, design their programs to enable these clients to become more capable of planning and directing their lives — often without the company of their partners. The other side of this ideological continuum might be represented by the religious shelters which also serve women caught in violent relationships. These shelters are founded upon a philosophy of love rather than empowerment. They are predominantly staffed by women who profess an abiding and deep faith, and who believe that through unconditional love (and religious devotion) battered women can be helped to find meaning and purpose in their lives. Interestingly, the issue of maintaining the marriage is minimally addressed, even among those religious sects that especially value the sanctity of the marital contract. Again, the focus is on enabling the woman to help herself in some manner. Clearly the means of self-help differentiates the various types of shelter facilities.

Despite the good intentions of these various services, a large number of battered women who use them in one way or another appear eventually to sabotage the objectives of the particular programs. Some, after taking what the shelter has to offer, seem to return impulsively to the same dangerous relationship from which they recently had to flee. Others who seek and obtain legal protection suddenly seem to change their original intentions to press charges and, in fact, drop the very action which was offered as help to them. These unpredictable reversals and shifts are not totally peculiar given the tumultuous nature of these women's lives.

Yet, it would seem that the effectiveness of a program designed to help the battered woman would depend on the extent to which it is tailored to this woman's inner needs, values, hopes, fears, and aspirations. This means that rather than creating a helping program that is based on someone else's preconceived notions (ideological, religious, or otherwise) such an effort should be personalized to take account of each woman's unique vision of reality. As Lynch and Norris propose:

> We must get back to basics — ask who we are trying to help, what kind of help is needed and if we are giving it to the right people ... then try to integrate our perceptions and experience with what can be learned from other programs and fields of knowledge. In this way we can attempt to impose a little order in the chaos around us. (Lynch and Norris 1978: 554)

The intent of this chapter is to outline a cognitive-humanist model of practice for battered women which begins with the basics of the subjective reality of the woman herself and incorporates theoretical positions that are consonant with principles of social work action. Such a program is designed to be of assistance to people like Mary who at last have taken the first step to reconsider the meaning of their lives and plan a course of action which includes "the birth of that which is ready to be born."

PHILOSOPHICAL AND THEORETICAL CONSIDERATIONS

This approach to practice with battered women is premised upon the assumption that people are very capable of change and growth in a productive manner. In Mary's case, her entry into a helping system is not seen as a simple reaction to a beating; rather, her behavior is appreciated as a tentative step towards a future that may possibly offer some sort of new beginning. The beating, per se, is of course not minimized. But in and of itself, this beating did not make her seek help. If this were the case how can we explain the fact that not all battered women seek help? Moreover, how should we understand why battered women who have been beaten countless times seek help for themselves at this point and on this occasion? Some writers propose that the episode preceding help-seeking probably differed from others; for example, the batterer may, for the first time, have used a weapon or struck a child. However, research addressing this "why now?" question discloses contradictory findings.

I would suggest that the plea for help at this point has more to do with the possibility that the woman has begun, in no doubt crude and

159

unformed terms, to redefine the meaning of her life in a way that impels her to reach out toward a more hopeful future. Statements such as "I'm just tired of it all," "I can't take it any more," or "There must be something better than this,"[1] more accurately represent an awakening of consciousness rather than a feeling of "enough is enough." Simply put, it is at this point in their lives that these women are no longer merely reacting, but are instead acting for the sake of something of value.

This belief in the proactive nature of the person is coupled with the idea that each person is her own best judge of her own reality — a reality that is the product of her own construction. This is not to say that she has made up, manufactured, or imagined her situation as difficult when in fact it is not so awful. Instead, it does suggest that her subjective view of her world, her definition of her situation, albeit construed through interaction with others and perhaps in conflict with others' abilities, is in fact her best rendition of her reality. Thus, Mary, like every other individual, is understood as a being with idiosyncratic hopes, fears, dreams, and intentions. If we were to get to know all the battered women sharing the waiting room with her, we would find that despite their common suffering, each woman perceives her situation as unique in some important way.

An existential view

This philosophical perspective is consonant with an existential view of humankind. Existential thinking suggests that existence precedes essence: one is born and given life, but the definition and meaning of that life are acquired and shaped throughout the course of a lifetime. The critical factor in self-definition is personal choice. Difficult times (or "life crises" in social work jargon) are, in existential terms, perceived as opportunities for growth and are therefore not denied. Each time an individual is confronted with a situation demanding critical life-choices, the possibility for a new beginning occurs.

Mary and others who present their stories to the Victim Services workers frequently say that they "have no other choice but to prosecute their partners." Prosecution is perceived as a last resort in this very emotionally complex and life-threatening situation: the "person of principle" is clearly manifested. The moral standards which compel the battered woman to choose to proceed with prosecution are couched in such phrases as: "I wasn't raised in a violent home." Brenda, whose husband repeatedly beat her with a vacuum-cleaner cord, expressed this moral principle when she said:

160

This is just something I cannot live with. I don't want to be a battered wife. They say "for better or worse," and I think we've been through better or for worse. But the physical thing I told him I won't go for. And now he says, "Well I haven't hit you in six months." That's not the point, even if it is six years, I don't want it to be at all. I prefer to have him prosecuted for the physical abuse he has already caused so I can go home, the kids can go home, and we can live a civil life for a while. I wasn't raised this way. It just isn't right. Marriage means more than this.

In choosing to take legal action against her husband, Brenda is beginning the process of rebirth, renewal, and a reaffirmation of the meaning of her life. This new beginning symbolizes an occasion on which she can reach toward the future and responsibly direct her life with feelings of power, not helplessness; with hope, not despair; with anticipation, not fear; with creativity, not conformity. For all battered women this perspective is most critical. Unless they come to appreciate the possibilities for personal choice, they will remain a "victim" which, by definition, implies hopelessness, vulnerability, and despair. The acceptance of personal choice and the belief about the worth of her life will enable a battered woman to accept the responsibility for her life's direction without the sense of continued victimization and oppression. The shroud of helplessness is lifted. But this step is not without anguish; for lying in the place of oppression is the spectre of isolation.

Once an individual accepts the ideal of self-responsibility, she also accepts the consequence of "going it alone." It is this point at which the meaning of existence comes into question; it is when the search for self-identity is initiated that anguish is experienced. Mary Daly states this idea well when, in referring specifically to battered women, she says:

The loss of self can be seen as a necessary and first step in a "death and re-birth" process which must take place in order for a new identity, new roles and behaviors to supplant the old. Becoming who we really are requires existential courage to confront the experience of nothingness. All human beings are threatened by this non-being. (*in* Ridington 1977–78)

Rejecting the nothingness of life requires acceptance of the possible solitary nature of one's life course. The risks a person takes in making life choices are laden with serious consequences; if we choose to determine for ourselves, this choice may involve having to face giving up a relationship. The unwillingness to go it alone was expressed by a young battered wife who said that if it took fifteen years of counseling for her husband to change his violent behavior, she would wait for him. "I kept thinking in my head," she said, "is it really that bad a hit to destroy my whole marriage and my whole life?" Other women symbolically speak from their person of faith when they suggest that "these rings were blessed" and "the sin would be upon my head if I were to divorce him." Yet if these women accept the power of personal choice, they also have to accept the consequences since credit or blame cannot be placed elsewhere. For these women, staying within the battering relationship while armed with the knowledge of other possible life alternatives demands their acceptance of self-responsibility for making this choice. It is this existential perspective that is the foundation and philosophy for this approach to practice with battered women.

Understandably, the reader may find in this philosophical perspective a somewhat over-romanticized characterization of the battered woman. After all, her life, to an outsider, may appear rather wretched; her relationship with the batterer scarcely invites much sympathy — given the way these partners seem to feed symbiotically on each one's push-pull attraction for the other; and the violence that results often spills over into and upsets other people's lives — family, neighbors, and community.

It is for these very reasons that it is essential that we keep in mind the fact that amidst the debris of the battered woman's life, a trace of sincere humanness, a longing for some sense of dignity, may still persist. Faced with the repulsive evidence of brutality — a bruised body, a bloodied face — and hearing the client's litany of mistreatment and anguish, sometimes stretching over years, the helper to whom this client has turned may easily become a partner in this woman's despair and hopelessness. On the other hand, the worker may reflexively elevate the battered woman to a state of sainthood or martyrdom. Clearly, we advocate neither reaction and, instead, encourage respect for any trace of dignity or responsibility that the search for help may symbolize.

A theoretical view

From a theoretical standpoint, there are a large number of perspectives that attempt to explain the phenomenon of domestic violence. They fall into three major categories which include intra-individual, social-psycho-logical, and socio-cultural theories. The intra-individual theories presuppose that the behavior of a battered woman can be best explained in intra-psychic or psychopathological terms. In this view, the masochistic personality structure of the woman is the key variable that explains her continual involvement in a violent relationship. The social-psychological theories posit that understanding of the battering relationship from the abused person's perspective requires that the psychological or personality factors be combined with variables in the social environment. These theories take into consideration the social, interactive nature of people. Finally, socio-cultural theories provide a macro-level analysis of domestic violence. They suggest, for example, that "socially structured inequality and cultural attitudes and norms about family and family relationships" are factors that explain the existence and continuance of family violence (Gelles 1980).

Our concern with the interactive nature of a person that involves the individual's capacity to self-define, self-determine, and responsibly function within a social system is consistent with the social-psychological orientation. This perspective is less concerned with the attempt to explain the existence of domestic violence (which is a doubtful undertaking) than it is with understanding ways to better help those women who request services that might possibly help them deal with their life-threatening situations. Most important in regard to a cognitive-humanistic approach, this orientation addresses the subjective reality of these women and their closely-held conceptions of meaning, intention, hope, and fear.

An understanding of the meaning of the battering relationship and the process of help-seeking is enlarged by aspects of George Mead's theory of symbolic interaction. The basic assumption of this theory points to the voluntaristic component of human conduct, i.e. the belief that people have some choice in their behavior. It also offers a dialectical conception of the mind or the idea that individuals have the ability to think and reflect upon the self and its motives: simply, one can think about what one thinks and believes in a way that may lead to new or revised thoughts or beliefs. As applied to battered women, it is assumed that they are capable of cognitively reframing their self-concepts through reflective thinking. This is critical since often these women have defined themselves not as distinct individuals, but as a fixed part of a complementary relationship with a battering partner. This emphasis on the relation between the reflective capacities of the individual and her self-concept reflects the existential nature of symbolic interactions: "Human beings, in part, are participants in creating their destinies" (Manis and Meltzer 1978: 8).

Another cognitive theme found in the theory of symbolic interaction is that human behavior and interaction rely on the medium of symbols and their meanings. Thus, to understand one's behavior it is necessary to comprehend the meaning the individual attaches to her social world — the interactional sphere that involves others (Manis and Meltzer 1978). The metaphors or symbols that the battered woman uses to describe her situation therefore offer some clues to the helping person about the meaning she is giving to the relationship with her partner. Statements like "I must be crazy to love this man," or "I'm so ashamed he beats me," give some indication of how she defines and symbolizes herself within the battering relationship.

Where symbolic interaction provides us with a way of grasping the reflective, cognitive, and transactional features of the battered woman and her situation, Lenore Walker's theory of bonding tells us something about the dynamics of the battering relationship itself (1979). Walker suggests this relationship is cyclical, which accounts for the "victimization" of the woman. Phase I, the tension-building phase, involves minor battering incidents. During this period, the woman legitimates these incidents, so to speak, by minimizing their existence and, in effect, denying the inappropriateness of this behavior. This minimization and denial on the part of the "victim" is similar to the cognitive gymnastics performed by the non-drinking partner in an alcoholic relationship. Beneath the denial is the hope that the relationship will improve over time. As a result, the batterer does not attempt or need to control himself and so the violence escalates. At the same time, the partner becomes even more possessive, jealous, and oppressive "in the hope that his brutality will keep her captive" (Walker 1979: 51). The "victim" learns she is powerless to prevent the rest of the cycle from occurring and, although afraid to stay, she believes that she is powerless to leave.

Phase II represents the more serious battering incident that is triggered principally by some external event and/or by the batterer's internal state. This phase is generally intense, relentless, and unpredictable. During this time the woman is often assaulted by verbal abuse as well. If it is the case that these women derive their sense of self-worth out of their transactions with their partners, it would be expected that whatever self-esteem they cling to would be systematically diminished — particularly if they have little opportunity to test their value in other environments and relationships. One woman, for example, who was battered for fifteen years, was routinely told to look in the mirror and see what an "asshole" she was. While she acknowledged that she learned to believe she was an "asshole," if only by subjecting herself to her husband's presence, at the same time she felt that other people would likewise believe she was a fool even if she left the battering relationship. Her self-concept, developed through her interaction with her husband, extended to what she expected others would think of her.

The battered woman often receives a number of mixed and conflicting messages from the very person in whom she has placed her greatest trust: at one time, her partner may proclaim her worthlessness or that she deserves this treatment because of her transgression; in the next moment, he may plead that this is his way of showing how valuable she is to him because he loves her.

Phase III is a period of loving kindness and contrition on the part of the batterer. He is apologetic, convinced that this will never happen again, and he seeks her forgiveness. His most charming Dr Jekyll self emerges in an attempt to bury Mr Hyde. Hope for the relationship is again rekindled and, within a short period of time, the woman might change from feeling lonely, hopeless, angry, and fearful to a happy, confident, and loving person. The trap has been set with the bait of hope, fear, and power. The bond between the partners is strengthened by these dynamics.

Experience with battered women indicates that they do indeed share certain similar patterns in their respective relationships with their battering partners. Moreover, they are often surprised when they discover that other battered women react to their own battering relationship in much the same manner. The isolation these women are subjected to, their separation from friends and family, contributes directly to their ignorance of the fact that other such "victims" share a common definition of their situations.

The observation of these more or less common and broad patterns of interaction in a violent relationship does not overlook the fact that the individual woman can and does formulate her own personal and unique definition of the situation (Stebbins 1978). It is this personal interpretation of the meaning of the battering relationship with which we are concerned since this subjective definition of reality, the woman's special way of conceptualizing her hopes, fears, and intentions is what makes her unique within the population of battered women. What may not be "that bad" to one woman may be "enough" for another. Again, this subjective definition implies that she alone is the ultimate expert and final arbiter about the meaning of her circumstances. In spite of how unreal, irrational, or incredible her definition may appear to an outsider, to the battered woman the relationship is her reality and is personally construed to make sense in a particular way. Ridington's findings support this view. She suggests battered women who enter shelters do so for immediate and personal meanings. "They are seeking to resolve problems they regard as only theirs. Their disillusionment is with themselves, their husbands, and their own marriage" (Ridington 1977–78).

Our interest in the meaning of the battering relationship to the abused woman and the ways in which she might learn to redefine her situation through the process of help-seeking can be summed up in the following assumptions that reflect the theoretical point of view of symbolic interaction and the philosophy of existentialism.

First of all, individuals are ever-changing and, in this process, are the best judges of their life situation and its direction. This assumption addresses the self-defining quality of the person and becomes the guiding principle in our work with battered women.

Second, the individual's growth is typically future-oriented. Thus, battered women are not seen as restricted or determined by their past lives. Such a position speaks to the self-determining and intentional nature of people.

Third, significant change becomes possible when individuals dare to confront the nothingness of their existence and so begin to question the meaning of life. More often than not, the battered woman who seeks help through the criminal justice system becomes thoughtfully quiet when asked what is good or redeeming about her relationship with the batterer. Typically, her response is "Nothing."

Fourth, individuals are not seen as helpless victims who are merely reacting to conditions in their environments. What has been said to this point suggests that they are capable of making their own choices about their own life's circumstances.

Other assumptions about battered women necessarily include the concepts of hope, self-concept, bonding, and meaning. We consider that the battered woman, like most women, first entered her relationship with her partner with some hope for its permanence. Moreover, in this population in particular, the battered woman's sense of who she is (self-concept) is shaped through the continuing interaction with her abuser. This relationship is cemented by a sort of bonding process where hope, fear, and powerlessness press her to accept her partner's definition of their relationship. Although others in her own family may argue that violence is not an acceptable part of living and loving, the woman's loyalty to and dependence upon her partner leads her to embrace his view. Finally, personal change becomes possible when the battered woman confronts the very meaning of *her* very own existence and comes to see the shallowness and danger of the relationship and the tenuous hold she has on her life with this partner.

These assumptions then lead to a theoretical perspective for a cognitive and humanistic approach to practice with battered women who seek help. The guiding principles of our approach are as follows:

(1) A battered woman is likely to share her partner's definition of their situation as long as her hope persists that the relationship will improve. In Mary's case, her husband began beating her two years before when she was eight months pregnant. The beatings increased, becoming more frequent and more intense as time went on. What precipitated her seeking help was directly related to a change in her feelings of hope for this relationship. Suspecting that her husband was involved with another woman, Mary eventually went to this woman's apartment. She found her husband there, and returned home, hurt and angry. He followed her and stayed long enough to beat her severely with a chain. He returned the next morning to continue the assault, this time using an umbrella as a weapon. The black eye, multiple bruises, fractured ribs, and chain marks on Mary's body became inescapable reminders of his involvement with another woman. Now hopeless, Mary sought help as soon as he left.

(2) When there is no longer a shared definition of the relationship, the battered woman must now question the meaning of her life and is painfully open to the need for new meanings. Mary now had to think about whether she truly deserved this type of treatment; at the same time she had to contend with questions about what living in fear, isolation, and helplessness would mean to her and her two-year-old son. Very tentatively, she began to feel some sense of confidence in her new belief that the marriage was destructive — this despite her husband's proclamation that she alone in fact brought this trouble upon herself.

(3) When a battered woman does question the meaning of life, any intentions she has to change her life circumstances depend on her perception of the field of possible choices she sees open to her. The Victim Service program offers battered women legal and protection measures which gave Mary the immediate choices of seeking a temporary protection order (similar to a restraining order), filing a criminal charge of domestic violence, and/or entering a safe place such as a shelter. She chose to obtain a protection order and press domestic violence charges.

(4) When a battered woman decides to take action, she must also be apprised in as helpful but direct a way as possible of the possible consequences of this choice. When Mary reappeared in the worker's office with new bruises (her husband refused to honor the protection order and beat her again), she was better prepared for the ensuing court hearings. Although she knew her legal actions had further enraged her

husband, she also recognized that none of her actions would ever guarantee a peaceful relationship between them. She felt the best alternative was to follow through with the hearing, leave town, and then dismiss the criminal charges in substitution for a civil divorce action.

The issue of choice needs special consideration when working with these women. Mary, like most battered women, was necessarily forced to choose the best option from a list of what are essentially poor choices. Clearly, going "on the run" with small children, little money and few, if any, personal possessions is one alternative most of us would not consider as favorable. Nor would we eagerly anticipate entering a shelter, crowded with strangers who, like Mary, are undergoing their own chaos and pain. Even the advent of a divorce is little comfort for these women as, all too often, the batterer simply will not sever his ties with her until *he* is ready to do so. Given that he apparently does not respect the law that says that wife-beating is a criminal offense, what hope is there that he will respect a civil order that this relationship is over? Hence, many women must leave their home state and be secreted in another part of the country in order to feel safely distanced from a divorced partner.

One option which on the surface may appear paradoxical is to choose to do nothing. If the battered woman consciously decides for the present to let life continue as it is, she can be helped to see that she is not entirely helpless and that her situation is not entirely hopeless: in choosing to do nothing, she can attain some sense of personal power. It is when a battered woman really believes that she has no choices at all that she feels doomed and despairing about her situation. Often phrases like "Death would be welcomed" speak to this reactive stance while the victim waits for the final blow, the ultimate act of battering to release her from the uncertainty of life of pain and despair. Doing nothing, then, may become choosing death. Within a cognitive-humanist perspective, we must give honest and open consideration to the possibility that this may be an active and responsible choice.

In the final analysis, these theoretical and philosophical suppositions and the principles of practice that logically follow are somewhat hollow if we overlook the way that *fear* contaminates every aspect of the battered woman's life — and most important, bears on the possibility of hope for something better, however "better" is defined. For a moment, consider what it must feel like to share your home, your body, your possessions, your dreams, and your future with a partner whom you fear. Consider what it must be like never to be assured that each gesture of caring, each hug, for example, can be accepted in and of itself as a loving contact.

Battered women live in a reality in which hugs quickly turn to hits, where a pat on the rear end can just as easily be a kick in the ass, and where making love can become rape. Yet within the personal, unique definition of the battering situation the elements of fear and hope must co-exist in some fashion if the woman is to have any hold on her sanity.

No doubt the battered woman experiences two types of fear — the fear of staying involved with her partner and the fear of leaving and having to face a threatening world of strangers. But battered women who seek help through the criminal justice system are faced with yet another fear, and that is the fear of reprisal. Consider that by seeking help the woman is explicitly revealing that she is extremely frightened of her partner's behavior. Once the battered woman initiates action to protect herself, she may become terrified that by this very action she may have put herself in greater jeopardy. If she believes out of past experience that her partner may become more angry when she is assertive, she will then anticipate that he will do greater harm in response to this particular action. Her sense of powerlessness is extreme. His power, on the other hand, seems almost magical. Typically the battered woman is afraid to face her partner in the preliminary court hearing. There he may be under police guard, yet she is afraid to meet his eyes since the look he might send her is forewarning of more bad things to come. The reassurance of the most well-meaning helping person may, at this point, appear empty and meaningless.

Yet, there is another side to this very poignant fear that we must not lose sight of — and that is the power of an emerging and tentative *hope* for herself and for a better life that makes it possible for this woman to make the first step beyond the paralyzing nature of this fear. It may signal that she has begun to give up the long-standing belief in the permanence of her relationship and the continued hope for its improvement. Moreover, it may mean that the battered woman has begun to consider that she is perhaps worthwhile and deserving of something more than the battering relationship offered. Hence, however we apply the aforementioned principles, the support that is offered, the action that is taken, must take serious account of the painful tension and the delicate balance that characterize the pull between hope and fear.

LINKING THEORY TO PRACTICE WITH BATTERED WOMEN

The guiding principles just outlined are designed to ensure an approach to working with these troubled women that is as free as possible of fuzzy and nebulous interventions — no matter how well-meaning these intentions might be. There is little room for random, trial-and-error methods in practice with battered women: too much is at risk. It is not just that her physical well-being (if not her life) is at stake, but that at this critical moment, a very special opportunity to do something meaningful about her definition of her life and future needs to be seized.

Lin suggests that "the utilization of models constitutes one effective way of constructing and evaluating potential theories" (Lin 1976: 42). Since our intent now is to translate the philosophical and theoretical propositions already outlined into a reasonable and responsive approach to working with the battered woman, the following model (*Figure 3*) offers a visual perspective on the process of help-seeking and help-giving following the woman's pursuit of assistance. As a heuristic scheme designed merely to capture the related elements of the process (a more detailed discussion follows), it does reflect what we know about how people learn to deal with their problems of living — with or without the assistance of professional help.

In this regard, the model shows the sequence of awareness, reflection, thought, and action that can lead to or impede the successful solution to, in this case, the problem of abuse. This is, of course, not a simple linear process that unfolds without stress or pain. At each point, the client confronts certain critical contingencies and choices, each having implications for the kind of progress or regress that bears on her existence. Hence, the model portrays the responsive role of the helper who, when alert to these critical contingencies, can provide the kind of climate, learning opportunities and incentives required by the client to find her way.

Hope and meaning

Although in real life one's feelings for or against something, one's hopes or misgivings, do not fall into mutually exclusive ways of thinking, this model points to the "more so than not" qualities of the woman's outlook on her circumstances. As to the concepts of hope and meaning, it is only when the battered woman begins to sense that her relationship is hopeless and at the same time begins to see that she does not need to accept her partner's definition of what her life with him will or must be like, that serious questions about the very meaning of her life come to the surface. Aware as she is of the inescapability of her plight, she may then be likely to seek help.

FIGURE 3   A cognitive-social learning model of the contingencies of help-seeking and responsive help-giving

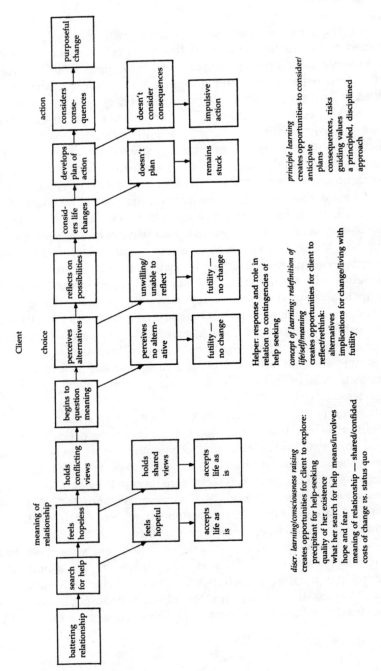

171

A delicate balance

Perhaps the most creative aspect of work with battered women is reflected in the practitioner's ability to strike a delicate balance between these many conflicting, opposing beliefs. For example, while the woman may indeed express her bitter disappointment with her partner, and indeed despair about his terrible treatment of her, she may still need to preserve her beliefs about his "basic goodness." She was, after all, drawn at one time to his qualities of charm, or attentiveness, or attractiveness, or whatever; vestiges of these attributes may still remain, or she may find it painful to acknowledge her past poor judgment. In either case, should the practitioner become critical of his Mr Hyde personality, nevertheless he or she must take care not to be overly critical of the Dr Jekyll. At the same time, the helping person cannot offer, even implicitly, any false hope that, as a result of the woman's assertive action to seek help, Dr Jekyll and Mr Hyde will merge to create a reasonable, well balanced, caring individual. All too often, in their zeal to help and to identify themselves with the suffering of the battered woman, practitioners will attempt to accept and to be very supportive of the woman's denigration of her partner — as if it were total. One must be mindful that in a battering relationship, denigration of the batterer implies, in part, denigration of the abused. Thus, during the initial phase of help-seeking, it is more reasonable to focus attention on the meaning to the woman of her immediate existence rather than on her partner's personality, motives, or character.

Although many women appear to seek help from what seems to be a position of vulnerability and helplessness, it is nonetheless essential to attend to the woman's strengths. Again the helper must cautiously balance the advice and counsel he or she gives to these women against the client's personal competencies — meagre though they may seem to be at the moment. Simply responding to the woman's request to "Tell me what to do" can dangerously replicate the dependent, one-down, relationship she has experienced with her battering partner.

One also needs to strike a delicate balance in one's response to the client's story about the violence she has endured. Hammond's[2] description of the four characteristics of a violent crime may address this issue. Hammond suggests, first of all, that dehumanization or the objectification of the victim occurs. For battered women, we find this generally begins on a verbal level. Carol, married six months and pregnant with Brian's child, graphically describes this process:

Well, the first time he called me names and I wasn't used to that. Real bad names and I said I wasn't gonna stay around while he called me names. It made me feel like a dirty dog and stuff. I figure, geez, he's suppose to love me more since we were married and have more respect, you know. Ever since I've known him he never called me nothing and it shocked me. The second time he pulled my hair and hit me in the back of the head. Now he beats me with a belt. I have bruises on my rear end and it's embarrassing, you know. It's like he doesn't treat me like a real person.

And Jane, married fifteen years, shamefully tells how each time she walked into a room her husband would announce "here comes the fat hog." Her thirteen-year-old son continues to refer to her in that manner even though Jane is no longer married to his father. To battered women, the dehumanization through derisive name-calling is more painful than the physical pain of the beatings. It is this emotional hurt that scars the woman's basic sense of self.

Second, in crimes of violence the victim experiences a violation of her physical and personal territory. Phrases such as "He gets right up in my face," "He jumped on me," and "He allows me no room to breathe," illustrate this point. Nothing is private in a battered woman's life. Her belongings, her telephone conversations, her friendships are all open to her partner's scrutiny. During the battering incident the woman's personal world is continuously invaded. Recalling these incidents, battered women's conversations are generously tainted with words like "trapped," "blocked," "cornered," and "imprisoned."

The third aspect is violation of the victim's integrity. Being forced to engage in behavior which is morally reprehensible to the woman is common. For example, one client shamefully described how her husband began his assault by referring to her as "slut," "whore," and "bitch." After a bout of this vilification, followed by a beating, he then demanded sex on his terms. When she refused, claiming she was menstruating, he demanded that she show him that this was indeed the case. Millet, although referring to child abuse, terms this "an invasion of the mind practiced upon the body" (1979: 77).

Finally, the victim experiences a loss of control. Her total being is subject to her batterer's whims. How she dresses, what she says, or who she likes, is dictated by her partner. Earlier we spoke of Jane who eventually left her abusive partner. Although the beatings went on for years, it was not until he demanded one night that she stay awake until he fell asleep that she decided to get out of the relationship; his demand was reinforced with a threat of death. Holding a knife to her neck, he told her that if she fell asleep he would slit her throat. Now even sleep was no longer a remaining sanctuary for her.

Hammond's paradigm offers important insights for the helper. Doing *for* the client, objectifying her bruises, directing her activities, or planning for her "new life" is just a kinder version of the previous assaults she has experienced. For helpers, "rescuing" the woman may in fact merely reinforce the helplessness and powerlessness she feels about her life in general. Again, attending to how she herself conceptualizes the meaning of her existence is the necessary first step toward helping her become "my own person."

Reflection and choice

The second stage of the model depicts the relationship between the willingness to think, reflect, and question and the perceptions of choices that might be made. To be sure, there is likely to be little incentive to break out of the abusive pattern if no alternatives are present in the woman's mind — no matter how much she ruminates about her difficult and sad state. And if her thinking is totally blocked, then she can only look forward to more of the same. We suggest that the battered woman's incentive to change her life is more likely to occur when she has critically considered the meaning of her existence and perceives that there are choices available for an alternative style of living. With this emerging consciousness, it becomes possible to creatively explore these possible choices with the client. Expanding the field of possible alternatives to the maximum is necessary.

When Sue sought legal protection from her abusive boyfriend, she expressed the futility of ever obtaining safety from him. She told how, on previous occasions, she had tried to get the police to protect her, and how she had moved out of his apartment and had sought shelter for a while in her parents' home. In spite of these efforts, he had followed her, broken into her bedroom through the window, and threatened her with death. Since he had already served a brief time for the murder of his former girlfriend, and he was "on papers" and conversant with the system of obtaining bond and how to delay court actions, Sue felt that legal action on her part would simply result in her death warrant. "After all," she said, "I'm worried about when he's out on bond, waiting to go to court. Him knowing that he's gonna be sentenced to the penitentiary doesn't seem like it would really be too much for him to come over and try to do something since he's going anyway." She believed she had no choices left because "He just isn't going to leave me alone." Yet when the helper asked how Sue could feel safe, she flippantly responded "Out of town." Although the worker indicated that a move out of state was possible if Sue desired this, she quickly discounted that possibility due to the lack of finances. The following day, however, Sue called wanting to talk about whether the worker could help her consider arrangements for her to leave the state. Ultimately, she was able to obtain bus money and, through the battered woman's network, the worker arranged for her to reside in an out-of-state shelter for four weeks until she could become employed and establish her permanent residence there. Until the alternative of relocation became possible in her field of choices, Sue was resigned to life with fear and pain. The new realization that she could choose to leave town and reconstruct a life for herself and her two children freed her from chaos and violence.

Motives and implications

Finally, our model links the relationship between the battered woman's motives or intentions to do something to escape or protect herself from abuse and the way she envisions the consequences of this intention. If after thought and reflection, her motives remain vague or unformed and she avoids any consideration of the consequences of her state, then it is likely that the problem will persist. Feeling unsure about what to do, yet realizing the implications of this way of being, will tend to ensure the same outcome but with the added burden of stress and conflicting emotions. Should she consider some specific alternatives but fail to give much thought to their outcomes, then possibly her action will be haphazard, if she decides to risk change at all.

Sue's circumstances exemplify the importance of some balance between action and thoughtful planning. When Sue intended to change her life, how she followed through depended on a degree of congruence between her plan and her ability to consider its consequences. At this point, it was incumbent upon the practitioner to ask Sue to anticipate and imagine the many possible outcomes of her intended move. Leaving her home state meant leaving everything with which she was familiar. On the other hand, moving could be seen as an adventure, a real opportunity to

Creative Change

begin anew. Employment appeared to be an obstacle until Sue considered the possibility of being transferred from her current employment to the same fast-food franchise in the south. Even the change in climate was discussed with all its advantages and disadvantages. In other words, until she had the opportunity to imagine the consequences, good and bad, of her intention to relocate, no action would be taken. When she was ready, she bought her bus tickets and left town. Congruence, then, must exist among what the battered woman expects to gain by reconstructing her reality, what she will need to do to achieve this change, and how she feels about what she must do to reach her intended goals. The consequences of her chosen alternatives must be apprised if this risk is to be successfully undertaken.

THE PRACTICE APPROACH: PRINCIPLES, GOALS, AND OBJECTIVES

Complementing the client's help-seeking process in *Figure 3* is a social learning model of practice outlined in *Figure 4*. Within a cognitive-humanist perspective it includes the learning stages of consciousness-raising or discrimination-learning, redefinition of reality or concept-learning, and principle-learning. Goldstein suggests that the concept of social learning "provides an explanation of the way people resolve problems ... and for the mere purposes of analysis, can be described as a logical and progressive series of stages" (Goldstein 1981: 257). Discrimination-learning enables one to experience a broadening of awareness of the situation under consideration and is the primary and necessary consciousness-raising level of learning. Concept-learning based on new awareness occurs as the individual reframes, reformulates, or redefines a problem situation. The ability to make sense of that situation in a new and creative way now enables him or her to reorganize reality so as to consider possible forms of action or change. Finally, principle-learning entails "movement beyond knowing (cognition) to include the influence of personal values ... if this learning is to be translated in consistent, personally meaningful and autonomous behavior" (Goldstein 1981: 257). We will show how this social learning model of practice can be translated into particular practice principles for work with battered women.

Consciousness-raising/discrimination-learning

Let us consider the significance and timeliness of the opportunity to expand one's awareness — particularly at the point where the battered

FIGURE 4 Linking propositional statements of help-seeking relative to battered women with a social learning perspective of practice

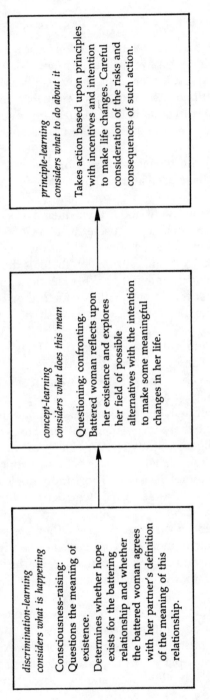

discrimination-learning
considers what is happening

Consciousness-raising:
Questions the meaning of existence.
Determines whether hope exists for the battering relationship and whether the battered woman agrees with her partner's definition of the meaning of this relationship.

concept-learning
considers what does this mean

Questioning; confronting.
Battered woman reflects upon her existence and explores her field of possible alternatives with the intention to make some meaningful changes in her life.

principle-learning
considers what to do about it

Takes action based upon principles with incentives and intention to make life changes. Careful consideration of the risks and consequences of such action.

woman has given up hope that things will improve and, at the same time, is very much alone in how she defines their relationship. For example, women who request legal and protective services and who see criminal prosecution as their last resort have probably discussed their painful situation before with other helping professionals such as their clergy, law enforcement personnel, mental health practitioners, and/or their family doctors. While one might assume that the woman's burgeoning awareness that the violence heaped on her is basically immoral and criminal might have been affirmed by such helping professionals, that is not always the case. In fact, some battered women are often more confused and ambivalent about their dilemma because of the doubtful responses of these helpers. Consider what a victim's reactions would be to a police response such as "I'm sorry but there is nothing we can do to help you," the clergyman's suggestion that it is the wife's duty to "make the best of it," or the mental health practitioner's attempt to help her explore her masochistic personality structure or other inner dynamics that are basic to her "need" to involve herself in such a damaging relationship.

Worse yet, uninformed practitioners may focus on ways of helping *her* to help *him*. There are two very dangerous implications in this orientation. First of all, many battered women are extremely empathetic; their desire to be understanding of their partner's abuse is rather profound. Rather than becoming outraged about his cruel and inappropriate behavior, a battered woman may attempt to explain and justify these outbursts. Gilligan's study (1977, 1982) of moral decision-making addresses this issue. She suggests that one's conception of self affects how one makes moral decisions. Those individuals who can "assume the role of the other" in Mead's terms, "tend to use a morality of care (sic) that rests on an understanding of the relationship" as opposed to a morality of justice employed by those who believe they are separate (Lyons 1983: 136). Hence, practitioners who support the "caring" battered woman's efforts to explore and discover explanations for the abusive behavior may be contributing to the injustice of subjecting another individual to physical harm.

Second, practitioners who collude with women to help the batterer are implicitly and subtly implying that if she is able to help him to stop the abuse then she must have had some control in the creation of the violent incidents in the first place. The logical development of this position, then, suggests that if the battered woman has control then she must be, in fact, allowing or soliciting her own "victimization." That one can be at the same time a victim and a perpetrator of one's own victimization defies explanation, however. Some writers have developed this perspective in yet another manner, suggesting that these partners, enmeshed as they are in the violent nature of the relationship, are both "victimized." We propose that none of these positions is very helpful in working with battered women. In fact, we suggest that such perspectives may contribute to prolonging the violence and risking the battered woman's life.

We must also be sensitive to the meaning of help-seeking itself. One must question if the battered woman perceives help-seeking as a way to threaten her partner in the attempt to change his behavior, whether she desires to help herself to become an independent and autonomous person apart from her partner, or to change herself so that she can live with her partner in a less violent way (Geller and Walsh 1977–78). The helper can make no prior assumptions about what help-seeking represents to the woman in this early stage. This must be carefully explored and spelled out.

Despite numerous false starts, however, those women who do seek help through the legal system have at least implicitly begun the process of discrimination-learning. What presses them to break out of the noxious relationship and to seek help is an emerging awareness — perhaps vague and unformed — that things aren't the way they were previously perceived. The woman may give a new credence to inner feelings she had suppressed up to now; she may come to terms with characteristics of her partner that she had formerly excused; or she may allow her values to surface in an undisguised way. Whatever this new awareness may be, it makes the prior relationship intolerable and so presses her to seek other solutions.

At the outset of the helping process, then, helpers need to take the time to develop, articulate, and underscore the battered woman's initial efforts to perceive the violence in a new and different light. This step may be overlooked by practitioners who are literally faced with a bloodied and hurting woman. In the helper's anxiety to offer safety, medical care, or legal protection to the battered woman (which should be done), the lack of attention to this new consciousness, this very important first step in her learning, may undermine the change process. One must be mindful that although the battered client is presenting the practitioner with a serious and life-threatening crisis, this crisis is but another in a series of chronic crises. Thus, without ignoring the immediate needs that the client presents, it is possible to help the woman deepen and broaden her new-found awareness of self and of what life might be. This novel discovery that being a woman does not entail abuse and travail needs to be given credence, but equally she needs to be pressed to expand and reaffirm this awareness.

Concept-learning

With this kind of affirmation of the client's consciousness, concept-learning, or the active intent to reframe and redefine self and situation, may quickly follow. Darlene's way of reflecting on her circumstances illustrates this new learning:

> I don't want to run into him and I don't want him to start pleading. I'm not saying I'll weaken and change my mind because my mind is made up. My mind is made up. I can't help him but I can help myself. If I don't do something now, soon one of us will be dead.

Darlene has "begun the process of restructuring her self image from victim to autonomous person" (Ridington 1977–78). She has begun to alter her perception of self from reactive and helpless to proactive and capable, which is evident in terms such as "I can help myself." Some principles of concept-learning bearing on practice with battered women include the following:

MEANING Attending to the meaning that the battered woman ascribes to her situation is a preliminary step in her process of self-redefinition and self-growth. Meaning is not found just in the factual rendition of how she sees this situation but also in the symbolic terms and images that give the definition its substance and depth. While a woman may with little overt emotion recount the pain and torture she endured during the violent episode, she may at the same time and with quiet insistence ascribe a special meaning to this relationship, even by means of a statement as basic as "Marriage should be more than this."

APPRECIATION OF THE CLIENT'S SUBJECTIVE REALITY Battered women need the opportunity to describe in detail their former and current realities. More than merely listening attentively, however, it is vital for the helper to believe what the woman has to say. These women are more than willing to involve themselves in the helping process, but only if they see that the helper respects their authority about their subjective truths. Often a great sense of relief is expressed by the battered woman when she is permitted to describe her reality without fear of the ridicule or criticism she has experienced before. Too often she has been told by others that what she has to tell is crazy, exaggerated, or contrived. More than one attorney, representing the batterer in a criminal domestic violence hearing, has asked the "victim" if she were absolutely sure she hadn't walked into a door. To her family and friends, what appears unreal and unimaginable is painfully real to a battered woman. And her partner may have minimized, ignored or discounted her perception of her life situation. In fact, the abuser may claim that "She just had one of her spells," or "She did this to herself." In effect he is denying her reality. What better way is there to foster feelings of craziness, confusion, and loss of contact with the real world than by denying what the woman says is her truth? These truths must be acknowledged by those who hope to help.

FOCUS ON THE PRESENT AND FUTURE The search for abstract explanations, or theoretical causes that might aid in understanding the battered woman's involvement in a battering relationship is not only an irrelevant luxury but potentially dangerous. Since her present relationship with her partner has been seeded with violence which will increase in frequency and severity as time passes, it is imperative that the battered woman turns her attention to her life as it is at this very moment. Time spent discussing or gathering her history rather than planning her destiny literally could cost her life.

The battered woman's immediate need is for safety, closely followed by some planning for alternative emotional, material and life needs (Lynch and Norris 1977–78). This focus includes an emphasis on future intentions, at least in terms of some immediate short-range goals that may be the basis for more permanent long-range goals. As already noted, the battered woman's situation, although critical in nature, is also chronic; thus applying short-term crisis-intervention strategies is necessary but insufficient. Planning for a yet unknown future also is imperative.

AUTONOMOUS CLIENT FUNCTIONING Support of independent, competent living must be offered with patience. The process of reconceptualizing a self that seems to be helpless, powerless, and hopeless in order to

181

achieve a sense of self that is a bit more confident and autonomous is especially painstaking for individuals who have never attempted this sort of redefinition. Since these women formed their identity through their interactions with their partners (often to the exclusion of other relationships), the actual physical separation from this relationship necessarily will be accompanied by some loss of self (Lynch and Norris 1977–78; Walker 1979). While battered women retain the basic human capacities to define self and determine their destinies, this process may be particularly slow and erratic. The power of and need for this relationship frequently haunt the woman even in the wake of its demise. Hence, the new identity will emerge out of the tensions produced by its relation to the old. And this will not occur in an easy, gradual fashion.

EXISTENTIAL DESPAIR/HOPE   Although the victim would not use such a term, existential despair nonetheless occurs when the battered woman confronts the emptiness of her existence within a battering relationship. Facing the nothingness, the meaninglessness of this relationship is the critical and transitional springboard into the future. The anguish of this experience, the giving up of hope for the continuance and improvement of her relationship with a partner whom she had once joined in good faith, is difficult and painful — even for a bloodied and bruised woman. Her anguish cannot be minimized. It must be accepted as a critical and uniquely personal experience.

Hope for self is manifested by the very process of seeking help. Without either hope for the relationship or hope for one's self, the battered woman is essentially choosing death. Help-seeking represents a step toward re-birth, a reaffirmation of the self-worth of the battered woman as a person. She is fanning the spark of the vital self and is once again risking her hope for a better future.

CHOICE   Choice implies that within the battered woman's "field of possibilities" are life alternatives and options which may indeed be maximized through the helping process. It is incumbent upon the practitioner to provide support and encourage creativity and imagination in exploring resources available to the battered woman. Provision of choices, however, is by itself insufficient unless the helper attends to the risk-taking element of planned action with the battered woman. Support and encouragement to take risks and face the consequences of personally-chosen actions are necessary components of planned choice.

Conflict, then, as a product of making choices, is considered a healthy impetus for personal growth.

Parting itself may take many forms and meanings for this woman, each having its own special implications — not only for her self-concept but for the process of re-adaptation. The contemplation of divorce or separation may, first of all, force her to think about what life might mean as a single parent. She might have to struggle with feelings of guilt if her partner tries to convince her that she is abandoning him. A batterer, for example, may threaten suicide if his partner plans to leave him, particularly if his sense of self is also dependently bound to his relationship with his victim. Without her, he may feel threatened, empty, exposed, or without purpose and meaning in his life. For battered women who have a very strong sense of empathy, a great amount of forgiveness, and a moral perspective about taking care of their partners, the possibility that their departure could shatter the abuser's will to live is very real and overwhelming.

Parting may also mean that she will have to begin to think of herself as an assertive or aggressive person — particularly if she plans to prosecute and, if necessary, incarcerate her partner. This redefinition of self may be somewhat painful and certainly alien to her. She would also have to consider the possible risks and costs including the risk of reprisal, the problems of relocation, financial and emotional suffering, and so on. And it is important to emphasize that the choice of something that promises to be better (although not yet proven) is all too frequently accompanied by the anguish of having to give up all that is familiar. Remaining may still symbolize loving and being loved while leaving may be equated with the loss of that love. Remaining perpetuates a certain self-identity while leaving creates a temporary loss of that identity. Remaining assures a measure of social approval and economic support, while leaving invites stigmatization and economic uncertainty.

Each meaning symbolizes an uncomfortable and frightening solution to the battering problem. After all, if the partner she chooses to spend a lifetime with, to trust and to love, mistreats her in such an unconscionable way, what can she hope for in the greater world of unfamiliar and non-loving strangers? Fear of the unknown must be addressed and hope for the future must be realistically considered. Throughout the helping process, the practitioner must gently but persistently challenge the client's reconstruction of her reality and her motivation and intentions to make life choices and changes.

Principle-learning

If the woman has achieved a new way of sensing and defining herself and her world and, out of these realizations, has begun to risk new ways of actively managing her life, then who she is as a person of principle that embodies her deeply-held values and beliefs must be given some regard. In short, what she has come to learn, what she wishes to be, and what she wants to do are given true substance and meaning when they are rooted in her secure and ethical principles of living. Therefore, the objective of this phase is to enable the client to make responsible choices, follow through with action, and assume the consequences of this new behavior. The worker helps the client integrate her competent knowledge (informed choice), the critical significance of her personal value system, and her subjective code of ethical behavior into, some form of planned action.

During this stage, the battered woman needs the opportunity to explore her personal and newly-defined principles of living. Such principles or guidelines for living may, for example, espouse a commitment to protect herself and her children from witnessing and/or becoming the recipient of any form of personally abusive or oppressive behavior in the future. In principle, perhaps, the woman may formerly have believed her children ought not be subjected to the disharmony, physical conflict, and emotional distress of a violent home. At this time, however, this more clearly articulated belief and commitment includes unequivocal action. It becomes more than a belief system about what parental practices and family life ought to be like. Such beliefs now demand the behavior which will uphold them.

Principles for living cannot be considered without attention to the battered woman's moral and spiritual perspectives on life. Despite research that indicates that most women who are battered do not subscribe to any particular religious preference (Straus, Gelles, and Steinmetz 1980), the lasting effects of legal, religious, and social philosophies which condone wife-beating cannot be summarily dismissed. Each battered woman has her own set of moral and spiritual convictions about life; concentrating attention on these during this time is therefore of great importance.

This phase of helping is not easily described. Certainly, our previous concern with the symbolic level and meanings of the client's thoughts and images, as well as her uncertain visions of her future, removes us from the realm of purely rational and analytic thinking. When it comes to understanding the ethical, moral, and spiritual principles that guide one's approach to self and the world, we will find ourselves attempting to make sense of images, visions, and convictions that are even more diffuse. Yet, if we were to limit our concerns to the client's thoughts and actions alone without regard for the personal principles that vitalize these thoughts and actions, we could not be sure that the client's attempt to take charge of her life would have any integrity or duration.

The stresses of helping

Throughout this chapter we have suggested that the demands of work with battered women pose special considerations regarding the worker's role with these clients. In particular, we believe the "delicate balance" mentioned earlier points to the kind of tension that characterizes interaction with these women. While workers must be both precise and cautious about their expectations of and hope for the battered woman, they must also be flexible enough to appreciate and welcome the personal power that these clients bring to the practice setting. Basically, if helpers are committed to the dignity and individuality of the client, then they must relinquish their control over how the helping experience ought to unfold. This does not mean that helpers should limit their investment in and concern about the client's life; to the contrary, their unrelenting interest and involvement offers the client a dependable ally and colleague in the pursuit of a better quality of life.

But such relinquishment of control is easier said than done. The fact that the worker is a professional does not diminish his or her essential humanness and vulnerability — for, in fact, it is this humanness that lends a spirit of collegiality and sincere mutuality to the helping experience. The worker wants "what is good" for the client — particularly escape from punishment and violence. The client wants "what's best for now" for herself: the two may be congruent at one moment and completely out of phase the next.

For example, within the justice system, the woman initially may appear adamant and unrelenting about her intention to prosecute. She and the worker may agree in fact that the injustice of a beating must not be dismissed, and the best solution for the woman is to prosecute. In this way she is publicly making her statement about her principles and beliefs regarding violent behavior and her intolerance for these actions. Marge, as a case in point, presented herself to the worker in just this way. Her

185

husband, John, had become drunk, hit her several times and held her and their three children at gunpoint throughout the night. When he finally passed out, Marge was advised by the police to prosecute. Marge announced to the worker that not only was she intending to prosecute on the criminal complaint but she also planned to begin the civil proceedings for a divorce. Quickly the worker enabled Marge to file the necessary criminal papers, have photos taken of her injuries, and to meet with a divorce attorney to acquire an emergency civil-protection order and motion for divorce. While it may seem premature to take action so quickly on these very important life decisions, the justice system demands immediate action if criminal proceedings are to be instituted. Marge and her worker spent four hours together during their first contact. When Marge left, she felt confident she had made the right decisions. The next day, however, during the arraignment on the criminal charges, Marge became very preoccupied with John's well-being. As John sat with the other prisoners in the crowded courtroom, Marge was aware of his cough and concerned about his health. She noticed he was without shoes and she worried about *his* embarrassment when he had to stand before the judge looking hungover, dirty and shoeless. When the judge set a high bond, because of the weapon involved, Marge was crestfallen. In spite of this, she did follow through on her divorce action in civil court two days later. The pre-trial date on the criminal charge was set for one week later.

When the worker arrived to meet Marge for the pre-trial, she was seated in the waiting room with John. Marge had made his bail and joyfully explained her current intentions. After John was released they had had a "long talk." He recognized that he needed help and agreed to pursue this if Marge dropped the criminal charges. Their reunion was reminiscent of adolescent first love. Magically everything between this couple was going to improve.

Marge did in fact drop all charges. After the court hearing, the couple walked out hand in hand. Both thanked the helper for her concern and interest.

How do we make sense of Marge's behavior? As noted, it would certainly be quite human for the practitioner to feel anger and disappointment after the many hours spent reaching out to this client when she was clearly frightened, in pain and requesting help. Or one might feel let down as if the client owed the worker something and had reneged on her part of the bargain. A cognitive-humanist perspective urges the practitioner who truly values personal choice and responsibility to accept if not anticipate the fluid nature of the battered woman's situation. From this perspective, Marge simply chose to change her mind for a number of reasons that were significant to herself. No fault-finding, blame, or rationalization of her behavior is warranted. By engaging in the battered woman's reality as a colleague rather than as an expert about her life decisions, the worker shares the joys of a woman's new life and understands as well the pain and hope of a reconciliation with the batterer. Most of all, the worker should experience the wonder of any battered woman who begins help-seeking and who, in spite of great adversity, can still entertain a bit of hope about creating a better life in some manner for herself. It is this small but vital sign that must be honored and nourished.

OUTCOMES

As with most of life's problems, there is no single absolutely right or wrong solution to the problem of domestic violence. Yet, given the wrongness, the criminality of the assailant's behavior, practitioners may easily become seduced into prescribing what they believe is the right solution for their battered woman clients; namely, to leave the battering relationship. Clearly Marge demonstrates how a battered woman may, in fact, repeatedly and happily return to her abusive partner. Separation is not necessarily the desired outcome for her. Instead Marge, similar to many others, simply wants the violence to end. What is of utmost importance, then, in work with battered women is to provide the ambience and the opportunities for these clients to maintain their prerogatives regarding responsible choice. In other words, although remaining in a battering relationship may not be the helper's choice, if the client wishes to continue with her partner, an important and necessary component of responsible practice with this client would be to help her construct a safety net of some sort.

Outcomes, then, can take the form of a number of creative solutions. For example, many women feel helpless and trapped during a violent episode. Their line to safety has been cut, often quite literally, when the batterer rips the phone from the wall. Anticipating and planning for the violent episode with the battered woman, as morbid and bizarre as this may sound to the non-abused helper, may be the best safety measure the battered woman can install. Developing a signal with a neighbor is an option so that when he becomes violent the neighbor will call the police. Keeping a cordless phone tucked away in the bathroom or bedroom, for example, or removing the bullets from the gun in her partner's absence may become the very measures which later can save the woman's life. The point is not, of course, that the practitioner in any way supports in principle the battering behavior but that she or he does indeed contribute creative options from which the battered woman can then choose. The woman's sense of helplessness, to a great extent, can be diminished when she becomes armed with a number of choices of useful solutions to the battering event.

Parting, then, becomes simply one answer to the battered woman's situation. And, as previously discussed, this solution is wrought with its own dilemmas. But parting may be but one of any number of creative solutions that the client and helper, together, may derive out of the process of learning described on these pages. What is important is that the solution is ultimately owned by the client herself and therefore becomes a dependable and principled alternative to her former depleted existence.

EPILOGUE

Mary's case encapsulates many of the vicissitudes and tensions of the process and outcomes of work with the battered woman. Clearly, this is not a comfortable or predictable process that culminates in the romantic solution we would prefer to look forward to. Yet, she did stick with the helping experience and, through the process of self-redefinition and rediscovery of her essential values and beliefs she was able, with the help of her family, to extricate herself from the battering relationship.

On the day of her preliminary court hearing, Mary arrived with her motion for a temporary protection order and bus tickets to leave town. When she went to the Clerk of Courts office to file her papers, her husband arrived. He convinced his young son to walk off with him, leaving Mary with papers in hand and no child. Her option, her choice as she perceived it at that moment, was to drop the charges, tear up the bus tickets, and return to her husband in order to remain with her son. The helper intervened however, informing Mary's husband that for Mary to drop the charges it was necessary for them both to attend the preliminary hearing. The couple agreed to this procedure and sat together in court with their child between them. Prior to the hearing, however, the worker informed the judge of Mary's dilemma. He in turn instructed Mary that if she chose to drop charges, he could not convince her otherwise. He essentially "got her off the hook." He then pressed the charges himself, set an extremely high bond and had Mary's husband held in jail until the trial. Knowing full well that Mary intended to leave town and then drop charges, the judge was buying the time and the protection for Mary to actively plan a new life for herself. When this was explained to Mary she was much relieved. She agreed to write when she was safely relocated and had secured a divorce attorney. When this information was received, the charges were withdrawn, her husband was "cooled off" and Mary was well on her way to starting a new life in another state. Mary was lucky. Her personal hopes, fears, and intentions were taken into consideration and although she could not remain with the man she had once loved, she did obtain the space and opportunity to begin anew with courage and conviction.

NOTES

1. All direct quotes in the chapter are derived from interviews and discussions with battered women who sought help through the Witness Victim Service Center, Cleveland, Ohio.
2. This material was obtained through conversation with Lynn Hammond, co-founder of Cleveland's Rape Crisis Center and current advocate at Witness Victim Service Center.

REFERENCES

Fromm, E. (1968) *The Revolution of Hope: Toward a Humanized Technology*. New York: Harper & Row.
Geller, J. and Walsh, J. (1977–78) A Treatment Model for Abused Spouses. *Victimology* 2: 627–32.
Gelles, R. and Straus, M. (1980) Violence in the Family: A Review of Research in the 70s. *Journal of Marriage and the Family* 42(4): 873–85.
Gilligan, C. (1977) In a Different Voice: Women's Conceptions of Self and of Morality. *Harvard Educational Review* 47: 481–517.
—— (1982) *In a Different Voice* Cambridge: Harvard University Press.
Goldstein, H. (1981) *Social Learning and Change: A Cognitive Approach to Human Services*. Columbia: University of South Carolina Press; pbk edn 1984, New York and London: Tavistock.
Lin, N. (1976) *Foundations of Social Research*. New York: McGraw Hill.
Lynch, C. and Norris, T. (1978) Services for Battered Women: Looking for a Perspective. *Victimology* 2: 553–63.
Lyons, N. (1983) Two Perspectives on Self, Relationships, and Morality. *Harvard Educational Review* 55: 125–45.
Manis, J. and Meltzer, B. (1978) *Symbolic Interaction: A Reader in Social Psychology*. Boston: Allyn & Bacon.
Millett, K. (1979) *The Basement: Meditations on a Human Sacrifice*. New York: Simon & Schuster.

Ridington, J. (1977–78) The Transition Process: A Feminist Environment as Reconstituted Milieu. *Victimology* 2: 563–76.

Stebbins, R. (1978) Studying the Definition of the Situation: Theory and Field Research Strategies. In J. Manis and B. Meltzer (eds) *Symbolic Interaction: A Reader in Social Psychology*. Boston: Allyn & Bacon.

Straus, M., Gelles, R., and Steinmetz, S. (1980) *Behind Closed Doors: Violence in the American Family*. New York: Anchor/Doubleday.

Walker, L. (1979) *The Battered Woman*. New York: Harper & Row.

Chapter 7

The Rural Poor:
Toward Self-Reliance in the Context of Family,
Community, and Culture

SUSAN VAUGHN

Practice with human problems of living is, by definition, not a technology that can be transferred intact from one cultural region to another. The term "human" embodies virtually an infinite range of personal characteristics. Likewise, "problems of living" take on their distinct meaning and characteristics only when they are studied within their own peculiar social, cultural, and environmental contexts. Within this perspective, the purpose of this chapter is twofold: the major intent is to show how cognitive-humanistic practice lends itself to modification when it is applied to individual members of a specific cultural population — in this instance, low-income, southern US, rural clients. The second purpose is broader — that is to encourage greater sensitivity and responsiveness to the variety of cultural conditions, idioms, customs, and belief systems that characterize each client so as to assure that the intent to help is indeed in accord with the client's world and reality.

Since the social and physical environment provides the context within which people live and work, an overview of some unique characteristics of the rural environment will be presented first. Against this environmental backdrop, we will consider the nature of low-income families. Finally, some specific practice principles will be outlined along with some case examples. A caveat is appropriate here: not every community, family, or individual will fit these generalizations. However, since a cognitive-humanistic approach does not prescribe set methods of practice and instead derives its form from an understanding of how clients view themselves, their concerns, and the world that surrounds them, the examples shown here should alert the reader to the needs and views of clients in other cultural settings.

The southern rural culture is a place of paradoxes. An outsider observing some of the attitudes, values, and behaviors in this culture might find them to be contradictory or incongruous. For example, most people are fully committed to helping out their unfortunate neighbors, while at the same time many would cheerfully abolish all social welfare programs. Another paradox is buried in the issue of school desegregation. Desegregation of schools was, as we know, a long, hard battle in which feelings ran high among both Blacks and Whites even though many of these same people had lived less than a mile from each other all their lives, worked together, and shared goods with each other — all with little or no open conflict and animosity. Moreover, they knew several generations of each other's families and attended each other's funerals as a natural matter of course.

Education in the rural culture is valued as a means for children to be able to live better than their parents, but only as long as it does not make the child "uppity." Although drinking may be as commonplace in rural areas as it is in urban areas, there are many counties that remain "dry" by choice. Families strive to be close and tight-knit, but should conflict arise, this rift or family feud may go on for years and even generations. Awareness of these paradoxes allows us to look at some other aspects of the rural culture with greater clarity and understanding.

Within the rural culture several generations of a family may live in close proximity and are in frequent contact. This rich resource of extended family is a source of love and support and provides a sense of belonging and identity to its members, even when they move away.

The place of the church in the rural community also is critical. The church provides not only spiritual guidance, but is an important source for social activities as well. Dinners on the grounds, revivals, tent meetings, singing events, and groups for adults and children are but a few of the varied events sponsored by the church. Some of the more fundamentalist churches provide an acceptable emotional release from the rigors, frustrations, and deprivations of routine daily living.

Rural schools provide another important source of social activities for families since the school's programs are open to all people in the community. In addition, teachers often know children's families and are willing to help them work out school problems should they arise. Unfortunately, this may have a negative effect when children are too readily labeled as dumb, unmotivated, or the kid from a poor family; through the informal school network, this label may follow a child and provide justification for a second-rate education.

People in rural areas prefer a concrete, down-to-earth way of talking and dealing with problems. They are not overly impressed with people who "put on airs" or who flaunt their education or money. In their terms, they prefer to get to the bottom of things and get on with doing something about it.

The rural environment has been described as a place where there is much face-to-face contact among residents of all classes and groups (Ginsberg 1976). As already suggested, this generalization is warranted. Whether poor people live next door to middle- or upper-class families or miles away from each other, there is frequent contact between them at such general meeting places as doctors' offices, grocery stores, and clothing stores. The poor are not as invisible as they often are in large urban areas. This face-to-face contact typical of rural areas may have both positive and negative consequences. It is not at all unusual for the more affluent residents of rural communities to extend aid to the less fortunate, either on a family-to-family basis or through formal groups such as clubs, churches, and women's circles. There is a caring concern for those in the community who are less fortunate, despite the skepticism evidenced toward social welfare (Farley et al. 1982).

People in rural communities may be quite sympathetic to the poor families they know personally, while being suspicious or derogatory of the "poor" as a general category. For example, it is not all unusual for middle-class families to identify with a poor family that lives nearby and to help them out with clothing, day work, or a much needed ride to town, while at the same time speak harshly about other "shiftless" folk. Hard work and independence are valued which often leads to the disparagement of those who are seen as being dependent and "unwilling to work." These people, including mothers who have no husbands and are on welfare, are deemed "unworthy" of social-welfare aid and services, whereas others, the aged and disadvantaged for example, are seen as "worthy." However, even those who are usually viewed as "unworthy" may be aided on an individual basis or on given occasions, such as Thanksgiving or Christmas.

We also find the working poor in the rural community, people who, despite their efforts to earn enough to support their families, never seem adequately to make ends meet. The working poor are not as looked down upon or stigmatized as the welfare recipient. Instead, they are viewed as people who try hard, but can never seem to catch up or get ahead. The more affluent members of the community lend these families a helping hand, and they may receive some help from formal programs.

When someone in a family dies, it is traditional in many southern communities for the neighbors and friends to bring food to the home and assume the household chores. These generalizations apply to the rural community as a whole, but more needs to be said about the rural low-income client in particular.

Rural low-income families

Anyone living in a state of poverty struggles, by definition, with the ceaseless demands of survival. Aside from deprivation, one is forced to cope with the mysteries of the various institutions one must turn to — educational, welfare, health care, housing — in order to secure desperately needed assistance. The stress that accompanies these ventures adds extra burdens to an already vulnerable family; repeated negative experiences increase the sense of helplessness and hopeless-ness.

When we talk about a lack of income and resources in the rural environment, it is important to note that this means these families often do not have what most other people take to be the necessities of life — an indoor toilet or running water, for example. The housing itself is often old, poorly constructed, and worn out, with holes in the walls, and floors, and the roof "big enough to throw a dog through." This means impossibly high heating bills in the winter and children who are often sick with colds. Transportation to town for those who live in the country is a major undertaking. It is often all a family can do to get to town once a week to buy groceries or make an occasional visit to the doctor.

Poverty fractures all facets of living. The daily grind of trying to make ends meet can wear down stamina and vitality. The constant frustration of trying to provide the essentials of life often leads to a sense of personal incompetence, hopelessness, or apathy. These families often suffer from health defects including hypertension, diabetes, "nerves," and dental problems. Most of these people are poorly educated and unskilled. There was a time in rural areas when the unskilled could pick up "day work" as a housekeeper or yard man, but now there are few middle-class families who can afford to hire these workers. Even if jobs were available, the lack of transportation, the absence of child-care arrangements for mothers who desire to work, or poor health may preclude working. Consequently, these people lose hope that things will ever be much better and settle for just trying to make it from day to day. These are the folks who are categorized as "living from hand to mouth," meaning that they never know where the next meal is coming from. They have little energy to expend on planning for the future as the struggle to survive dominates their existence.

All too often these people have been viewed by helping professionals as helpless victims — victims of society's lack of equity or as a result of their own past deprived lives. Few will deny that poverty can have deleterious effects, but the fact remains that not all families who find themselves poverty-stricken perceive themselves as helpless victims, nor does it help to categorize them in this way. Eliminating the concept of "victim" then demands a very different view of the individual and family. It is our conviction that people are not merely reactors to or captives of either their past or the noxious societal conditions that surround them. Even the poorest of the poor have choices that they can make and must make for, if nothing else, these choices are necessary to maintain a degree of dignity and independence. The choices and options are certainly much fewer in number than those available to the more privileged middle class, but choices are still available and decisions must be made in daily living to achieve improvement in the quality of living.

As already noted, there are many supports and benefits within the rural culture that can soften the harshness of poverty and that, if exploited, would bolster the clients' choices and strivings for a better way of life: the extended family networks, the give-and-take among neighbors, the faith in a better future derived from an affiliation with the church.

The helping professional and the rural community

Some of these characteristics of the rural environment have a direct impact on the helping professionals and the delivery of human services in the rural environment. The first thing to be noted is that the professional distance, anonymity, privacy, and confidentiality that characterize practice in larger urban communities are scarcely typical of practice in the rural setting. The helper's contact with clients is not restricted to an office. Helpers often find themselves meeting clients in stores and on the street.

The visibility of people in small towns and rural areas makes it probable that anyone who receives services from a social service agency will be known by the larger community.

The role of the worker in the rural area is more that of a generalist than a specialist. The worker must be able to relate to people of varying ages, with diverse problems. In addition, he or she must be able to relate to both the formal and informal helpers within a community. It should also be noted that the human-services worker usually is quickly identified and is often approached informally by members of the community who are concerned about an individual or family's well-being.

Professional helpers often know most of the other professionals as well as the informal helpers and therefore find it possible to mobilize resources in both casual and formal ways to aid individuals and families in times of distress. The scarcity of formal social services within the rural community makes it necessary for helping professionals to depend heavily upon the voluntary efforts of local churches, clubs, and other informal resources. These groups provide much-needed emergency monetary assistance as well as other forms of aid including medical care, food, and clothes.

As noted, transportation is a chronic difficulty for low-income clients. The family that has its own "rattle trap" car or truck is fortunate indeed, particularly if the family can afford to buy gas for it. This means that office visits are rather rare; most helping professionals ordinarily will visit the clients' home. This gives the worker a more accurate perspective on what the clients' home and community environment are really like since the worker has the opportunity to observe first-hand what goes on within the family and between the family and the community, as well as the degree of isolation from or proximity with the town, neighbors, and churches. This awareness has implications for the client and worker relationship.

Outside of the comfortable borders of the scheduled appointment and the fifty-minute hour, the worker often must "catch as catch can" on a home visit. The interview may be conducted on the front porch with children playing in the yard or neighbors stopping by to speak or "chew the fat" a minute with both client and worker. It is not unusual for the worker to arrive at the house and find neighbors and other family members present. Clients will often encourage the worker to proceed with the interview explaining that "She's my friend or sister and knows all about me anyway." Most important, many workers in rural areas have lived there some time — some for all their lives. They may know several generations of the client's family and most of their relatives and neighbors. In times of crisis, therefore, it would be quite natural for the worker to call on these friends and family to offer aid the client requires.

The relationship that develops between the client and worker in this open environment can be a major impetus and support for client change. Clients no longer feel alone with their problems. Many clients do not perceive the worker as an expert to begin with, but as a "co-worker," one of "us" who is there to aid and help find solutions, not to prescribe them. By discarding the expert role and actively engaging with the client, the workers encourage the clients to begin to believe in themselves as people who are quite competent and capable.

The "therapeutic" relationship between client and worker that is typical of urban practice may not be very successful with rural clients, particularly if the client who appreciates a concrete, down-to-earth approach cannot figure out what the talking relationship is all about. Thus, acting *with* the clients and connecting them with others in their world who can aid them is far more appropriate. This in no way implies that rural clients should receive a second-class kind of service; rather, the delivery of services must be in tune with the values and orientation of the specific group with whom the helper is working.

Practice with low-income rural families

The emphasis given in the previous pages to the social and cultural environment presages an approach to practice that gives particular attention to the transactions of clients and their contexts of living. In this perspective, the humanistic element of a cognitive-humanistic approach embodies the general values, belief systems, moral and spiritual idioms, and cultural patterns that characterize the community and lifestyle of these clients. Balanced against these factors are the specific perceptions and cognitive functions that allow us to understand individuals and families in their own unique terms.

This transactional perspective not only captures the give-and-take of the low-income client's way of life, but also allows us to understand this way of life as something more than a collection of severe problems. This view is therefore not limited merely to problematic areas but includes as well those interactions with others which may be helpful, supportive, and satisfying to the client. If we utilize a transactional perspective in work with clients, we are in effect attempting to ascertain the action that is transpiring between members of the family and between the family and its social environment. A transactional perspective focuses on the exchange and activity between the person and the community and thereby connotes interdependence as well as dynamic and reciprocal relationships. We are not just concerned, for example, with the fact that there may be extended family members that live close to a client, but instead with the quality of the relationships that exist between these people. For example, do they help each other out more than they fuss and quarrel with one another, and more important, what does this relationship mean to the client?

Many low-income people perceive themselves as having "a hard row to hoe." They are aware that their own situation may never be drastically altered in economic terms, but most maintain the hope that their children will do better than they have. Depending upon where they live, they may or may not view themselves as contributing members of the community. If they live close to other low-income people or have good relationships with their neighbors, they may perceive themselves as active members of the community. Others may perceive themselves as stigmatized and as outcasts. Some perceive themselves as singled out by God and people for lives of misfortune and thus feel their lives are beyond their control. Others assume that they will not be given more than they can bear and face the struggle of daily living with equanimity.

These generalizations about rural families and their environment provide the backdrop for our work. What is now needed is a structure that will enable us to understand the particular family and its perceptions of and interactions with the world around it. In other words, how do we begin to try to understand what is peculiarly "real" to them? The four frames of reference described in the first chapter are useful in guiding our efforts. These frames of reference include the psychological (person of the mind), socio-cultural (person of the community), ethical and moral (person of principle), and spiritual (person of faith). In order to have as full an understanding and appreciation of the client as is humanly possible, we engage with the client in an effort to comprehend what is occurring within these frames of reference, their meanings and the interactions between them. Two case examples are illustrative of these four frames of reference.

It should be noted that both of these families came to the attention of a human-service agency because of community complaints that they were neglecting their children.

Ms Smith and her five children live in a small, rural, southern town. She has a small, inadequate income from public assistance. Mr Smith was living with the family until recently when he got "fed up" and left. Over the years, the Smiths have become known as trouble-makers in the community. Ms Smith continuously has disputes with her neighbors and her children are always in trouble with the school and the community. She appears to have little control over her children, either in the home or outside the home. The family has no close ties with the community. Ms Smith appears to just make it from day to day with no particular goals or hopes for herself or her children. She concludes that all of her troubles are being caused by "bad children," and that her neighbors and community people "pick on" her. When she talks to the worker, she dwells on all of the bad things that have happened to her in the past. The Smiths might be known in the community as "poor white trash."

Ms Jones, like Ms Smith, has five children, lives in a small southern town and also receives an inadequate income from public welfare. The Jones family originally came to the attention of the public welfare department five years ago because the children were destroying property and the community accused Ms Jones of neglecting to supervise her children. The children's father and mother did not marry and the father has never been an active participant in the daily family life. Since the original neglect complaint, Ms Jones has from time to time contacted the social worker for assistance with various problems. The children have been in no further trouble. Presently, Ms Jones is attempting to enroll in a training program in order to prepare herself for a job, as she knows that when the children are grown, she will not be able to depend on public assistance. The Jones family has close ties within the community, predominantly through their church. The children attend school regularly and do well. Ms Jones does not complain of her past troubles, or her "lot in life," but instead is very concerned with the future for herself and her children. She is, overall, optimistic in her outlook and despite innumerable barriers, she continues to look for other alternatives. She often makes the comment that when things are really bad she "takes them to the Lord" and He gives her strength to carry on. The Jones family is known in the community as a "welfare family," but no other negative labels are ascribed to them.

These case examples illustrate the importance of meaning and intention in the lives of our clients. Both women have similar descriptive or factual life difficulties: low income, poor housing, sole responsibility for several children. However, the meaning they attach to these problems, the meaning they attach to the past, their hope for the future for themselves and their children, and their willingness to assume responsibility for attempting to find solutions to problems are quite different. They also differ markedly in their attachments to others within the community. And the spiritual aspect of their respective lives stands in some contrast. If the helping person depends too heavily on the "objective" facts without attempting to understand the ways these facts are perceived and given meaning, these two families would probably be given similar prescriptive sets of "solutions" to their dilemmas. However, should the helping person begin to try to understand these families in subjective terms — i.e. through the clients' own vision of themselves, the meaning they attach to their lives, and their approach to life — very different patterns of working with each must then follow. The helper, given this approach, is not the expert who must tell these women how to "straighten out" their lives, for only they "know" their lives. Instead, the helping person will attempt to search for and to understand the meaning clients have given their lives. The four frames of reference mentioned earlier can now be explicated in light of the case examples given.

When we think of the person of the mind, we begin to wonder how the person perceives him- or herself, how he or she perceives others and the opportunities available to them, and last, but certainly not least, if there are possible goals that might motivate them to begin to deal with hurtful life issues. Here we are talking about a very personal construction of the personal and social world. Does the client see him- or herself as lacking in strengths or as one whose strengths are not utilized? Does one perceive oneself to be helpless in the face of daily adversity? Does the client feel hopeless, seeing so few opportunities and alternatives in the environment? Is the future dreaded as something that will unfold over which the client will have no control? Is the client's life pervaded by helter-skelter attempts to cope with things as they crop up or are problems approached in a planned, thoughtful way?

In the socio-cultural arena, do the clients view the people with whom they have intimate face-to-face contact as hostile, demanding people or do they perceive their intimates as supportive and nurturing? Is the larger community seen as a threatening and condemning or as a friendly and concerned place? How do they react to other people waiting in line at the grocery store when they pay for their purchases with food stamps?

In the ethical/moral area, how do clients define their obligation to others? How do they perceive the rightness or wrongness of certain beliefs or courses of action? Does a belief in something greater than themselves (spiritual or divine) lend a sense of hope and optimism of eventual reward for continuing to struggle with life? Does a belief in a higher being provide a source of comfort in times of stress and trouble? These are only suggestive questions which, if nothing else, touch on the complex inner world even of people that, to the casual observer, may appear to be drab, constricted, and routine. More important, an appreciation of the subjective experience of clients in relation to their view of the world, their conceptions of their place and status in the community, their notions about personal obligation, choice, and matters of right and wrong, and their attachment to a divine source of inspiration and hope may truly help us make some significant and helpful distinctions between clients who, in objective terms, seem to share the same factual world. Consider how this way of understanding begins to distinguish ideas about practice with the Jones and the Smiths.

Although she probably could not express things in this way, Ms Jones seems to have things in place; there is a degree of congruence between perceptions, beliefs, and actions. Ms Jones evidences a degree of self-esteem, takes her place in the community, and acts in accord with her values and commitments. The role of the worker would be to enable Ms Jones to make these strengths more explicit — not necessarily through words but through helping Ms Jones identify possible alternatives and goals and the active means of achieving them. Basic to this process is the respect for her dependence on God as the source of her optimistic hope for some sort of fulfillment.

Practice with Ms Smith would have to begin on a more elemental level where she might be helped to sort out a few meaningful goals. The intent here is not just to achieve these goals but to discover some personal meaning and worth in the experience. The goal may be as simple as "getting the welfare people off my back," or as complex as the desire to "take hold of my life." The worker must help Ms Smith to understand that despite the hassles from the community, she has some part in her difficulties and the responsibility for her actions and those of her children. The worker will help her reframe her present situation so that she no longer feels a captive of her past or uses it as an excuse for present behavior. The worker will help Ms Smith to redefine her sense of helplessness to enable her to see herself as a person with strengths or potential, since she is not without some capabilities. After all, she dutifully sends her children to school, which indicates at least a minimal amount of authority and control over them. She buys food and prepares meals, although somewhat haphazardly, and pays the bills — or at least pays some of the bills each month. She feels and shows affection for her children, although discipline is delivered in an erratic manner. Neither a victim nor a pathological mess, Ms Smith can begin to think and generalize about these strengths and see that they can be transferred to other daily life difficulties.

Finally, despite (or because of) her miserable existence, somewhere in her being must be a shred of hope, a vision or image of a better life or a source of comfort. It may be necessary for the worker to resist dwelling on the endless procession of daily problems and, at least occasionally, shift to questions of what Ms Jones once hoped for, how she wanted things to turn out, her ideals, and so on. If this spark can be brightened, perhaps she can move from resignation to meaning.

THE HELPING PROCESS

Beginning the helping relationship

The apparent realities of a family's problems often are almost too self-evident. Immediately, a worker is struck by the sight of ramshackle housing, tattered clothing, unkempt children and adults, and dirty rooms. However, what is not at all self-evident is what these circumstances mean to the family itself. Almost reflexively, the tendency of some workers is to inject resources into the situation to ameliorate some of the more disquieting problems. Goldstein suggests:

> Clients who feel trapped by their privation need to be helped to reconsider their claim to a more humane way of life — a claim that takes on meaning only when their enduring sense of despair and hopelessness is challenged. Rather than smothering anguish with some momentary aids, the human services worker needs to seek and arouse the traces of outrage that still linger within his client.
> (Goldstein 1981: 339)

All too often, families have allowed workers to do *for* them while expending little effort themselves, largely because no one ever asked them what was most important to them and what they would like to see accomplished. More important, no one has ever credited them with the ability to do something about their lives.

What I am suggesting, essentially, is a little less ardor for doing *for* and more time spent *with* the family, first to try to get some kind of understanding of their world as they see it. The worker must in some ways suspend his or her preconceived ideas of how this family got to be this way, how they ought to be living, how they ought to feel about this situation, and what they think is the appropriate solution. These presuppositions must be put aside in the attempt to understand the client's world from his or her perceptions. Familial perceptions that are critical in our work with these clients are centered around the following perceptions and meanings: (1) their goals — as they relate both to specific solutions for their difficulties and as they project themselves into the future; (2) their problems; (3) the strengths they can bring to bear on problems.

In the cognitive-humanist perspective, the worker is involved with clients to help them to relearn or discover that there are choices which they can and do make daily and for which they can and must assume some responsibility. Compared with the "big" problem, these choices may seem insignificant. Yet even within the dreadful environments where many of our clients find themselves, some options and choices do exist. We might suggest that helping professionals have unwittingly contributed to the client's sense of hopelessness and helplessness. When helpers resign themselves to the belief that there is little hope for change because of a client's wretched past or because the environment is not supportive or even harmful, we close off hope, and limit for ourselves and our clients some potential areas of change. The client must then be seen as one to be done for, pitied, and/or consoled.

The ongoing phase

Assuming that the worker is convinced that there are some small but progressive choices that can be made by the client based on the goals that the client defines as significant, co-operative work on specific problems can begin. All too often, clients fail in their attempt to resolve a constantly recurring and painful difficulty because they insist on falling back on the same worn-out solution. This may be all they know and all they can think of, but despite repeated efforts, it does not work. For example, Mrs Smith has stated consistently that she cannot control her children after school. All she can do in her attempt to control them is to scream at them when the neighbors complain of their unruly behavior. Long ago, the children learned that once their mother vented her anger, she would take no further action or not even appear concerned until the neighbors once again complained.

Effective problem-solving begins when the client is helped to reframe the baffling problem in a way that will open other possibilities for action.

203

Given what has been said about the significance of community rural life, the most logical place to begin to search for these possibilities is within the client's immediate environment — that is, the family, the extended family, neighbors, and community.

Problem-solving efforts with clients that begin with an exploration of their world and its potentials accomplish several other aims. First, we keep the clients and their culture — all that is known to them and valued by them — at the center of our work. Second, if clients learn to identify and use their interactions and relationships with others in their immediate world, they will begin to redefine their roles and thus come to see themselves as competent and capable, if only in certain areas. Finally, as the clients redefine their role within these immediate relationships they depend less on outside help as the community circle becomes more meaningful. The helping professional needs to determine how neighbors, family and church members can be marshalled on the client's behalf, if only because of the scarcity of formal resources as well as the desire to foster autonomous functioning among all members of the community. If asked, the client may hesitantly identify the people within his or her world who might have the potential to be helpful in different ways so that the worker can begin to appreciate the human potential that is available but not openly apparent.

In the case of Mrs Smith, for example, Mrs Wilkes, an elderly neighbor has, in the past, shown concern for the Smith children. The children seem to like and respect the older woman. Perhaps it is possible to enlist Mrs Wilkes to help with the children when Mrs Smith must be away from home in the afternoon. Mrs Wilkes might also become someone with whom Mrs Smith could share her concerns and from whom Mrs Smith might learn some new ideas on child rearing.

If the worker can pose the proper questions, the client will disclose the neglected values, beliefs and principles to which some small part of self is still committed. It should be noted that we are not talking about potentials in a total or absolute sense; rather, we suggest that there are different levels of potentials and strength as they may be perceived by the client. Clients may find themselves in situations which, to an outsider, would appear to be bereft of positive possibilities. Nonetheless, from the client's standpoint, his or her environment may be rich in possibilities for helping in the problem-solving process. Mrs Smith, for example, is not nearly as disorganized as it initially appears from her statements and those of her neighbors. Let us not overlook the fact that she does get her children up, feeds them, gets them off to school, keeps her house spotless and never fails to cook an evening meal. The question then arises, can we begin to help Mrs Smith recognize what she does well and generalize these skills into the area of supervision of her children.

In practice, then, we are concerned with whatever the client can demonstrate by word or action. Once we appreciate areas of strength, we have the basis for identifying new areas of learning which will give the client additional sense of capability and mastery and bring forth new alternatives for solving life difficulties.

As clients begin to redefine themselves and their circumstances, it may become clear that they do not have all of the resources necessary to deal with their difficulties. Thus, the worker must act as a resource to such clients in expanding the transactional arena to include other community supports and networks of which their clients may be unaware. This necessitates the worker being familiar with both the formal and informal resources within the community. The Williams family provides an illustration of how a worker can help clients connect with needed resources.

Mr and Mrs Williams and their two children live in a small, rural community. The community considers them to be a family who was doing well, but then fell upon hard times. Mr Williams had always supported his family, but a year ago he was diagnosed as having terminal cancer. The Williamses had always prided themselves on being independent, hard-working folks. After a year, the family was barely surviving. Mr Williams' condition was deteriorating rapidly and Mrs Williams was just about at the "end of her tether." A neighbor suggested that she call the local social service agency. The worker helped Mrs Williams to begin to think about and explore others within the community who could help relieve the strain imposed on her by the twenty-four-hour care she had to provide for her husband. Several neighbors and church members were more than glad to help from time to time to allow Mrs Williams to rest. The neighbors also took turns in looking after the children after school and included the children on their family outings.

The worker was also able to help Mrs Williams secure services from the formal helping agencies. They arranged to have transportation to the hospital paid for, to obtain medical supplies for the home, and procure a home-health aide to care for some of Mr Williams' physical needs. The worker modeled means by which one could obtain services and helped her rehearse the actions to be taken. The worker consistently reinforced the caring concern existing within the nuclear family and supported the close relationship between the family members and the members of the extended family, who also helped out when they were apprised of the needs of the family.

As in the case of Mrs Williams, once a plan of action has been mutually decided on, the client endeavors, with the support and encouragement of the worker, to risk a new solution. This new solution is bound to feel risky to the client if only because it is new, untested, and unpredictable. In the Williams case, the idea of asking for help from friends, neighbors, and agencies was a totally new experience for Mrs Williams. As she attempted to approach other people and found them willing to help, her sense of power over her situation and her feelings of being able to cope grew. If the client hesitates to move forward, this should not be labeled by the worker as a sign of resistance or as a lack of motivation. Rather, the worker should attempt to understand what the client views is at stake or at risk in attempting such a venture.

The reasons for this seeming inability to move forward may be numerous. Many assertive actions that may seem completely natural and harmless to successful middle-class people may be perceived quite differently by low-income clients. For example, the need to ask an officious physician to explain how to care for a sick child may be somewhat threatening to many poor clients. Something as simple as workers suggesting a list of questions that can be asked, rehearsing with clients, or assuring them of their right to know may be enough to convince clients to break through their reluctance.

For people who have failed time after time to cope with various situations, the idea of another failure or rejection also may be a barrier to risk-taking. It should be noted that these fears are often well-founded. In some instances, the worker may have to extend active support by accompanying clients when they attempt to reach out to community agencies for resources that are needed. For example, one family with thirteen children was not receiving the ordinary services and benefits to which they were entitled. The father could not read well and the mother was totally illiterate. Hence, they avoided any contact with an agency that had a detailed application form they would have to complete. The worker worked very carefully with the family, helping them to fill out applications, making appointments, and continuously reinforcing and monitoring their right to services. One major service was procured, to the delight of the mother, father and worker. They then bravely set forth in the attempt to receive an additional service. Careful preparation of the family by the worker as to exactly what they should do and what they needed, including the appropriate documents, preceded the actual visit to the agency. All should have gone well. However, when the worker next visited the family, the father did not come out on the porch to talk as he usually did. The mother informed the worker that he was quite angry as the worker in the agency had been very ugly to them, had talked down to them, and denied them service. This family's original fears and reluctance to attempt to secure needed services had again been justified. And so this helping process had to be carefully reworked.

Clearly, not all solutions in the problem-solving process are successful. This does not mean the client necessarily is or even perceives him- or herself as a failure. Some problems may indeed be unsolvable given the limited nature of resources, yet clients may need to take some pride in the fact that they have given it their "best shot." It is more reasonable, therefore, to think about degrees of resolution that the client finds acceptable rather than total solutions (Klein and Hill 1979).

Ending phase

Once a solution has been tried, the worker and client then begin to reconsider the problem-solving process to help the client begin to see that he or she owns these changes. To encourage future autonomous functioning, it is important that clients are able to understand or at least have some grasp of the process in which they and the worker have been engaged. Although workers and clients often summarize the problems they have solved in their work together, the process in its entirety and the client's emerging strengths are not always examined. The client and worker must identify within the client's own idiom the progression of their work, from defining life goals, to specification of goals for the working relationship, to review of strengths and resources, to formulating possible solutions that are consistent with these goals, to appraisal of consequences to implementation of an alternative, to a final evaluation of the solutions. Learning how this process works is in many cases as important as arriving at a specific solution since it becomes a source of strength the client can turn to as new problems arise.

A case illustration

Mr and Mrs Allen live with their five children, who range in age from three to thirteen. Mr Allen is a pulp wooder who works sporadically (when the weather is good) and makes far less than a family of seven needs to make ends meet. Mrs Allen has virtually no skills as a homemaker and has only a fifth-grade education. She is a shy retiring woman, in contrast to Mr Allen who is quite verbal and outgoing. The children seem friendly and unafraid of strangers.

The Allens come to the attention of a local child protection agency about once a year when a member of the community calls to complain that they are not sending their children to school or when the public health worker calls to report that the children have lice or have not been taken to the dentist. Occasionally, the local hospital social worker calls because Mr Allen and his wife have had a fight and he beat her up. And from time to time various neighbors call to complain about the wretched condition of the Allen home and to insist that the agency remove the children from the home. All the children have difficulties in school. Mr Allen's family lives close by and is very critical of Mrs Allen and the family's constant involvement with the public agencies.

The Allen family is seen as a "problem family" in the community and is known to all of the existing social and voluntary service networks in the community (mental health, hospital, public health, churches, and public welfare). The children were placed in foster care on a previous occasion because of neglect.

Clearly, the Allens have no shortage of difficulties as this brief inventory shows. The persistence and variety of their problems would tempt any well-meaning helper to plunge in and begin to do something about these dreadful circumstances. A cognitive-humanistic perspective does not overlook these conditions; yet, a dialectical view that considers that every state of affairs contains its opposite alerts us to the fact that this family must at least have some survival instincts or some wish for something better since they continue to keep trying. In other words, those of us who have a more fortunate existence have to expend much less effort in getting by, whereas others such as the Allens must truly scuffle and toil just to get through the day. Consider, first of all, that despite all of the problems and stresses this family has managed to stay together. Mr Allen does continue to try to make a living. Although the extended family is often critical, we see that they do help out "in a pinch." When help has been proffered by an agency, it has been utilized by the family and in fact, the parents worked diligently to have their children returned to them from foster care. Although the family appears to be a "mess," we see that they are not totally bereft of strengths.

Within the context of the community, they persist despite the fact that they are anything but well-respected. Although the official institutions provide assistance, other folks do little in the way of extending themselves to the Allens — and in fact seem to take every opportunity to make life more difficult for them.

This perspective, which attempts to appreciate the Allens and their circumstances in a holistic sense, resists the tendencies either to reduce them to the classification of the "multi-problem family" or to idealize their strengths. Rather, we want to know them as they are in their struggle to survive and to cling to a trace of dignity. More important, our work with the family begins with the premise that these circumstances, problems, and strengths are *theirs* and not *ours* to take over and solve. This does not mean that we should ignore their material needs or the oppressive conditions that surround them; yet, in the final analysis, it is the Allens who must begin to define and act on the critical issues in their lives if they are to discover a greater sense of power and independence.

This principle of practice leads us, at the very outset of our work with this family, to ask them to help us understand what is happening in their lives as they see it. What are the needs that are of greatest concern for them? What would be their ideal resolution to these dilemmas if they had their "druthers"? Only when we have given full credence to the clients' perceptions and meanings, only when we have done our best to see their situation through their eyes, only when we have some glimmer, dim though it may be, of what they long for, can we begin to ascertain how we should begin to help. Through the clients' sharing and owning their feelings, hopes, and aspirations, they begin to assume responsibility for these and begin to build a commitment to work toward their goals — whether these be immediate relief from distress or a serious alteration in the life situation.

Mr and Mrs Allen, we find, do have some hopes and dreams. The most immediate hope is that they will be able to maintain their family and keep the children at home. Mr Allen has hopes that his children will finish school and "not have to break their backs pulp wooding" as he has done. The Allens realize that they do not have the niceties of life, but feel it is no small accomplishment if they can "get by," which for them means a little food on the table, clothes on their back, a roof over their head, and an old rag-tag car in which to go to town. The Allens do not spend a lot of time complaining about their "lot in life" as they are busy "just trying to make ends meet." Clearly, this family has not given up on itself.

Amidst these hopes, problems persist. One night after he had been drinking, Mr Allen beat his wife and she ran away from home. The next morning, Mr Allen called the sheriff's office to report what had happened and asked them to look for his wife, saying that he was concerned for her safety. He also called his social worker to tell her that his wife had left and that he needed to talk to her about keeping and taking care of the children. He stressed that he wanted more than anything to keep his family together.

Mr Allen now face numerous problems. He needs to work, but has to care for the children. In addition, he is very upset that he has caused his wife to leave home and is quite anxious for her safety. How can we work with Mr Allen? Mr Allen has a commitment to keep his family together. Now what can we do to help him reach that goal? It has long been a premise of practice that we should build on client strengths — yet we persist in dealing only with the problems. If we can begin to help Mr Allen to discover for himself his strengths, his family's strengths, and the potentials within his network of friends and kin, he might then become aware of some possible alternative ways, some fresh approaches to dealing with his troubles. For example, as we talk with Mr Allen, we find that he understands the rudiments of household management. He suggests that the oldest daughter can help him out and that his parents might be willing to care for the baby while he continues to work. We also discover that the Allens do have one neighbor who, in the past, has extended herself to the family. Sure enough, she is also willing to work with Mr Allen and the daughter and watch the children three days a week after school. As Mr Allen begins to weigh these strengths and resources, the worker encourages and validates his efforts. The worker also takes every opportunity to help Mr Allen recognize that his attempts and ability to grapple with these problems can be applied to other of his problems as well.

Bit by bit, Mr Allen begins to put his life back together, although many problems remain (and may continue to be) unresolved. There is the basic problem of an inadequate income as well as the health and educational needs of the family. The stigma imposed by the community has not decreased markedly, and last but not least, the mother of the family still has not yet returned. But what has occurred is that Mr Allen has indeed taken command of his life — at least in the areas where the control is in his hands. He has assumed responsibility. Granted, the Allens may never be considered model members of the community, but we do have a family that is beginning to pull together. Mr Allen has some new-found competencies, and the relations between the family and others in the community are improving in small ways.

The fact that the Allen case is relatively typical of the circumstances of practice in the rural culture gives rise to some pertinent questions. We ask why social workers merely give lip service to the profession's commitment to concepts of client strengths, cultural factors, and clients' values when they insist on "therapizing" the individual who they assume bears the problem? In the Allen case as in so many others, the many workers who passed through this family's existence automatically assumed that it was mother who needed to be treated in order to help her become more appropriate in her functioning. There is no doubt that Mrs Allen required some help, but would these workers' efforts have been more effective had they put aside their presuppositions and started with a clean slate, as it were, in the attempt to understand the balance of strengths and lacks in the family as a whole, in its members, and among others that make up the total life situation? Is it possible that the singular focus on Mrs Allen may have unwittingly contributed to the disruption in the family since this focus ignored (and perhaps demeaned) what others, including Mr Allen, might have contributed to a better life?

The emphasis in this chapter has been on working with individuals and families to help them maximize their functioning through interaction with others as they reach toward their goals. Emphasis has been placed on utilizing the positives within the family and their transactions with others in their immediate environment to ameliorate difficulties. It is imperative to note that we are aware of the structural changes and the involvement of the profession that are needed at the societal level to ensure adequate income, health care, education and child care so all families can have the basic necessities of life. In the meantime, rural helpers must do the best they can to help these low-income families improve their lot in life and, without retreat to accommodation or resignation, discover their own sense of dignity and power.

REFERENCES

Farley, W., Griffiths, K., Skidmore, R. and Thackery, M. (1982) *Rural Social Work Practice*. New York: The Free Press.
Ginsberg, L. (1976) *Social Work in Rural Communities*. New York: Council on Social Work Education.
Goldstein, H. (1981) *Social Learning and Change: A Cognitive Approach to Human*

Services. Columbia: University of South Carolina Press; pbk edn 1984, New York and London: Tavistock.

Klein, D. and Hill, R. (1979) Determinants of Family Problem Solving Effectiveness. In W. Burr, R. Hill, F. Nye, and I. Reiss (eds) *Contemporary Theories about the Family Vol. I*. New York: The Free Press.

Chapter 8

Self-Help Groups:
A Cognitive Approach to Ritual Participation

MICHAEL L. BLAUNER

In this chapter, a cognitive-humanistic approach takes on a form somewhat different than that portrayed in other sections of this book. In many respects this approach is reminiscent of what social work practice was all about in the profession's earlier days, the time of settlement house and neighborhood work. The context of practice in this case is the group — more specifically, the self-help, or mutual aid group comprised of people who voluntarily join together to partake of the mutual assistance needed to cope with a particular problem and/or to foster social change and personal growth. As will be shown, it is the role of the committed humanist that most clearly characterizes the helper's relationship with this type of group.

Although the roots of self-help groups can be traced to the reform movements of the late nineteenth century, the notable re-emergence of these groups in recent times appears to stem from the heightened consciousness of consumer activists, minorities, and other grass-roots movements that have come to find that traditional social-welfare agencies and systems are unable to provide the services required to deal with their special concerns and problems. Thus, we find citizens uniting to grapple with such issues as unemployment, tenants' rights, or crime, or to form food co-operatives or neighborhood block associations.

Our focus in these pages, however, will be on self-help groups that are occupied with the physical and emotional concerns that are related to specific health problems. Such groups are created not only to provide education for their members, to aid in the development of coping skills, and to offer various types of support, but also to increase the awareness of society-at-large about the special problems with which the group's members must contend. It should be noted that the purpose in focusing on this type of group is twofold: first, the growing number and power of these groups should alert traditional health and welfare agencies to the fact that self-help and mutual assistance can be an alternative model of service; second, it is believed that the basic principles of practice with health-oriented self-help groups are eminently transferable to a range of other types of voluntary groups.

SELF-HELP AND PROFESSIONAL HELP: A COMPARISON

The significance of the self-help group becomes apparent when it is contrasted with more traditional forms of practice such as the therapeutic group that is organized and led by a professional. For the most part, the latter group is responsive to the decisions, philosophy, and expertise of the professional whose right to intervene is legitimized by his or her acquisition of expert knowledge (Papell and Rothman 1980). How the therapeutic group develops and in fact persists depends on the leadership role of the professional. The self-help group, by comparison, is far more egalitarian in structure and action and depends more on the sharing of the experiential knowledge provided by its own membership. Face-to-face social interaction is the rule as is the assumption of personal responsibility by the members for the group's well-being and continuity. The participants provide both substantive and affective resources for one another as they strive to cope with the mutually shared problems that first brought them together (Katz 1980).

The concepts of positive and negative freedom described by Wilkes (1981) offers yet another way of differentiating self-help from professional help. Concerning the former, the notion of positive freedom, consonant with the values of western societies, gives workers the entitlement to invervene in the lives of people so long as they exercise proper responsibility in carrying out their duties. In Garvin's terms, the "worker has the sanction to act in ways that benefit the group as a whole as long as harm is not done to any individual member" (Garvin 1981: 460). Although the worker endeavors to convey respect and to enhance self-determination, he or she nonetheless assumes the role of the expert.

Negative freedom refers to freedom from interference and the expectations of others; in this case, responsibility for one's life is assumed by the individual. In the more ideal circumstances, this sort of freedom characterizes the workings of self-help groups. First of all, these groups are not dependent on any one model of change and are more pragmatic in the way they go about managing their concerns. Often their origins have no societal sanction or impetus; in fact, the overwhelming life problems that they are struggling to manage may have been ignored by existing health or welfare agencies. The subjective world of the member is of the essence and, within the sharing of a common problem, individuality and personal freedom is valued. Basically, it is either implicitly or explicitly assumed that through mutual assistance, rather than by the imposition of direction, each member will find his or her particular way.

In this regard, the self-help group, as a medium by which people may achieve greater control of their lives, expresses the philosophy and tenets of cognitive-humanism. As will be shown, the humanistic element is evident in the respect that must be accorded to the values and beliefs that have aroused people to unite in the pursuit of goals of their own making. And from a cognitive standpoint the self-help group is seen as the social context within which people can achieve not only the heightened consciousness and knowledge that is needed to enhance coping abilities but also the opportunity to redefine self and circumstances in ways that can enlarge the meaning of their existence.

These qualities have profound implications for professionals who wish to assist medically-oriented self-help groups. Ross (1977) for example, described the tensions in a French retirement community that chose to pursue its own interests. The professional staff's attempts to develop leadership qualities among the members of the community were ignored; instead, the group's leaders were chosen by the residents themselves on the basis of characteristics that they perceived to be desirable (Ross 1977: 81). In addition, the group formed norms of its own that were distinct from the rules imposed by the staff. Since the staff could not relinquish control, overt conflict between residents and providers was destined to become an inherent element of the social life of that community (Ross 1977: 104).

The very nature of self-help groups requires that the helper reverse his or her accustomed professional role: rather than imposing control and direction (albeit benign), the peer-to-peer context of this group calls for the absence of outside control; rather than pressing for the ideal of self-determination, the emphasis must be on a shared concern for others; and instead of the professional hosting the group, he or she must accept the fact of being a guest of the group. Hence, the professional must learn to be comfortable in a more or less ambiguous role that is devoid of the rules and protocols of traditional practice.

In these circumstances, it is quite possible that professionals can easily become befuddled. Not only are they attempting to be helpful without a mandate to intervene, but they also find themselves working with an alliance that does not have the usual societal sanctions or clear definitions of roles, policies, and procedures. In the attempt to allay this confusion, some practitioners and researchers have merely redefined the professional role with self-help groups as a variation or extension of practice with the more traditional, worker-led small group (Papell and Rothman 1980; Garvin 1981). This role may involve: linking members to traditional service systems; acting as consultant to the group; educational planning; and initiating and planning new groups (Cole *et al.* 1979; Coplon and Strull 1983; Gwyther 1982; Nurco and Makofsky 1981; Todres 1982; Toseland and Hacker 1982). For the most part, these roles are largely pertinent to the initial planning stage of the group's formation; it is assumed that the practitioner will disengage him- or herself as soon as the group is on a strong footing and capable of shaping its own directions.

Katz (1980: 379–80) offers several warnings about this way of thinking. First, self-help groups are not really extensions of traditional professional services; if they are perceived in this way there is the risk that the providers may also become the arbiters of who should join and use the groups and of what the groups ought to accomplish. Second, in acting as a consultant or advisor, there is the additional risk that the provider will urge the group to make decisions that support the values, beliefs, and behaviors that professionals deem important. This attitude contradicts the very definition of a self-help group as well as the forces that lead people to start and join these organizations.

Given the current political and economic climate in which it is apparent that self-help groups and professionals need each other, we suggest that an accommodation between these points of view is possible. To be sure, an affiliation with a social agency and its professional staff offers the group such benefits as a source of referrals, advertising and marketing resources, and other types of expertise. Reciprocally, human-service agencies can profit from their affiliation with self-help groups — particularly in times when new governmental policies and financial restrictions force some rethinking about normal ways of delivering services. More than just a reasonably inexpensive way of reaching a larger clientele, self-help groups offer an alternative and innovative means of enabling people to manage their problems of living.

The balance of this chapter offers a practice model which attempts to reconcile the traditional professional role with that required for effective work with self-help groups. We will consider first how workers begin to involve themselves with the group as well as the forces and conditions that come to shape the group itself.

CREATING ACCESS: UNDERSTANDING THE RITUAL PROCESSES

Let us say that a hospital, health, or social agency comes to learn that a number of people have banded together out of a shared concern about a troublesome condition or problem that is of interest to the organization itself. In the agency's desire to extend its services to a broader clientele, or because it believes it has some expertise to offer this embryonic group, a professional is asked to determine if he or she might be of assistance in some way. Such workers, on considering how their entry into the group might be achieved, face a vexing dilemma: they have not been invited; they have no sanction to offer their talents; the group is not of their making; and no apparent need for their services has been voiced. Assuming that they have, at least, the permission to attend a meeting, how do they begin to define their role and purpose in relation to these strangers?

Good sense tells us that when we enter another's habitat or domain (whether it be someone's home or another country) it is wise to be rather circumspect while we attempt to understand the values, rules, idioms — the rituals, as it were — that may tell us something about the spirit and cast of the setting. In this instance, the worker surely wants to "fit in" and feel comfortable but, of greater importance, also needs to understand a great deal more about these people and their relations if he or she is to have any value relative to the group's purposes. A method of achieving this depth of understanding — not entirely unknown to group and community workers but more concisely developed by anthropologists — is participant observation. As stated in a manual for anthropological field workers:

Participation-observation is field research in which the ethnographer is not merely a detached observer of the lives and activities of the people under study, but is also a participant in that round of activities. By becoming an active member of that community, the anthropologist need no longer be a somewhat formidable "scientific" stranger, but can become a trusted friend. By doing, insofar as is feasible, whatever it is that the people he studies are doing, he can have a first-hand experience of what such activity means to the people themselves. He

217

loses his natural ethnocentric bias by gradually immersing himself in the day-to-day facts of life of the people with whom he is working.

(Crane and Angrosino 1974: 63)

It needs to be said, however, that a worker who enters a self-help group as a participant-observer should never resort to deception or pretense; this is morally wrong and discovery of his or her hidden motives would be far more of a threat to future assistance than would be the risks in giving an honest presentation. Admittedly, this form of entry into a group assures that helpers will need to assume a more modest role than the one their professional title usually affords. But experience has shown that an honest explanation on the part of the worker that he or she is sincerely interested in understanding and, if possible, offering whatever help may be needed relative to the common problem that unites the members of the group, will allow for more genuine access and acceptance.

From the outset, workers must remember that ownership of the group rests with the members; again, the status available to workers will not be of leadership caliber. Yet, if they are comfortable enough to put aside their professional cloak, this can be a benefit rather than a hindrance. By sensitively allowing themselves to become assimilated, they can both experience and observe the interpersonal processes and stages by which the group comes to shape its own integrity.

Within these processes, deeper meanings find expression in the symbols used by the members in their expression of their mutual concerns. Any social group can be characterized by its peculiar symbolic language and interaction. And in the case of the group that is voluntarily formed to cope with a health problem, physical disorder, or disease, it is likely that the members' symbolic themes will embrace not only their personal meanings about the specific bodily condition but also their impressions about how society in general sees this condition. In a sense, this symbolic process translates the biological reality of illness or disability into a personal metaphysics of the disease (Taussig 1982). Hence, if the observer-helper pays careful heed to this level of discourse, he or she might begin to appreciate a bit more about how these members define themselves, their suffering, and their relationships in spiritual and moral as well as physiological and psychological terms.

Such symbols become truly significant when they reveal something about what the members hold in common in the challenges they face in coping with their physical and social environments. For example, physically handicapped people must cope with a world built for others who are unimpaired, whereas laryngectomy patients have to find some adaptive means of communicating in a society that depends upon verbal interaction. Such interactions between the individual group members and the external world are often transformed into personal constructs and meanings which, in turn, express the way these people demarcate themselves from society.

Two experiences bear this out: one, a group organized by a hospital social worker for families of severely injured head trauma patients; the other, a group devoted to disseminating information and developing other new support groups for the families of patients stricken with a chronic degenerative neurological disorder. Each group symbolized its problem in different ways. Some families of the head trauma patients focused their hopes and fears on the medical equipment that supported their patients' lives. The apparatus of pipes and tubes that gave different forms of sustenance to the patient came to represent the hopes of both patient and family about leading a normal life. To other families, the same medical equipment bore mute testimony to the possibility that they might have to give interminable care to a permanently disabled individual.

In contrast to the families of head-trauma patients, the families of patients afflicted with a neurological disorder tended to use other symbols. Realizing that there was no hope for recovery, their cognitive patterns of understanding embodied the daily tasks that would occupy their time for many years to come — changing bed linens, putting fresh adult diapers on the patient, and feeding an invalid for example.

Alert to these symbols and their meanings, the worker begins to gain a deeper appreciation of how each disorder or disease creates its own special challenges and demands upon those directly affected by it. The unique value of the self-help group truly emerges as it then becomes apparent how the need to find ways to cope with this threat to existence impelled these individuals to find their way to the group in the first place. The opportunity to discuss and share their respective problems with others who are enduring similar hardships accomplishes at least four purposes. First, the new relationships that arise within the group serve to bolster each person's own personal relationships. Second, the reciprocity that is encouraged by the group restores a sense of self-worth which in turn has a great impact on the member's own physical, mental, and emotional well-being (Garbarino 1983). Third, it is possible to obtain the kind of fresh and practical information which aids in increasing

Creative Change

understanding of the shared problem and adds meaning to the disease process (Blythe 1983). Finally, the personally-held symbolic assumptions of the members are affirmed and strengthened as the group resurrects the feeling of individuality that the physical disorder had shattered (Taussig 1980).

This tendency to create personal symbols can be understood in yet other ways. Prior to the onset of illness or disability, the members of the self-help group were more or less ordinary and functional members of society who, like others, were unaware of the stigma that a state of illness invites. However, the imposition of illness changes their status in society from one of integration to that of marginality. Arnold van Gennep (1960) explained this process as a passage from one culturally-defined status to another in which one moves through rituals involving separation, marginality, and reintegration — each involving certain symbols.

In this view, members of self-help groups might well be using the group to escape their marginal status and to prepare for reintegration into society by learning new ritual codes. Not only might they feel victimized by a severe medical problem, but they also discover that their expectations about how they ought to be treated by society are violated; they may perceive others' attitudes and behaviors toward them as threatening and mendacious (Wortman and Dunkel-Schneider 1979). As a means of coping with this dissonance, patients and/or their care-givers are likely to mobilize symbols having great emotional meaning and power which they can share with other people who are experiencing similar suffering. Many of these abstract images will embody the sense of a shared fate in a form that is unique to the particular group.

For example, a group affiliated with a hospice organization shared their love of the Bible and a sense of spirituality that transcended denominational boundaries. No matter what their prior religious beliefs happened to be, they were able to merge traditional theology with various unorthodox credos to create a belief system that served as a barrier to the pressures of the ordinary world. At the same time, these symbols buttressed the unity of the group itself. Victor Turner (1969: 176) calls this the "rituals of status reversal" wherein symbolic and behavioral patterns are aroused to reorient socially the group's members without noticeably disrupting the fabric of the larger society.

To summarize, medically related self-help groups are composed of people who find themselves in the interstices of social structure and who have had to organize an "underground" structure in order to conduct rituals they feel will assist them in becoming reintegrated with society. Because of their borders, rituals, symbols, and myths, these groups constitute smaller communities within society. They are more like the communitas of Victor Turner (1969), which have a spontaneous, immediate, concrete nature, than the more norm-governed, institutionalized, abstract nature of community. Moreover, communitas contain an existential quality with its emphasis on "I–Thou" relationships, which allows the members of these groups to develop intense friendships based on a spirit of egalitarianism. In turn, the problems with which these people must contend erase secular distinctions of rank and status. These relationships often symbolize the moral value of communitas as opposed to the oppressive power sometimes held by people of high status in the normal social structure. This inherent egalitarianism extends Buber's dyadic relationships to "a community of several independent persons, who have a self and self-responsibility....The WE includes the THOU" (Buber 1961: 213–14).

"We-feeling" is expressed by members of a group as a sense of distinctiveness, of shared fate, or of experiences in common. The members of these groups have views of their own world that are at variance with the views of others; these contrasts are seen clearly in the oppositions often made by members between themselves and some outside "they" (Ross 1977). We-feeling also arises from mutual expectations about interactions, especially when these interactions are regular enough to be identified as roles. In addition, we-feelings develop from sharing of mutual knowledge about group boundaries and categories, norms about the way members ought to behave in certain circumstances, and in beliefs held in common about the workings of their social world.

An example

The neurological group previously noted provides an example of many of the elements that coalesce into symbolization and meaning and their importance to the helper's role. The patient (John, aged fifty-six) in question was in the early stages of the disease process, but was intermittently losing comprehension of reality. He was married with six children, all of whom had either married or had moved on to other areas. John had many lucid moments during which he was aware that mysterious changes were occurring somewhere in his body. These moments were frequent enough for him to exhibit contradictory processes of denial. For example, he continued to drive whenever possible despite the dangers to himself, his passengers, and other drivers. At the same time, he gave up fixing things around the home; this attitude thrust an unaccustomed new role on his wife. At times, these alterations in lifestyles impinged on their children who were called on to assist their parents through countless emergencies. All came to the group meetings (with the exception of the father who was trusted enough to stay at home alone) in order to convince their mother that she should immediately commit her husband to a nursing home.

This narrative reveals two contradictory cultural themes. The children conceptualized the disease as an objective entity that was eroding the tissues and brain of their father. In their minds, the only people qualified to handle cases of this nature were trained professionals. Commitment to a nursing home was their solution to the problem posed by their parents' perceived dependence. Although they were concerned, this reaction is not out of accord with current American mores that involve escaping from reminders of aging, disease, and incapacity.

The wife, on the other hand, understood the disease in other terms. She realized that increased social support would not restore her husband's health but she could not fathom how physical deterioration might be connected to the phenomenon of her husband's rapidly disintegrating personality. She attributed the illness to the work of an invisible deity who was exacting retribution for wrongs committed during her husband's youth. She conceptualized social support as something children do for their parents, actions that might prevent the same mysterious illness from striking the same family again. Social support was not just a matter of maintaining the independence of a sick, elderly couple, but rather the kind of aid bearing on the existence of a family that ought to remain a cohesive, supportive, and integrated unity. Here the force of her spirituality (person of faith) and her sense of morality and obligation (person of principle) took precedence over all else.

As the worker in the group became aware of these symbolic differences, she suggested, with the support of other members, that the family not sit together as a unit, hoping that this would allow for their exposure to a greater variety of ideas and to prevent the group itself from being monopolized by a single family's difficulties. As the group progressed, each of the children listened to people speak about a variety of problems and the coping strategies they used to overcome them. During breaks, the family often came together and the worker took this time to sip some coffee with them. These breaks created opportunities for the helper to comment on how fortunate this family was to have each other in contrast to the isolation suffered by so many other people. In addition, the worker attempted to sit with the wife in the same discussion group. The conversation in these sessions reinforced her belief that she did possess a very rich network of resources. As it turned out, she began wondering openly how she might use these resources in such a way that everyone might not be overburdened. Another member suggested that she should draw up a reguar weekly schedule so that each child would be on call one week out of every six. The family gladly accepted this idea. This plan succeeded in keeping the father out of a nursing home until the final stages of his illness. Without underestimating the impact of John's condition, it was apparent that the family could maintain its own worth and integrity, and at the same time, provide for the father's needs.

This example demonstrates the ambiguity which professionals inevitably encounter in the context of medical self-help groups. Workers in these settings are constantly observing what Taussig has called "the archaeology of the implicit" (1980: 51). In order to restore the wholeness of persons of mind, community, principle, and faith, the meaning of disease must be demystified both for the sufferers and their caretakers. This demystification frees these people from disturbing misconceptions and allows them to cope with the contradictions inherent in their own social relations as well as in society.

PARTICIPATING IN GROWTH AND CHANGE

Active participation-observation, appreciation of individual as well as a group's belief systems, and a thorough knowledge of the physical liabilities imposed by the disorder with which the group is concerned should enable the worker to have become an accepted insider within the group and to have gained some understanding of what the disorder means to each of the members. Reciprocally, the professional may now have the opportunity to encourage the members to begin to reconceptualize their dilemmas as a means of opening some pathways that will enable them to move beyond mere accommodation to their disability. More than having to live with the condition, the members may also discover that their crisis can indeed be a motive for the discovery of strength, growth, and power.

Consciousness-raising

Virtually any experience in which people congregate for some purpose offers a multitude of opportunities for people to achieve greater sensitivity to themselves, others, relationships, the environment and so on. A group — and particularly a group made up of people uniting out of some common cause or concern — is particularly endowed with possibilities for expanding and deepening awareness. To be sure, recent times have witnessed the emergence of great numbers of groups whose purpose it is to raise the consciousness of people who, without this experience, would remain oppressed and hopeless. Women's rights, gay liberation, welfare rights, and veterans' rights are but a few of these groups.

Since the major need of the members of self-help groups is to learn, know, and understand in the hope that new knowledge will support the mastery of a physical condition that is felt to be overwhelming and demoralizing, such a group, from its very outset, is rife with opportunities for consciousness-raising or discrimination-learning. The provision of facts about the illness or disability itself enlarges one's comprehension of the condition with which one is battling. Just knowing the progression of the disease or the symptoms that might be expected gives the individual a sense of readiness and preparation for what lies ahead: the notion that we might in some way anticipate the future can give us a sense of control.

Facts alone are useful. But the ideas that we can glean from others' actual experiences and trials are even more powerful. In this instance, the exchanges that occur between members, the accounts of "What I tried," or "What did or didn't work," provide other members with real-life, vicarious experiences by which the individual can, in his or her own mind, visualize and rehearse these novel and untried approaches. Hearing and picturing how another reacted to or dealt with pain, with the loss of a bodily function, or with stigma stirs images and ideas that the individual could not generate alone. And as one idea conceives others, new pathways of knowing are opened.

As the members reveal themselves in their many persons and dimensions, another form of consciousness becomes possible. Beyond the narrative experiences, each speaker, in relating his or her story, tells something more intimate about him- or herself and thus in the observer's eye becomes a model of sorts. That is, beyond the account of "What I did," or "What I know," the narrator is saying something about "Who I am." Other members in their respective ways can discover something more about themselves as they balance their own selves against the self of the speaker—for example, that they are not alone with their own thoughts and feelings; how they are like as well as different from the other; what they might risk or fear in relation to the narrator's experience, and so on.

Without exhausting the potentials for learning on this basic level, the group can readily provide the members with the emotional support and confirmation that are lacking elsewhere. This awareness arises not only out of the aura of communion and caring that the group offers but also from the differences and conflicts that are likely to arise.

The concern of the helper during this phase is not with interventions that will generate this kind of consciousness but with the climate of the group that will allow this awareness to evolve. In other words, the worker acts as a catalyst of sorts, one who, on one hand, strives to diminish the conditions that would impede the free flow of exchange and learning and, on the other, seizes every opportunity to enrich the existing potentials that the group experience provides.

Beyond this involvement in the transactions that characterize the particular group, the process of the helper's participation and observation should reveal something about the collective needs of the group itself. This perspective might well encourage the helper to extend some suggestions about a particular program or activity. These suggestions can range from bake sales to in-service programs for local agencies, but should be tailored to fit the group's needs as well as the distinctive talents of the individual members. These activities, if willingly undertaken, should provide the group with increased satisfaction, a sense of worth, and undeniable evidence of their strengths and capabilities.

Two examples of these programs come to mind. A nurse in an eating-disorder group found that many members were ignoring others in the group who had the special problem of being unable to digest grains. One of the patients of the latter group, rather than disrupting the meetings, spoke to the nurse about the possibility of organizing a subgroup for those people with the specific disorder. The nurse supported this willingness to assume the initiative and, in addition, suggested that the splinter group take on its own independent identity. As a catalyst, she encouraged the original group members to assist their peers in some of the tasks involved in setting up the new group. Both groups continued to join together for educational activities but otherwise became separate entities that continued to flourish.

In the second case, a worker assisting an Alzheimer's group heard about a health fair to be presented at a local shopping mall. The members were excited about the idea. Several organized their own presentation about the disease and contacted the mall manager to arrange space. Many shoppers stopped by their table to chat, look at the literature, and buy some books. Needless to say, the members' ability to communicate something of significance to ordinary people who knew so little about their health problem contributed a great deal to their conceptions of self as individuals as well as to the value of the group itself.

Despite the apparent differences between the two groups' activities, from a cognitive standpoint both were engaging in consciousness-raising or discrimination-learning. By no means do we discount the explicit importance of the activities themselves; on a more lasting dimension, however, the members gained increased awareness — if only in experiential or symbolic terms — about their own strengths and the potentialities in their relationships with others. The worker's role in this first stage of learning and growth is perhaps somewhat different than that found in other helping contexts. Again, the helper's role does not derive from his or her sanction or expertise but from the extent to which he or she has been assimilated into the group as "one of us" — even though there is a shared recognition that this person has not or is not undergoing the penalties of the health problem. It is not enough merely to say that the helper is an "enabler" or "facilitator." This person has achieved this role by enduring an apprenticeship in which he or she willingly became a naive learner — an outsider who wished to understand the subjective realities of the members. It can be assumed that the worker also had to undergo the experience of consciousness-raising within which he or she had to confront the threats of vulnerability and mortality as something was learned about what it is like to be afflicted with a chronic illness or disability.

It needs to be said that the intent to create opportunities for consciousness-raising is not without some risk. Clearly, not all ventures to step beyond accommodation or "adjustment to the condition" will be successful. However, even the activities that do not fare very well provide the occasion for the worker to help the members move beyond their frustrations and recriminations. Dialectically, the extent to which people feel that they have not succeeded gives some indication of their standards and values — in a sense, their expectations about what they ought to be able to be and achieve. Bringing these expectations to light is yet another opportunity for deepening awareness of self and what that self really stands for. To be sure, awareness of such commitments and values is of no small importance for people who could easily resign themselves to a state of powerlessness or helplessness in the face of an unexpected affliction.

Redefining reality

As awareness is enriched in these or other ways, it now becomes possible for members of the self-help group to begin to reframe some aspects of their former conceptions of what they, their relationships, their lives are all about. This can occur quite naturally when new-found consciousness prompts the individual to risk new ways of acting — the product of which is a novel way of defining one's self. For example, a member of a group had long endured what he felt was inadequate care and interest on the part of his physician. It was not that he felt powerless to do anything about this state of affairs — more to the point, he had never given any thought to the prospect that he merited anything better. Listening to others' similar complaints and experiences, the germ of the idea that a patient indeed could demand something more came into being. Confronting this idea, he now realized that he had a choice to make: either to stand up for his rights or to succumb to a state of helplessness. No longer able to resort to passive resignation, he chose to act — although with fear and hesitation. To his astonishment, his plea for better attention elicited an approving response (even if it had not he would have learned something about his assertive self). Altogether, this process evoked at the very least novel conceptions of self and how to deal with authority. Clearly, the group with its potential for generating new insights and encouraging (if not sometimes demanding) risk-taking behavior, is a potent source of learning of this sort.

The group context can provide a climate for learning wherein members with special problems can surmount the obstacles that had been disturbing their reality. The helper, as an accepted member, can rely on the group process to reveal the motives and causes that persistently trouble some members. This dialogue should help the troubled individual to reconstruct a more productive worldview so that maladaptive and illogical behaviors and interactional patterns will be discarded in favor of ones that produce benefit for the concerned person.

Cancer, with its life-shattering implications, has given rise to self-help groups that are particularly effective in assisting patients and their families to reframe their concepts of living as part of the process of adapting to the contingencies posed by the disease. Quite often, these members are burdened by the vicissitudes of age as well as the disease. Sam and Hilda, for example, belonged to one of these groups. Both were over seventy years of age and lived on a modest retirement income. Hilda was in an advanced stage of bone cancer; her only trips out of the house were to her physician's office and to meetings of the self-help group. Despite her physical frailties, Hilda appeared to have adapted in fine fashion but Sam was another story. He not only accosted every female home-health aide that visited his house as part of his wife's treatment, but also the unaccompanied women who attended meetings of the self-help group. When his wife became bedridden, these activities increased. Finally, at one meeting, a worker who belonged to the group found the opportunity to bring this problem up for discussion. Almost spontaneously, other members proceeded to role play with the errant husband, playing the part of the critically ill patient. Sam left the meeting in a subdued emotional state. He never again made overtures to the people helping his wife, he stopped drinking, and became a devoted care-giver. Two years later, after his wife died, he became an exemplary volunteer helper for his local hospice organization.

In Sam's case, his obnoxious behavior appeared to represent his reaction to a crisis situation. The re-creation of the crisis in another perspective by the group forced him to see himself in terms that, for some reason, he had been able to ignore, thereby bringing his behavior in closer accord with his new reality. This is, of course, a condensed example of how such changes occur. More often than not, the process whereby an individual comes to reframe his or her conceptions of self and others is far more complex, involving the social, moral, and spiritual values that are basic to one's intentions and goals. Frequently, these personal goals are not only in conflict with those shared by the group as a whole but may be seen as self-defeating. The inventive helper again can depend on the qualities of the group to initiate conditions that may lead to a redefinition of these goals.

A group of supporters of Alzheimer's-disease patients provides a telling example of this process. One of the most recent participants in this self-help group joined the association after he had committed his wife to a nursing home. Although Frank suffered from a terrible depression, he joined the program committee at the behest of a close friend. During one of the committee's meetings, he expressed bitterly negative attitudes about activities of the sort being considered by his peers. In response, a worker-member attending the session joined with other members in a long discussion with Frank during which, among other things, they found out that Frank was a retired druggist; he closed his drug store when he realized he had been using both drugs and alcohol in an attempt to forget his responsibilities. He had also given liberal quantities of these substances to his wife in futile attempts to quiet her nocturnal wanderings. When that didn't work, he contemplated a murder-suicide. At that point, his physician arranged for his wife to enter a nursing home. During this revelation, the group began to understand Frank's loneliness, a fact to which they could all relate. The ensuing dialogue enlarged the entire group's comprehension of their own realities and enabled them to understand what new conceptions Frank would have to learn in order to get along with the rest of the world. They grasped the moral and spiritual conflicts that had driven Frank to the brink of committing a desperate act. They also felt that Frank's basic intuitions were correct; as evidence of that, they pointed to his joining the group and his work on the program committee. This process was helpful to all of the participants in the discussion since they got to know each other not merely as individuals but as possessors of a certain unique worldview that was symbolized and expressed in individualistic ways. In this process, true mutual support began to develop within the group context. The session led to Frank's reassessment of his resources; he found that there was plenty of faith and love in the world to which he could respond. He soon learned that those who give trust and affection rarely lack reciprocal human companionship. This alone provided him with the basic resources he needed to begin to master his situation.

This group experience, like other persuasive events in self-help groups, was unplanned and spontaneous — fully in response to the perceived needs of the member. Unlike the protocols of traditional practice, assessments of Frank's problem were not made nor were interventions planned. A kind of intuitive awareness of or an identification with Frank's feelings, symbols, and actions alerted the various members to Frank's anguish; more to the point, these members, perhaps more so than any expert and objective observer, were equipped to understand how the disease process which was destroying Frank's wife had also stripped Frank of the moral and spiritual values that previously had been the bulwarks of his life. His many lonely hours absorbed with his wife's empty meanderings and senseless babblings led him to question the meaning of his religion and his faith in God. As these formerly dependable beliefs drained away, murder-suicide became a

229

reasonable alternative. It was not insight or intervention that altered his course; rather, it was a restoration or a redefinition of his faith and personal worth that made the difference — all this a product of human dialogue and compassion.

Goldstein (1981) distinguishes mutuality from mutual assistance. Mutuality is a form of redefinition of reality or concept-learning and arises during group processes as individuals realize they are not alone, begin to trust their peers, and appreciate their differences as well as their similarities. The degree of openness and honesty in a group is an important ingredient in building mutuality. A free and open dialogue between members will result in the revelation of members' cognitive style, the degree to which they are coping with the situation, the strengths of self-concept, and sense of their personal history. As seen in Frank's example, participants gain an understanding of their peers' inner selves, how each of them views their relationships, and other aspects of their existence. When relationships progress to this degree of mutuality, mutual assistance will follow.

For example, the neurological group encouraged the development of other neighborhood support-groups. The worker who was assisting in this project noted how members who regularly attended sessions progressed from exchanging experiences to disclosing their thoughts and feelings. In one of the discussion groups associated with the neighborhood support-association, several people were always engaged in a heated discussion with an elderly man whose wife was confined to a wheelchair. When the husband was hospitalized with a heart attack, each one of the care-givers with whom this man had debated banded together to offer mutual support of their own. They visited the hospitalized patient on a regular basis and took care of his wife. They claimed they were just paying their friend back for the cookies he always baked for their meetings! For these people, the relationship had progressed beyond mutuality to mutual support. The honesty and openness of the group experience moved these people to make personal sacrifices to each other outside of the group context.

Obviously, the crucial element in encouraging the processes that lead to new conceptualizations is to see that the group has open lines of communication between its members. For this to take place, a worker who is an accepted member of a group has advantages over other professionals who chose to be leaders of, or advisors to, self-help groups.

Many members do not wish to bother designated professional leaders of groups with what might seem to be trifling matters; occasionally, political factors might also prevent issues from being openly discussed. As an equal member, however, the worker can more readily have access to this knowledge and can therefore encourage modes of communication between the participants that should lead to the rich interactions so necessary for new and more functional conceptions of self, relationships with others, and how these notions influence the capability of coping with disability or the disease itself. Indirectly, and within the natural flow of the group experience, the worker can assure that the following attributes of a climate that fosters learning and change are achieved: (1) clarity of communication and the reduction of ambiguity sufficient to allow thoughts and feelings to be expressed and understood; (2) achieving the kind of balance between personal viewpoints and others' beliefs that will ensure each individual's commitments to his or her own convictions and values; (3) opportunities for people to pursue a particular topic without interruption or digression; (4) maintenance of the basic relationships that give the group its integrity.

In the attempt to help people redefine or discover a more rewarding conception of living in the face of a chronic or disabling ailment, the self-help group offers its own advantages. Primarily, the group can actually "start where the client (member) is" since the other participants are either at the same point or have, themselves, experienced similar circumstances in the past. This, of course, does not obviate the need for the direct help of a professional when one requires the intimate attention of the counseling relationship (see the chapter on chronic illness). In its own way, however, the self-help group with its shared concerns invites the new member's reality as it is; this acceptance provides the firm ground upon which the troubled member can, through dialogue, activities, and shared values and goals, begin to contemplate a new cognitive orientation and its consequent alternatives. Not to be overlooked is the distinct possibility that members of the group are more likely to be attuned to the moral questions and spiritual losses that are endured by someone seeking refuge from the pain of an affliction. Those who undergo this sort of anguish may at first need a quiet hand much more than psychological study; awareness that other people can and are willing to understand and comfort them, that they are not alone in their suffering, in itself may restore faith and hope.

CONCLUSION

As medical or other types of self-help groups and their members work through their problems, what are the specific roles and tasks of the worker? The answer is simple: nothing and everything.

There are no specific roles and tasks for the professional because if he or she were to assume a particular status this would violate the integrity of the group by pre-empting its ownership and demeaning the abilities of its members. At the same time, there is a great deal open to the worker's talents — particularly if he or she is flexible and comfortable enough to lend assistance wherever and however it is needed. As the group comes to value and appreciate the worker's sincere concern and involvement, a path is opened for the worker to contribute to the climate and strengthen the patterns of interaction that will encourage people to reconstruct their beliefs and principles of living in more gratifying ways.

This function is accomplished not by deliberate professional interventions but by what might be called *presence*. In this regard, what makes the difference is not what the worker *does* but how the worker *is* within the ebb and flow of the group experience. Within the cognitive-humanistic perspective, the humanistic dimensions of the worker's involvement are apparent in his or her acknowledgement of the members' values and beliefs, in respect for their rights and goals, and in the expectations that they will find ways to cope with their distress. The cognitive aspect is evident in the worker's talents for encouraging the expression of personal or shared beliefs and conceptions and for enhancing the conditions within which the members can begin to revise, test out, rehearse or otherwise discover fresh existential solutions to their suffering.

In more matter-of-fact ways, the helper who becomes part of the group can introduce proposals for projects and activities that may serve to energize the entire membership. The group, of course, has no obligation to accept these suggestions; they are offered with the group ethos in mind and can be rejected by the same ethos. With this understanding the worker is able to make supportive contributions that create an active climate for social learning.

In yet other ways, the worker's knowledge about group processes equips him or her to participate in the human experience in a way that helps maintain the integrity of the group — by keeping communication open, explicit, and free, by concern for the continuity of leadership, and by regard for conditions bearing on the group's morale. The helper is also alert to the stresses that arise when new members enter or others leave and therefore attends to the integrative functions of the group. Not the least of the worker's activities within the group is his or her ability to serve as a link between the group and the community, thereby enlarging the opportunities for greater mutual understanding, for growth experiences, and for access to other services.

Self-help groups offer a vast reservoir of benefits for people who, individually, lack the power, identifications, or shared knowledge that they require to grapple with their problems of living. Such groups could not have increased their numbers so dramatically and demonstrated their staying power if all they provided were social contacts or information. Self-help groups include but exceed these functions: not only do they empower people to act on their own behalf and provide a sense of identity, but they offer beleaguered individuals the havens that they need while they struggle to reconstruct the moral and spiritual dimensions of their lives.

REFERENCES

Blythe, B. J. (1983) Social Support Networks in Health Care and Health Promotion. In J. K. Whittaker, J. Garbarino, and Associates (eds) *Social Support Networks: Informal Helping in the Human Services.* New York: Aldine.

Buber, M. (1961) Between Man and Man. R. G. Smith (translator). London: Fontana Library.

Cole, S. A., O'Connor, S., and Bennett, L. (1979) Self-Help Groups for Clinic Patients with Chronic Illness. *Primary Care* 6(2): 325–39.

Coplon, J. and Strull, J. (1983) Roles of the Professional in Mutual Aid Groups. *Social Casework: The Journal of Contemporary Social Work*: 266–69.

Crane, J. G. and Angrosino, M. Y. (1974) Field Projects in Anthropology. Morristown, New Jersey: General Learning Press.

Garbarino, J. (1983) An Introduction to Social Support Networks in the Human Services. In J. K. Whittaker, J. Garbarino, and Associates (eds) *Social Support Networks: Informal Helping in the Human Services.* New York: Aldine.

Garvin, C. (1981) Social Group Work. In N. Gilbert and H. Specht (eds) *Handbook of the Social Services.* Englewood Cliff, N.J.: Prentice Hall.

Gennep, A. V. (1960) The Rites of Passage. M. B. Vizedom and G. L. Caffee (translators. London: Routledge & Kegan Paul.

Goldstein, H. (1981) *Social Learning and Change: A Cognitive Approach to Human Services.* Columbia: University of South Carolina Press; pbk edn 1984, New York and London: Tavistock.

Gwyther, L. P. (1982) Care-giver Self-Help Groups: Roles for Professionals. *Generations* 4: 37–9.

Katz, A. H. (1980) Self-Help Groups and the Professional Community. In A. S. Alissi (ed.) *Perspectives on Social Group Work Practice: A Book of Readings.* New York: The Free Press.

Nurco, D. N. and Makofsky, A. (1981) The Self-Help Movement and Narcotic Addicts. *American Journal of Drug and Alcohol Abuse* 8(2): 139–51.

Papell, C. P. and Rothman, B. (1980) Social Group Work Models: Possession and Heritage. In A. S. Alissi (ed.) *Perspectives on Social Group Work Practice: A Book of Readings*. New York: The Free Press.

Ross, J. E. (1977) Old People, New Lives: Community Creation in a Retirement Residence. Chicago: University of Chicago Press.

Taussig, M. T. (1980) Reification and the Consciousness of the Patient. *Social Science and Medicine* 14B: 3–13.

Todres, R. (1982) Professional Attitudes, Awareness, and Use of Self-Help Groups. In L. D. Borman, L. E. Borck, R. Hess, and F. L. Pasquale (eds) *Helping People to Help Themselves: Self-Help and Prevention*. New York: The Hayworth Press.

Toseland, R. W. and Hacker, L. (1982) Self-Help Groups and Professional Involvement. *Social Work* 27(4): 341–47.

Turner, V. W. (1969) The Ritual Process: Structure and Anti-Structure. Chicago: Aldine.

Wilkes, R. (1981) *Social Work with Undervalued Groups*. London: Tavistock.

Wortman, C. B. and Dunkel-Schetter, C. (1979) Interpersonal Relationships and Cancer. *Journal of Social Issues* 35: 120–55.

Chapter 9

The Mentally Ill Client in the Hospital and Community: Regenerating Personal Dignity and Value

MARCIE C. TAYLOR

Quiet desperation, isolation, unconnectedness, feelings of inadequacy, and nothingness — all these frightening sensations characterize the experience of too many persons discharged from mental hospitals. Testimonials to such emotional depletion abound in the personal accounts of both these individuals and those with whom they interact most intimately (Laing 1960; Plath 1971; Sartre 1956; Reed 1977). The resultant stress that falls on family members and friends of discharged mental patients is a factor to be reckoned with. In addition, the literature is replete with discourses on the diverse problems which these persons face in adapting to life outside of the mental hospital (Chu and Trotter 1972; Hynes 1977; Mechanic 1969; Bachrach 1976; Bassuk and Gerson 1978; Burnes and Roen 1967). Factors such as economic insufficiency, the presence of symptomatic and/or dysfunctional behavior, and recidivism are repeatedly cited as indicators of unsuccessful adaptation to community life (King *et al.* 1981). The "revolving door" syndrome (repeated recidivism) has received much attention and caused much alarm. Although subsequent to the Community Mental Health Center's legislation of 1965 there has indeed been a decrease in the number of persons residing in mental institutions, this fact in isolation is misleading: the probability of a person being re-admitted to a psychiatric hospital within two years of discharge is between 40 and 60 per cent, and from 15 to 25 per cent of those re-admissions ultimately require long-term care. In 1975, over two-thirds of public mental hospital patients in the United States had a record of previous hospitalizations, and this figure continues to increase. Although Solomon and Doll (1979) warn against the use of recidivism figures as solitary indicators of adaptation to the community, when these data are considered in conjunction with the other factors mentioned (clients' self-reports, behavioral patterns, interactions with relatives and friends), they can be useful in creating a picture of what life in the community is like for many discharged mental patients.

Clearly, the difficulties experienced by the discharged mental patient, by family members, by other relatives and friends, and by deliverers of mental-health services are problems to be confronted. From a pragmatic, cost-benefit perspective, former mental patients who return to the hospital, who are incapable of being economically self-sufficient, and who continuously drain social-support services, are expensive and problematic. From an interpersonal perspective, all parties, including family members, friends, casual acquaintances, and the community-at-large, experience stress when a particular individual is not coping well or adapting adequately to community life. From an intrapersonal perspective, each discharged mental patient is daily confronted with his or her feelings of distress and experiences of failure.

SOME BASIC PRINCIPLES

As was noted in the introductory chapters, a cognitive-humanistic approach to human services is based on two prime assumptions. First, a cognitive orientation suggests that clients and workers are capable of discovering, understanding, and then using the personal, subjective definitions and meanings of their experiences in efforts to change. A humanistic perspective encourages clients and workers to examine their values and ethics; to determine the salience of such values and ethics in relation to individual experiences; and to apply those values and ethics in pursuit of autonomous, personal goals.

These assumptions translate into several practice principles: (1) workers should help to create opportunities for clients to determine and reflect on their own premises; (2) workers should help to expose clients to alternative premises; (3) workers should help clients to compare and contrast the similarities and differences between their own premises and those of others; (4) workers should help clients to consider the ramifications and the salience of their premises, based on the results of their behaviors; (5) workers should respect clients' values and personal

236

meanings, and enable clients to pursue goals which contribute to their autonomy and selected self-concepts.

Practitioners in the mental health field often have sorely neglected the principles noted above. Thus, clients who display emotional and cognitive disturbances are too readily deemed incompetent and incapable of making sound judgments for themselves for reasons which, from a detached, objective viewpoint, appear logical and defensible. In addition, the "irrational" and often convoluted nature of these clients' thought processes frequently precludes the helper from engaging in meaningful or lucid verbal exchanges with them. Consequently, mental health professionals are often quick to define their clients' problems for them, and even quicker to determine the "right" ways for clients to resolve problems, meet needs, and achieve happiness. This argument unfolds so neatly that most mental health professionals are hard pressed to question it. I contend that the personal, idiosyncratic, often symbolic, and disjunctive acts represent something more than evidence for the popular belief that such persons (the mentally ill) cannot help themselves; rather these behaviors and verbalizations are the very basis of a cognitive-humanistic approach. In the realm of mental health practice it is especially critical that workers truly listen to their clients. By "getting inside their clients' heads," and by "taking the role of the other," practitioners may be able to understand the client's perspective and reality. Only by first allowing mental health clients to guide and teach us about their definitions, their meanings, their needs, their intentions, can we as mental health professionals possibly expect to develop and offer beneficial services which will be to the client's advantage.

In the present chapter, then, I will spell out this approach to practice with mental health clients, describe "case" vignettes, and share personal experiences in order to demonstrate how a cognitive-humanistic approach is particularly useful in relation to mentally ill persons, especially those residing in the community.

MENTALLY ILL PERSONS IN THE COMMUNITY

To imply that "the mentally ill in the community" is a homogenous group is to commit a serious error; at the same time this would do a grave injustice to the persons being considered. In addition, such an orientation runs counter to the very principles of uniqueness and individuality which are central to the cognitive-humanistic approach;

each person who wrestles with mental/emotional problems experiences very singular and personalized reactions to his or her own life events. Yet in spite of the very individual and specific ways in which a person perceives and copes with various circumstances and stresses of living, some common characteristics can be found among the types of issues which are problematic. It is these similarities that allow us to make a few generalizations which are grounded in people's real situations and their very real responses to those situations. Thus, being careful not to oversimplify or stereotype mentally ill persons and their situations, it is possible to delineate a few critical themes, questions, and adjustments which tend to shape their existence for them.

The institution

To understand the person in the community, let us first sketch the rather typical, yet all-too-accurate daily routine of an individual residing in an institution for the mentally ill. The time of waking up has some leeway: one either rises within a set time-period or pays the consequences — missed breakfast or the revoking of some privilege.

Normal morning hygiene becomes anything but normal in an institutional setting. Any sense of self-pride or dignity that one may have had is quickly stripped away by the lack of privacy and the paternalistic manner in which clients are "taught" or "reminded" to take care of personal needs. To decide to have a leisurely breakfast is not within one's range of choices, for this would conflict with the needs of the staff to get everyone fed efficiently, medicated, and off to their morning programming. Medications are dispensed after breakfast; here again the regimented standing in line and expected compliance do little to instill any sense of individuality or choice for the clients.

The remainder of the day either is highly structured or completely unstructured, depending on one's psychiatric status, position in regard to the privilege structure, or the environment.

Residents can participate in structured activities such as physical exercises, current events, or other group discussions; or they can elect to create their own ways to pass the time. If one does choose to become involved in unit activities, typically there is no explanation as to why one is expected to do a certain thing: one may well conclude that "I have to participate in this activity because I've been told to do so. Someone else has the power here and I do not."

For clients who have privileges and are able to leave the unit, usually there are a range of off-unit programs to attend. Depending on the philosophy of the staff, individual clients may have either considerable or little choice concerning off-unit activities. The types of activities available tend to fall into four categories: vocational rehabilitation or training, educational classes, socialization/interest groups, and recreational/leisure activities. Most common to these activities is that little or no explicit connection is made for clients regarding the relationship between their participation in the activity and their mental health needs or, for that matter, the reason for being in the institution in the first place.

Following the evening meal which is frequently quite early, there is typically very little organized activity for clients.

Occasionally a client may get to spend a few minutes with the doctor though more often than not, it is those clients who "act out" or present management problems who receive a disproportionate amount of "clinical" time. On a periodic basis (every few months) clients may be requested to participate in a treatment team meeting. The purported intent of such meetings is to draw information from the client to aid in his or her assessment and to engage the client in participating in his or her own treatment plan by being involved in the decision-making process, primarily with regard to program participation. Often, however, the actual purpose is to obtain agreement from the client to a plan which has already been determined by staff. Many clients receive some psychological attention upon admission, due to the requirement of psychological testing and assessment; subsequent contacts are often reserved for those clients who present the most interesting "cases," or who seem amenable to "talk therapies."

Although there are certainly exceptions to these generalizations, what is important to note are the patterns and routines which tend to characterize the daily life of the institutionalized mental patient; issues such as lack of control, structure, and direction become critical factors when we look at the daily routines of discharged mental patients living in the community.

The community

Among the several different options as to where a discharged mental patient may reside after leaving the hospital is the growing trend toward residence in some sort of community group setting. Such group residential settings represent an array of services and arrangements — from the very structured and supervised to those that are virtually unstructured and without supervision. For the sake of brevity and illustration we will consider a typical setting which falls approximately in the middle range of the continuum of structure/supervision.

Our typical group residential facility is located in a rather run-down, marginal, urban neighborhood that is of mixed racial and ethnic composition but is predominantly Black. The typical socio-economic status of local residents may be called blue-collar, among whom are a disproportionate number of unemployed persons. The physical structure often is a large, old house which has been renovated to meet health and safety standards. Specific floors or sections of the house may be designated for male or female residents. The number of persons residing in this building varies, with twelve to sixteen being a common range. There is usually an effort made to balance the group composition by sex, race, and age, but most settings fall short of this ideal; the preponderance of clients are White and ages range from early twenties to early fifties with the greatest concentration in the mid-twenties to mid-thirties. These residents generally have experienced several psychiatric hospitalizations; most have never lived any place other than in their family's home or the hospital. The majority of residents did not complete high school, but have from ten to twelve years of education. Most are not employed.

A usual day begins with the alarm going off for one of the two or three people sharing a room. At least one of them would probably need to get up and get ready for work, school, or day treatment. The remaining roommates tend to sleep on until they awake naturally. The individual going to day treatment, vocational rehabilitation, or to school no doubt will endure a day which is structured and dictated to some degree by others.

After sleeping late, residents remaining at the group home might watch TV for several hours, snack on "fast foods," make or receive a few phone calls, and perhaps take a walk. Once or twice a week a resident might be involved in some structured activity at the group residence such as learning how to cook a meal, creating a shopping list, or working on a budget — all with staff involvement. Counseling or discussion about personal matters is noticeably absent.

The evening meal generally is shared. Mid- and late-evening activities usually include watching television and playing cards. Occasionally a special activity or outing planned by staff will occur. Bedtimes vary, ranging anywhere from 8.00 p.m. to 1.00 a.m., depending on the effects of medication and depression.

Life in the hospital and in a group home: some contrasts

Let us now compare and contrast the daily routines of mentally ill persons living in institutions with those living in group residences in the community. One striking difference between the two settings is the type and amount of structure built in. Life in an institution is characterized by either of two extremes — tight structure within which clients are told precisely what to do and when, or no structure, with many hours of time left open to spend idly. In the group after-care setting, a portion of the day is programmed and structured (those hours spent at day treatment, school or vocational rehabilitation) while the remainder (approximately two-thirds) remains unstructured. Intimately related to the issue of structure are two other factors: time and choice. If one's day is highly structured and programmed, it follows that most of one's time will be occupied in some way. Conversely, if one's day is unstructured, time seems boundless.

Institutionalized individuals find themselves at one end of a conti-nuum characterized by large amounts of externally imposed structure, leaving them with few choices about their daily routine. At the other extreme are discharged clients living in the community who are often thrust into relatively unstructured settings where they are faced with numerous choices for which they must be ill-prepared.

Another difference between institutional and community settings is the amount of freedom of movement available. Freedom of movement within the institution is largely externally controlled, while mobility in the community appears to be more a function of an individual's motivation. Yet, this difference may be more apparent than real since the individual's freedom may be restricted in the community for another reason — that is, public attitudes which serve to isolate discharged mental patients in run-down, unsafe neighborhoods, and which succeed in reinforcing a negative self-image. Indeed, this more insidious process of being labeled in a way that supports a conception of self as different, incompetent, crazy, or bad may really be at the root of the seemingly self-imposed immobility of discharged persons living in the community.

Conceptual issues

The differences between the institutional and community lifestyles of mental patients point toward some significant conceptual (though nonetheless real) issues that bear on practice with the situation of persons living in the hospital or, later, in the community.

Goffman and other symbolic interactionists have successfully employed the concept of *career* to delineate the dramatic and rather all-encompassing changes in a mental patient's life and his or her tenure in a mental institution. Perhaps the most pervasive and poignant transformation which an individual in a mental institution undergoes is the change in identity. Consider that prior to entering a mental institution you were considered to be a person more similar than unlike others around you living out their daily lives. Possibly you may have acted in a way that made it difficult for others to relate to you; your actions may, in fact, have been odd enough to suggest to others that you needed psychiatric help. You were, nonetheless, functioning in some marginal way, at least in the community, and with the same rights and privileges as others living in the community. Upon entrance into the mental institution, you are abruptly stripped of the rights and privileges which you used to take for granted, and you are treated as if you were seriously different from those with whom you used to share similar status and position. You are accorded the identity of mental patient or crazy person, and people begin to act towards you in ways which insist on validating their perception of you as a mental patient.

In the meantime, what is happening to your own sense of identity? You wonder who you are, whether you are the same individual you were a few days earlier. Judging by the behavior of others, you wonder if you have suddenly become an imbecile, a criminal, or a child. You may question your competence in even the simplest of tasks, yet for a while you may continue to assert yourself so as to prove that you can do something and that you really are the same person that you were a few days before. Linked with the myriad of behavioral and attitudinal changes are the great shifts that occur in your feelings. Many newly-labeled mental patients experience confusion and disbelief which passes quickly into anger or even rage. Following these initial emotions you may succumb to feelings of loneliness, grief, depression, despair, and perhaps, ultimately, complete apathy.

Close upon the heels of these changes and confusions comes an additional array of problems. Being in the mental institution demands that you adopt a new role — that of the sick person. You are denied the opportunity to make decisions and choices for yourself, primarily because it has been assumed (or determined) that you are incapable of doing so. You are also required to become dependent on others and to display the deference, respect, fear, passivity, or obedience that is proper in your relations with those who control your new life. Failure to comply with such expectations and to assume your new role will complicate your life; non-compliance merely provides further evidence that you are really a troublemaker or a sick person. Thus, there is no way to escape the sick role: compliance affirms it; non-compliance proves it.

It is also important to note that since one's identity and role are tied to one's reference group, a prolonged stay in a mental institution will leave you with extremely limited choices in regard to the groups with whom you will identify. With the opportunity for continued contact between yourself and the community completely denied or at least severely curtailed, it is unlikely that you will be able to maintain your familiar associations for more than a brief period of time. In fact, any contacts which you do have with the outside world probably will only serve to reinforce the growing perception or definition of you as one who is more like other people in the institution than those in your community. Isolation and lack of identification with any group is an alternative, one which is elected by some patients. Those who do choose to be part of a group are left with not much choice other than to identify with the other patients around them. Thus one is not only seen by staff and other clients as a patient, but one ultimately perceives oneself as a patient. And as "patient-like" behaviors become more and more frequent, these behaviors are approved of by both staff and other clients. This behavior is thus reinforced and likely to recur even more frequently and become more entrenched in the individual's behavioral repertoire. Eventually you yourself may act as if there were no other choices for you and with this cycle and patterning of behavior comes a changing perception of the individual, both by others and by yourself. You have now "become" a mental patient — you yourself believe it, act the part, and accept the role and its consequences and rewards.

Such a change in role is enhanced by the effect of institutionalization in that all of an individual's daily needs are met within one setting — interpersonal, intrapersonal, vocational, recreational, educational. Thus, not only the availability of choices, but even the necessity to make choices, is extremely diminished if not obliterated for persons residing in total institutions. This often results in the individual client adopting a completely new stance in life: in part created *by* him or her and in part created *for* him or her, it is tantamount to a whole new lifestyle — a "career" if you will.

Within the psychiatric institution the transition into such a lifestyle or career may not be a particularly troublesome one. This is not to say that individuals do not reject their new situations or struggle to maintain their former identity, but only to acknowledge that most people sent off to psychiatric institutions slide into their new roles without obvious prolonged resistance. Living in the community while maintaining a career as a mental patient, however, often necessitates some skillful maneuvers on the part of the individual. Consider, for example, your own response to the question, "What do you do?" Like most people, your reply would give some information about your job — "I'm a teacher," "I work for a car rental agency," "I'm a homemaker," "I work for IBM," and so on. Since the majority of mental patients living in the community do not have jobs, such a fairly straightforward question becomes problematic for them. Most clients I have known who are confronted with this query also respond by stating what it is that they do, but they have to say such things as: "I go to day treatment," "I'm in a training program," "I go to the center a couple times a week," "I don't have a job right now," "I mostly visit my neighbors and watch TV." But to the unsuspecting ear such responses may be offered so smoothly as to hide any signs of hesitance or discomfort on the part of the respondent. Arriving at such "smooth" responses may not be as "easy" as it seemingly appears.

The maneuvers necessitated by the acknowledgement of the discrepancy between wanting to present oneself as "normal" yet having to adopt a lifestyle which earmarks one as a mental patient, are tricky, to say the least: people will attempt to present themselves in ways which they believe will convince others of their "normality," while not really lying about their daily routine. As can be imagined, this is nearly impossible to effect. What mental patients end up doing is alternately trying to act the role of mental patient and the "normal" person, the outcome often being that they do not convince those they are trying to convince, although they may "convince" or fool themselves. If they fool themselves only temporarily, then they are faced with the confusion of a constantly changing identity and the attendant emotional stress which such flux brings in its wake. If one is such an accomplished actor that one fools oneself permanently, the result is that one "becomes" whatever type of identity one performs the best — and that becomes one's "real" self. Usually one's best performance will be in the role of crazy person, since one has already been labeled and others are therefore predisposed to perceive one in that way.

Thus, accommodating to the role of mental patient is one way of adapting to life outside the mental institution. It is incumbent upon the individual who takes on this role either to play it "to the hilt" or not at all. In order to obtain the "benefits" of being a mentally ill person living in the community, one must enact the role so convincingly that others will take care of one's needs since, as a mentally ill person, one would not, of course, be able to meet one's own needs. In exchange for having these needs met, one will have to endure ridicule and discrimination. But if vestiges of the former "pre-mental patient" self exist, such ridicule and discriminatory treatment also will be cognitively painful and difficult to endure. One is then caught in an insoluble emotional struggle trying to decide whether or not the benefits outweigh the disadvantages of being mentally ill: the extent to which one's self-image as a "normal" person is at stake may compete with the wish to continue to accrue the benefits of being mentally ill. To be sure, some individuals do manage to obtain a tenuous sort of homeostasis — a delicate balance between acting mentally ill yet still retaining the self-identity of a "normal" person. Yet the effort to maintain this balance is itself not without some psychological cost in the forms of confusion, depression, or worse. Another possible outcome, as was noted earlier, is to "buy into" the role of mentally ill person so completely that one is actually convinced oneself of this new identity. If one can no longer detect the difference between "crazy" and "normal," between self and others, between the times when one is "acting crazy" and when one is not, then chances are one has *become* "crazy."

A CLIENT'S VIEW

The preceding discussion attempted to convey something *about* the experience of becoming a mental patient and the necessity to create a new existence as a mental patient in the community. But what is it like for the individual who undergoes this experience? Subjectively, what has it all meant and what does it now mean? What has "my world" become? Where do I fit within it? What do I value?

Gracie (a pseudonym), formerly a hospitalized patient and now living in a group home, gives us some sense of what this experience is like — and, by implication, how things might have turned out differently had someone listened. I know Gracie well: I was her roommate in the group home during the months that I conducted a study there.

Gracie is a thirty-four-year-old White woman. Her sandy blond hair frames her face in a loose, unstyled manner, while tired blue eyes peer out from beneath the strands which fall across her forehead. Gracie's skin is sallow and the extra weight she carries girds her middle and appears to hang on her like discarded clothing on a rocking chair. Her physical presence, combined with her usual attire of misfitting, unmatched, outdated clothing, gives her a dowdy appearance, making her look much older. In addition, the many years of taking psychotropic medication have left their effects — in her rocking, unsteady gait, in her bent-over posture and in her uncontrollable shaking of hands and legs.

Gracie would tell me stories of her younger days when she had a boyfriend and went to the junior prom while showing me pictures of herself when she was thin and pretty. The prom was so important to Gracie because she felt that she had never been very popular in school and didn't date much. She wasn't sure whether her lack of social life as a teenager was a result of her over-protective parents, her strict Catholic upbringing, or something inherently unappealing or "wrong" with her. As the oldest of six children she had been given much responsibility for raising and overseeing her younger brothers and sisters. Because her mother and father both worked (her father in an auto factory and her mother in a drycleaners), she developed many homemaking and parenting skills at an early age. But her parents never seemed to be pleased with her; what she did was never enough or was wrong in some small way. Gracie never could figure out why her parents gave her all the responsibility of caring for her siblings, but at the same time didn't trust her to go out with friends. School kids used to tease and call her "Gracie the hermit," or "slow Gracie." She now realizes that she wasn't very good at socializing — she never seemed to have much to say, nor did she have much in common with other teenagers. That's one of the reasons why being asked to the junior prom was such a thrill for Gracie. And when her date wanted to sleep with her, well, that was the most exciting part of all, for surely it meant that she was pretty and appealing and just like all the other girls.

Unfortunately, her resultant pregnancy was not something that Gracie was emotionally prepared to handle. She recalls that school kids ostracized her and word got around that her date for the prom had been a "set-up." Girls chided her about being so ugly and weird that they had to pay someone to take her, while the guys mercilessly spread the reputation of her as an "easy make." Gracie's parents called her evil and told her that she was full of the devil. They allowed her to live at home, but their embarrassment further isolated Gracie from the outside world; they thought of her and treated her as if she were weird, different.

The pain and confusion which Gracie said she experienced led her to withdraw at times and spend hours in her room just humming and talking to her baby. At other times, she'd sneak off in the middle of the night and go out with boys to drink, try drugs and to have sex. She felt that it was almost as if there were two different Gracies emerging.

That's precisely what her parents thought when they felt that they could no longer handle her, and went to the priest for help. He suggested that Gracie see a doctor. An appointment was made but before she was able to keep it, Gracie leaned out her bedroom window one night, yelling and screaming obscenities at the neighborhood and was carted away to the psychiatric hospital by the police.

At the hospital Gracie was diagnosed as schizophrenic and was given medication and told to go to the arts and crafts group. As she described it, her daily routine at the hospital was structured with few opportunities for her to decide what she wanted to do. She felt that her parents abandoned her when they said that the doctors knew best what to do, and that they really couldn't help her. Weeks passed and due to her apparent lack of improvement, Gracie was transferred to a long-term state hospital. There she apparently melted into the background for years; she was co-operative but fairly delusional and dependent. With the push to discharge people, Gracie was released to a family care home. Her life there was tumultuous. She was ridiculed and taken advantage of by other female clients and by the husband of the woman who ran the home. Gracie returned to the streets, and drugs and sex once again. Her frequent run-ins with the police led to her being kicked out of the family care home. There was no place for her to go but back to the hospital.

After several more years in a hospital, a social worker and nurse successfully got Gracie out and into a group home. Upon entering the group home Gracie was instructed that she was expected to do something constructive or therapeutic during the daytime. She had no idea what to do and confessed to me that she was quite confused and angry about this rule. She didn't think she needed anyone to tell her how to spend her time, and furthermore, it wasn't what she was expecting; it was too much like being in the hospital and always being told what to do. Arrangements were made for Gracie to attend day treatment at the same mental health center where she received medication. Three times a week Gracie took the bus to the center and spent most of the day there.

Frequently Gracie would complain about how boring it was at day treatment since all they ever did was to take walks, do arts and crafts, play volleyball and talk. When I inquired what they talked about, Gracie's typical reply was: "Oh nothing, really. Just stuff. I mean it's really nothing. Nothing at all important." Once in a while she would tell me that they talked about problems and feelings and that she didn't like that. "After all," she said, "I'm not sick. I'm certainly not crazy and I don't need to talk about those things. Anyway, all that talk about feelings and problems makes me nervous. I don't have any problems. I don't need to talk. I'm not like them. I mean sure I have some problems, we all do, but I'm not like *them* — I don't need help." I used to ask Gracie why she went if she disliked it so much. Her reply usually served to remind me that we had to in order to live at the group home. She would add that even though she was lonely and missed her family, it was better to be in the group home where she could be on her own.

In spite of her repeated complaints, Gracie's other actions seemed to contradict her protestations. For example, the day treatment began at 11 or 11.30 in the morning but Gracie usually got there at 9.30. When she got home at the end of the day and I would ask how her day had been, she would almost always reply that it had been real good and that it was a lot of fun. She said that the people at day treatment were her friends and that she liked seeing them. Because of her previous complaints, I suspected that these acclamations were only "socially acceptable" answers to my questions. But Gracie did get together with people from day treatment on her own, and she always seemed to be cheerful and excited on the mornings that she was getting ready to go. With further questioning, I was able to discover just how Gracie actually felt about day treatment — ambivalent. On the one hand, she didn't like going to day treatment because she was told that she had to, because it was intended to be therapeutic, and because by attending she was labeled "mentally ill." In addition, it was difficult for Gracie herself not to continue to "buy into" that label and to perceive herself as strange or different, if not mentally ill. Also, Gracie claimed that she was bored by the types of activities which went on at day treatment and that she wanted to work and do something meaningful like everyone else. On the other hand, she actually looked forward to day treatment, as it broke up the monotony of an otherwise uninterrupted existence, and gave her a reason to get up a few times a week. In her own words:

I don't *do* anything. I just sit around all day watchin' TV or cookin'. I'm not really sure why I'm here except that Miss Simpson said it would be good for me and there was no other place to go. But I'm not like these other people. They're weird. They talk to themselves and act strange. I used to do some of that too, I guess, but not any more. Now don't get me wrong — they're nice people. They're okay. But there's really nobody to talk to here. I get so lonely sometimes. I wish I had some friends — some regular friends outside. 'Bout the only people I ever talk to are Dorothy and Don [staff] and the people at day treatment. But they don't really understand me. And I don't really understand why I have to go there, but I guess I do.

Gracie's feelings about moving away from home and living in the group home were equally confusing. She recounted to me how she loved to spend hours at a time at home, in her room, not being bothered by anyone but having all her needs met. When she felt like having company she could always talk to her mother, whom Gracie said was always good to her. Yet Gracie would also complain about feeling restricted at home and claim that it was good to be in the group home because here she was on her own and could make her own decisions. Interestingly, Gracie spoke to her mother several times a week, asking for advice and then getting angry when it was given, feeling she wasn't treated like an adult. In addition, she asked to be picked up to spend the day at her parents' home almost every Sunday; she always appeared full of excitement as these Sunday afternoon visits approached, and truly depressed and lost if her parents did not allow her to visit.

Some of Gracie's previous domestic abilities began to return. Gracie admitted to me that the reason she cooked so much was because there was nothing else to do and it kept her from being bored. She also gave away much of the food which she made and thus she was fairly "popular" with the other residents. Staff viewed Gracie's cooking as functional and therefore encouraged it, not being privy to the fact that she was giving so much food away and that she often felt exploited by other residents. This was confusing to Gracie because in one way she knew she was angry, resentful, and sad about being used, but in other ways also realized that her cooking not only provided for some contact with others but it resulted in approval from staff.

Aside from visits to our apartment by hungry residents, Gracie was rarely sought out. Most of her interactions within the group home were a result of her initiating contact with others; but even at these times Gracie was ignored or openly mocked. Hence, she would often withdraw by becoming silent, getting a glazed look in her eyes, or by physically leaving the situation.

Gracie felt that she was defined and placed in situations by others. She wanted to get out and do something more, but had no idea what to do or how to do it. She did mention to staff a couple of times that she might like

249

to work. Appointments at the local vocational rehabilitation bureau were set up for her, but when counselors asked what she felt were probing questions, she became angry and left. Gracie confided that when people asked a lot of questions, it reminded her of how she used to be able to do a lot more things and lived at home like other people, and this made her sad and angry. This same display of anger at other community agencies was interpreted as a sign of her unreadiness for help, and she was subsequently refused entry into their programs. Gracie acknowledges that she is angry, hurt and confused. She certainly doesn't think of herself as crazy, and yet, she knows that she is different from most other people. Her lifestyle attests to it.

Despite her despair, Gracie passively accepted the niche carved out for her by others. She knew that change is what she wanted, but she had no idea how or what to change. Gracie sadly noted how she once used to be responsible for a whole family and how she now has to tell others of her comings and goings. Though she doesn't understand nor can she assimilate this perception of herself, she acquiesces and acts accordingly most of the time. Gracie sometimes admits that her existence is pretty meaningless and futile, but not too often because when she does, she feels like killing herself and that really frightens her. As bad as her life is, she's afraid to die, doesn't want to die.

When my study was completed and I was preparing to leave the group home people were asking if they'd ever talk to me again or if I'd come back to visit. I said that I would. Gracie's response sums up her perception of her existence quite dramatically:

I'll still be here when you come back to visit. Maybe I'll have a different dress or some new towels, but I'll still be here, the same old Gracie. It doesn't seem like there's much chance for me to ever get out and be the old me again. So say hello when you come — I'll still be here.

Gracie, in fact, is no longer at the group home. She was asked to leave due to violent behavior and an inability to get along with others. I later discovered that she tried to live in several other communal arrangements but was again asked to leave. Gracie currently is living in a roominghouse and is barely managing to survive as a marginal person. She explains, or understands or gives meaning to her "antisocial" behavior by stating that she is merely standing up for her rights and telling people how she feels, rather than being used by them. Gracie has also enmeshed herself in her latest attempt to be attractive, "normal" and ideal — she has become anorexic.

Understanding Gracie

A cognitive-humanistic perspective may help to elucidate some of the seemingly contradictory and perplexing behaviors and feelings displayed by Gracie. For example, Gracie's physical appearance is not atypical of those of other mental patients living in the community. Her unmatched, ill-fitted clothing; her general unkemptness; her poor posture and awkward gait; and her over-done, clown-like make-up; all these draw negative attention to her and single her out as someone who is weird, different, sick. However, Gracie's comments about herself reveal that she does not always perceive herself in the same way that others do. On numerous occasions Gracie told me how she had lots of guys who were after her, how they'd whistle at her when she was at the bus stop, how they'd always ask her to go for rides with them. She'd go on to tell me how "those other women at the bus stop look at me real funny-like. I know it's 'cause they're jealous. It's 'cause I get all the whistles and boyfriends and they don't."

Common mental health parlance would label such behavior as a lack of reality-testing ability on Gracie's part. That analysis is certainly not erroneous, for Gracie did, in fact, perceive a different reality than that of others around her. But we need to ask if such an analysis adds much to our understanding since the conclusion that she lacks reality-testing ability may be more jargon than helpful information. What is crucial is an understanding of Gracie's behavior from her own perspective to illuminate her own subjective meanings. Rather than categorizing her behavior as a symptom or a deficiency we might find that it represented a purpose — the attempt to make her appealing to men; she dressed the way she did *in order to* be pretty. And to Gracie being pretty meant having boyfriends, going out on dates, and doing things that other people did — "normal" people. In turn, this understanding of her subjective intent would open the way for discussions with Gracie about her self-image and the troubling and felt discrepancies between the Gracie she perceives and the Gracie she might wish to be; the possibilities are numerous for the emergence of new meanings and potentially new understandings and interventions.

The point to be made that bears on understanding is that it is not always necessary for the helper to probe or to ask for explanations (recall Gracie's aversion to such questions). Rather, the willingness to put preconceptions aside and simply to listen with sincere care and regard may be all that is required for the moment. At the root of things, few people have offered this basic human concern. Listening to Gracie, she, perhaps inadvertently, interpreted the intentions of her own behavior to me on many occasions. I can remember her telling me that she'd do such and such a thing to try to imitate her sister-in-law whom she praised endlessly; or she dressed a certain way in order to look nice, like everybody else; or she went to day treatment because it was like going to work; or she didn't carry on much conversation because she didn't have a job and so there wasn't much interesting to talk about; or she hung around with the gals upstairs because she was better off than them and they needed her; or she spent time with the women next door because they were more like "regular" people; or she tried to be like me because she thought I was really "pretty together." One or two of these "explanations" taken alone or in strict comparison might only serve to confuse and mislead. From a cognitive-humanistic perspective, however, which seeks to understand the world from the client's view, these apparent contradictions and paradoxes begin to make sense. In some way, everything Gracie did was geared towards one goal and was motivated by one desired outcome — the wish to live a normal life like everyone else, to be normal, and to perceive herself as normal. All that Gracie did, in spite of the apparent discrepancies and contradictions, she did in order to prove her normality to herself and to others. She acted for the sake of becoming the way she thought she should be. So deep and fervent was her desire to be normal that she unwittingly created a closed system within which she could convincingly (to herself) explain any of her behaviors, no matter how out of the ordinary, "unrealistic," or "dysfunctional" they appeared to others.

COGNITIVE-HUMANISM IN THE PSYCHIATRIC HOSPITAL

This study of Gracie's career as a mental patient casts a brighter light on the overwhelming hazards that a troubled and insecure person might encounter on entering into and departing from a mental health system. Paradoxically, the well-intentioned endeavor to stabilize the client's reality may achieve the opposite effect. This is particularly the case when conditions in the hospital and the community become an assault on the individual's sense of time, space, identity, purpose, usefulness, meaning, or other subjective processes that are the building blocks of a substantial reality.

Gracie persuades us that she can indeed be understood. Now, understanding doesn't grant her rationality or rightness — her conceptions are certainly twisted and often futile. But understanding does tell us something about what the world is like for her. And her behavior, which would otherwise be categorized or dismissed, now takes on intent, purpose, and meaning. This awareness provides the common ground within which effective helping can begin. Another example, perhaps even more challenging and occurring in the hospital setting, is offered to illustrate this thesis.

Mrs W. spends a large portion of her day sitting in a wheelchair in whatever room she happened to be transported to by an aide, nurse, or social worker. Being quite frail, most of her physical environment is controlled and structured for her in the interest of protecting her from any danger or physical harm which might befall her. Similarly, it appears that extensive attempts at controlling and structuring Mrs W's emotional and psychological environment are also made, purportedly in the interest of protecting her from the potential dangers of viewing her life in an improper perspective. What is the "proper" perspective? you ask — why, the one held by those in control: administrators, helping professionals, and society-at-large. In this particular instance, the "proper" perspective is that deemed appropriate by the director of social work at the psychiatric hospital where Mrs W. resides. Before enumerating the specifics of this "proper" perspective, however, a bit of Mrs W's history as she tells it will be helpful.

Mrs W. is an eighty-two-year-old Jewish woman of Polish descent. She grew up in a small, isolated farming village outside of Krakow. Her husband and three sons farmed a plot of land large enough to support the family needs with a bit of food left over to exchange with others in the village for goods and services. In addition, Mrs W. did some embroidery in her home and this brought in a little money. She and her husband had grown up together in this village and had known no other life-style.

During the Second World War all of Mrs W's family members were killed in concentration camps. She alone managed to escape with a nearby family. They lived in refuge in Switzerland for a few years and then eventually made their way to the United States. Mrs W., not having any relatives left, moved in with her friends. She took a job in a bakery and assisted with the homemaking and raising of her friend's children. She led a fairly isolated existence, and when the family she had lived with decided to move away and Mrs W. chose to remain, this further sealed her aloneness.

A few years later, Mrs W. came to the attention of the welfare department and then the Visiting Nurse Association. Her neighbors reported not seeing Mrs W. for several days at a time and when they finally got her to let them in to check on her, they found her without food and quite dirty. Mrs W. was not very able to respond to inquiries regarding the last time she had eaten or bathed and whether she was all right. Rather, she sat by the window and talked out loud, as if to someone passing by outside. Ultimately, someone at a local psychiatric hospital was contacted in regard to Mrs W's "condition" and she rather passively allowed herself to be admitted.

For years Mrs W's behavior in the hospital did not change. She continued to spend hours sitting and looking at her arms and legs, talking out loud as if carrying on conversations. Her condition was diagnosed as involutional psychosis, and the treatment plan consisted primarily of the attempt to eradicate her delusions and get her to face reality. Every year, this particular hospital took social work students for their field practicuum. Mrs W. had become a favorite "learning case" for the social work supervisor; therefore, year after year she was "assigned" to one student social worker and then another. Since Mrs W. was viewed by staff as being resistant, uncooperative, and difficult to work with, the task given to the student social workers always was to help rid Mrs W. of her delusions, so that she would be more amenable to participation in the programming and activities which were offered to make her "better." All types of therapeutic approaches with Mrs W. failed and, with each year that passed, staff and students became more frustrated and angry, while Mrs W. became more "entrenched in her delusions."

An analysis of the interventions directed at Mrs W., and the assumptions underlying those interventions, may illuminate the situation. A psychological interpretation of Mrs W's behavior yields senility as an explanation of why she was not in contact with reality. The underlying assumption is that there is one known and valid reality — the reality that is identified only by professionals or people in power. Consequently, if one does not act in accord with that one reality, one is viewed and labeled as different or deviant or crazy. Interventions were thus aimed at helping Mrs W. to acknowledge this "objective" reality.

A sociological interpretation of Mrs W's behavior focuses on her years of relative isolation that deprived her of the ability to live effectively and functionally in a social world. One might even say that she had developed her own closed system — a microcosm within which she was able to exist without much contact with others. Interventions were aimed at teaching Mrs W. appropriate modes of social interaction and to encourage or to force her to participate in opportunities made available for such social interaction.

A cognitive-humanistic approach to Mrs W. is based on rather different assumptions. By stepping inside Mrs W's world it would be possible to establish some basic communication with her — communication that would be within Mrs W's own framework and therefore meaningful to her. Her private conversations would be respected rather than assuming that she was "merely hallucinating." This eventually occurred when a more patient and creative student social worker actively participated in Mrs W's conversations and attempted to understand the "sense" which the conservations held for Mrs W. The result was rather astounding. Mrs W. eventually explained in great detail how she was talking to different people from her past. Her arms and legs represented the streets and alleyways of her village in Poland, and her discourses were not, to her at least, mere babblings and hallucinations, but conversations with neighbors, the butcher, the rabbi, the schoolmaster. Mrs W. had reconstructed for herself scenes from her life in Poland — a life that was rich and meaningful. When Mrs W. trusted that someone was really listening to her stories about herself, her family and friends, when she was no longer confronted with the "pathological" nature of her "delusions and hallucinations," she was then willing to acknowledge that she was of course aware of the "objective" reality around her. She explained that back in Poland everybody in the village knew her, that she was a somebody, an important person. Here, at the hospital, she was a nobody — because others saw her that way. The fact that others constantly challenged and attempted to negate her own beliefs led Mrs W. to conclude that those same persons could not place any value on her reality, her experiences as she knew them and, in sum, her self. So here we have a cycle of Mrs W. "retreating" (as some clinicians would say) to her own world, being subsequently labeled and either ignored or inundated by attempts to get her to "see" reality. This led to her becoming further enmeshed in her world, thereby losing social contact with others.

As Mrs W. revealed many of her feelings of isolation, worthlessness, and purposelessness, she also became less socially isolated. The practitioner elicited some clues as to how to spread Mrs W's new openness to others in the hospital as well as how she might increase the amount of time spent in the actual world around her. Eventually she was helped to join a story-telling group in which some participants spoke of their treasured experiences and memories of the past, while others recorded those stories to preserve them in a collection of autobiographical sketches. Mrs W. also rekindled her interest in embroidery and became an active member of a sewing group.

Undeniably, dramatic changes occurred in Mrs W's behavior. Ironically, these changes were exactly those that had been hoped for by staff in the previous years. And, as Mrs W. shared her deeper feelings with the worker, a richer portrait of Mrs W. emerged. For example, she could actually confide that she really didn't like it there at the hospital. She complained of feeling lonely and isolated, like she was "in the army." When asked about this metaphor, she explained that everyone told her what to do and when to do it. She wasn't a child, she insisted. She had lived her entire life caring for others, raising her friends' children, giving advice to the young women in the neighborhood. Having found herself in an environment which was truly foreign to her, she had had to find ways to modify it and make it more tolerable. Thus, her behavior, seen as "sick" from an objective standpoint, takes on sense and meaning. Sitting in her chair and talking to people from her village who passed by on her arms and legs was Mrs W's own way of creating a setting, a niche, an experience that was meaningful for herself out of what was otherwise alien and incomprehensible. The potency of this new meaning was most evident in the extent to which she maintained her world, her reality, against all clinical attempts to "free her of her delusions and hallucinations." In this more humanistic and positive view, the client's behavior can be seen as having purpose and more function. Since the worker could not create another new reality as a substitute for the hospital environment, and could not have offered Mrs W. a "better" reality than the one she had created for herself, the only other reasonable option was to participate in Mrs W's own reality. This meant accepting Mrs W's world, focusing on her strengths as they emerged, and "following" wherever she was willing to lead.

Participating in the story-telling group encouraged Mrs W. to begin to participate in others' worlds a bit more. As she spoke and interacted with others around her then, and not just with her arms and legs, those around her responded accordingly. A new and growing spiral emerged and her image of herself began to change. As she became a respected, desired member of the hospital community, other residents saw her as friendly, interesting, and full of energy and life. Staff perceived her and began to respond to her as "healthier" — no longer delusional, but socially appropriate, compliant, in other words, a "model resident." And Mrs W. viewed herself differently. "I don't feel lonely, cranky, and worthless anymore. You never really knew me. But now I'm the someone I've been trying to be. I was that person all along, but none of you saw it, and none of you wanted to let me be me." What is fresh in this instance is the idea of a permissive, accepting arena, advanced by a cognitive-humanistic approach, within which one can reflect on and develop one's vital conceptions of self. It is the commitment to the various aspects of self which contributes to the richness and utility of this approach. In Mrs W's case, the practitioner gave credibility to her motives and goals (intentional self) — that part of her which was somewhat hidden by her actions and buried in her thoughts, but present nonetheless. Mrs W's intentional self embodied the array of feelings, desires, and energies which had been walled up inside of her, needing some outlet. Placed in a setting where no outlet seemed apparent to her, Mrs W. had created her own. With the help and respect of the practitioner, Mrs W. discovered new outlets that were pleasing to herself and certainly more acceptable to those around her. She finally became important again — the person she had always been in her own eyes. Others now saw her in the same way. And so a new cycle was set in motion that was based on growth and being rather than pathology and cure.

This account of practice with Mrs W. adds the creative dimension to the five principles of practice outlined at the beginning of this chapter. We see that such principles can provide the general guidelines and direction for practice, but they cannot prescribe specific methods or interventions: how these principles are applied depends on the uniqueness of each client's situation, the worker's perceptiveness, and ultimately, his or her own creative imagination.

REFERENCES

Bachrach, L. (1976) A Note on Some Recent Studies of Released Mental Hospital Patients in the Community. *American Journal of Psychiatry* 133:73–5.
Bassuk, E. and Gerson, S. (1978) Deinstitutionalization and Mental Health Services. *Scientific American* 238:46–53.
Burnes, A. and Roen, S. (1967) Social Roles and Adaptation to the Community. *Community Mental Health Journal* 3:153–58.

Creative Change

Chu, F. and Trotter, S. (1974) *The Madness Establishment: Ralph Nader's Group Report on the National Institute of Mental Health*. New York: Grossman Publishers.

Goffman, E. (1959) *The Presentation of Self in Everyday Life*. Garden City, New York: Doubleday.

—— (1961) *Asylums: Essays on the Social Situation of Mental Patients and Other Inmates*. Chicago: Aldine.

—— (1963) *Stigma: Notes on the Management of Spoiled Identity*. Englewood Cliffs, N. J.: Prentice Hall.

Hynes, C. (1977) *Private Proprietary Homes for Adults: An Interim Report*. Albany, NY: New York State Deputy Attorney General.

King, J. (1981) *Institutional Services: The Community Adjustment Experience*. Columbus, OH: The Ohio Department of Mental Health.

Laing, R. (1960) *The Divided Self*. London: Tavistock.

Mechanic, D. (1969) *Mental Health and Social Policy*. Englewood Cliffs, N.J.: Prentice Hall.

Plath, S. (1971) *The Bell Jar*. New York: Bantam Books.

Reed, D. (1977) *Anna*. New York: Penguin Books.

Rosenhan, D. (1974) On Being Sane in Insane Places. *Clinical Social Work Journal* 2(4):237–56.

Sartre, J. (1956) *Being and Nothingness*. Translated by H. E. Barnes. New York: Philosophical Library.

Solomon, P. and Doll, W. (1979) The Varieties of Readmission: The Case Against the Use of Recidivism Rates as a Measure of Program Effectiveness. *American Journal of Orthopsychiatry* 49(2):230–39.

Chapter 10

The Vietnam Veteran: Working with Moral Anguish

HARVEY C. HILBERT

The purpose of this chapter is to present an approach to practice with Vietnam veterans. Although the aim is to help veterans begin to make some sense of their experience as soldiers of the war in Vietnam — and subsequently as citizens — the implications of this approach extend toward all clients whose problems are concerned with a principled, moral way of living.

In a sense, we are all "veterans" of the war. We all share to some extent the burdens of that era. Very few of us have not experienced, directly or indirectly, many of the traumatic effects of that war: it was indeed a national trauma. Yet, it is the *veteran* who lives and re-lives this experience. It is the *veteran* who is targeted as the "victim-perpetrator" of the war. He has been held accountable as the person responsible for our national shame over losing the war. It is often the veteran who is blamed for his loss of his own innocence.

The veteran comes to the social worker with problems that often have no name. They are vague and undifferentiated. They are often a well-kept, tightly tucked away secret — so tightly kept that the veteran often cannot talk to anyone. His wife complains there is a "wall" between them. He feels guilt, anger, sorrow. Or he feels cold, distant, or somehow different from everyone else. The veteran doesn't understand. We do not understand. As a nation, we have attempted to forget him. As a helping profession we attempt to explain his affect and behavior as a consequence of a traumatic stress. He becomes a likely candidate for the psychiatric diagnosis, post-traumatic stress disorder (PTSD).

As a nation, we seem to be living in a world that has lost its sense of virtue (MacIntyre 1981), or a world that has misplaced its "gyroscope"

259

(Morison 1980). People seem to be discovering that their tried and true guides to living no longer apply to their life-problems and, as a result, there seems to be a need on their behalf to discover some new guidelines, new principles for living. The Vietnam veteran provides a vivid example of this need. Yet, as Peter Marin has pointed out, "the prevailing cultural wisdom, models of human nature, and modes of therapy" are inadequate for explaining or dealing with the veteran's "moral pain" (Marin 1981: 68). This chapter will provide some ideas for practitioners to think about in their attempt to meet this need and to initiate a creative search for guidelines to a better and moral way to live.

THE NEGLECTED PERSON OF PRINCIPLE

It has been suggested here that it is the "person of principle," that aspect of self addressing the moral and ethical dimensions of our existence, which has more often than not been neglected by our technologically oriented approaches to the human services. It is this aspect of the person that is most difficult to grasp, to understand and deal with. The person of principle, because of its moral basis, is resistant to any attempt at separating and classifying its nature. It belongs to the world of ideals, personal values, and subjective metaphysics. As such, the person of principle is an anathema to the empirical sciences and scientifically grounded models of practice.

One outcome of an empirical orientation to practice is an increased focus on effectiveness, that is, on doing the job well. Insofar as our clients obtain better care as a result of this orientation, I would have little argument with it. The difficulty arises from the empiricist's need to quantify with objective measures that which the client is experiencing. Such a need, when misplaced, may lead to the ignoring of those client problems which cannot be empirically measured with any real sense of reliability or validity. In some cases, as Wilkes has suggested, entire populations may be "undervalued" as a result (1981). This leads to a "dominance of controlling over caring, doing over being" which seems to typify scientific approaches to the human services.[1]

It is difficult, if not impossible, to quantify and measure moral feeling, to control moral ambiguity, and do something with the ethics of the soul. How do we go about deriving measures and proposing concrete solutions to the problems of personal moral anguish? What I sense, and this chapter contends, is that there can be no "resolution" possible for moral anguish. I suggest that the practitioner give up the quest for solutions to moral perplexity and, instead, attend to what Rychlak calls the "ethical motive" to practice with people (1981). This would mean paying attention to the meanings that clients' anguish hold for them and to be with them as they attempt to construct and reconstruct a worldview that would enable them to make the living of their lives more meaningful.

A fundamental assumption of cognitive-humanistic practice is that being a human being is in itself a moral activity. People cannot live in a social world without human interaction. This interaction consists of a series of human choices — to engage or disengage, to choose for or against, to do well or poorly — all having implications for the definition we give to ourselves as moral beings. In short, we persist in making moral judgments about ourselves and others, judgments that either enhance or depreciate ourselves. It is in this very activity that the veteran is caught.

THE WAR AND ITS AFTERMATH

Vietnam was a bewildering place for most American soldiers, filled with traps and other dangers that were both man-made and natural. Not only did the American soldier have to contend with the ever-present danger of Viet Cong rifles, but he also had to live with the fact that he neither knew where or even what his enemy was. The enemy could be a child on the side of the road, a woman in a village, or a bamboo stick honed to razor-sharpness and hidden in the grass of a peaceful meadow. The clash of these images constantly confronted and confounded the soldier.

Moreover, the soldier rarely knew his comrades well. He arrived "in-country" alone, endured alone, and left alone. The soldier knew that he needed only to survive until his DEROS (Date of Expected Return from Overseas). On that date he would be ordered back to Saigon and flown with a group of other soldiers back home. It was very possible that he could be killing "VC" Wednesday and walking the streets of San Francisco on Friday. For the sake of survival, the soldier often burrowed deep within himself, pushing aside the confusing horror, only to have it slip out at home years later.

A total of 1,647,000 human beings died in the war. Some 57,000 of that number were Americans, 900,000 were enemy, 182,000 were South Vietnamese combatants, and 420,000 were civilians. The remaining 83,000 were killed after the war had "ended." The counting stopped in 1974 (Pilisuk 1975).

From 1964 through 1975, an estimated four million Americans served in Indochina. Twenty per cent of these, or 800,000, are said to be suffering from difficult war-related psychological problems (Blank 1982). An estimated 300,000 American soldiers were wounded (Shatan 1973). Some authorities, such as Wilson (1980) and Egandorf (1982), suggest that due to the nature of the war and the effects of combat stress, we will not see the peak of war-related suffering until 1985.

When soldiers returned from the war zone, they were not greeted with the respect their fathers were granted when they returned from Germany or Japan. Vietnam veterans often were openly despised, even spat on and jeered at. They were called baby-killers and maniacs. Frequently, the result was a quiet withdrawal from any involvement. They learned rather quickly not to identify themselves as ex-soldiers.

What does this all mean to the veteran? What is it like for the person who felt he was doing his part for his country only to have the people he fought for despise him for his commitment? For many veterans it meant living with a deep sense of pain, alienation, and disaffection. For others it confirmed a view of the world they had learned in Vietnam: trust only oneself in order to survive. Playing by the rules seemed only to result in suffering, or worse still, in death. Moral concepts such as duty, justice, fairness — these became hollow words, devoid of meaning in the contemporary world.

It was not until 1980 that the psychiatric community gave official recognition to the recurring problems of veterans of Vietnam. This took the form of post-traumatic stress disorder, a medically-defined and official mental disorder. This diagnosis is applied to the veteran who presents the following symptoms:

The existence of a recognizable stressor; the re-experiencing of the stressful event; a numbing of responsiveness to the external world; and any two of the following:

hyperalertness, sleep disturbance, guilt over surviving, memory impairment, avoidance of activities that would facilitate recall of the event, or intensification of symptoms when exposed to events that symbolize or resemble the event.

(American Psychiatric Association 1980)

What is overlooked here by the clinical eye is the deep and often profound sense of moral falsity and error that the veteran may feel. The tremendous anger that the veteran can manifest toward himself and others may be understood as an expression of man betrayed. He may righteously see himself as having been used as a means to an end — only to be callously thrown aside at the war's end. By psychologizing the problems veterans face we, in effect, ignore their moral dimensions. The issues become medical, the veteran becomes a patient, and the community is absolved from its part in the trauma.

The veteran is no wiser nor more ignorant than any other human being. However, he is, by virtue of his experience with warfare, more aware of the frailty of life and the grotesque ease with which civilized man disrobes himself of his moral and cultural finery. There is often, on the part of the veteran, a profound sense that some of our most cherished traditions and esteemed values are really a sham. The veteran may suspect that they are true for us only so long as they are easily lived and not too severely tested.

Seeing our traditions and values as transparent, the veteran may challenge them and watch with a smug sort of glee as they are pushed aside. It is this sort of iconoclasm that is often very difficult and taxing for his family, friends, and others. The veteran's intention, however, may not be for the purpose of destruction for its own sake, but rather, for the sake of gaining or insuring a new clarity about these values. The veteran may also be attempting to regain a sense of authenticity about living to make sense of it all again after the Disneyland of Nam.

The case of Johnny G.

For the social work practitioner engaging in practice with a veteran client, there must be an awareness of and respect for the client's story as a real one that is charged with great emotional energy and moral ambiguity. Johnny G. is not unlike many other Vietnam veterans. He first saw a social worker because he felt he must be doing something wrong in his relationships. Johnny had been married two times; each marriage ending with the complaint that Johnny never opened up — that he was emotionally distant. What precipitated his first visit was the fact that he had fallen in love again, seriously so, and he felt he had better do something about this problem. With that said, Johnny's eyes began to cloud over and he started crying. He said that ever since he had been discharged from the army he had trouble talking to people. He felt very much alone and was afraid that he would never be able to love anyone completely. He added that he felt that he frightened the women he had loved. It seems that every once in a while, mostly at night, Johnny would get depressed and begin to cry. He would tell, in choppy phrases and oddly juxtaposed images, of the pain in his heart, his memories of the war, of his difficulty in re-adjusting to civilian life. These stories were told with power and emotion and Johnny felt they were scary to those near him.

When asked what story he thought of most, Johnny told it quietly, almost coldly, until the last sentence. At that point he fell apart again. It was the story of how he was injured.

Johnny had been in Vietnam for about six months. He had seen some combat during that time. It was the rainy season and his company had just returned from a search-and-destroy mission. He was very wet because he hated to use his poncho. When asked why, he said that it was because a few months before he had to wrap the body of a dead sergeant in it. Johnny said the sergeant had died trying to cross a river that his company didn't have to cross in the first place, so the sergeant had died a "stupid death." No sooner had he begun to dry out when his company was ordered back onto the choppers. The "sister" company in his brigade was pinned down and under heavy fire. Johnny's company commander, a Captain who shaved his head and carried a pearl-handled pistol, had volunteered his company for a rescue mission. As he flew toward the LZ (landing zone), he watched the bomb craters passing underneath the belly of the chopper. He was ashamed that a land so beautiful was becoming so ugly.

The LZ was "hot," meaning there was enemy fire coming in to the area as they jumped from the choppers onto a bed of saw-grass. The North Vietnamese were all around them and the troops had to scramble to any available safety. The ground was stony and water lay in pools. The enemy was hidden and it was difficult to get any sense of where they were. They stopped shooting when it got dark and he used the time to find a fallen tree to give him shelter. The Captain ordered three FNGs (Fucking New Guys) to go out some distance from the perimeter. They were to become the company's listening post (LP). The job of the LP was to listen for enemy movement. At this, Johnny had become angry. He felt there was no sense sending out an LP when they already knew where the enemy was. Johnny directed much of his anger toward his company commander adding additional reasons to prove the commander was "stupid." When, for example, the enemy began its assault on Johnny's position, the Captain called in illumination rounds from an artillery unit. Since Johnny's company was exposed and the enemy was well-entrenched, the illumination only served to show the enemy where Johnny's unit was.

The men in the LP found themselves caught in the crossfire. They became panic-stricken, ignored the passwords they were supposed to use, and broke into a run toward their lines. Johnny, not seeing anything but muzzle-flashes, caught the shadowy, charging shapes of men with

264

rifles. He began firing at them. He feared his position was about to be over-run. He said there were mortars and grenades exploding everywhere, but these figures kept coming.

Johnny began to cry, telling the rest of his story haltingly. But he went on. As the figures approached, he emptied a magazine into the body of one of the soldiers. The soldier spun around from the impact of the bullets, stumbled, then dove across the trunk of the tree Johnny used as shelter. It was then that Johnny discovered that he had shot one of his own guys, a "kid" the same age as himself.

Shortly after, Johnny himself was shot in the head. He did not lose consciousness and was awake for the rest of the night. It seemed that he could not be evacuated from the area until morning and he lay on the wet ground for several hours, listening to the death-screams of the fellow soldier he had shot while the rest of his company were fighting for their lives. Much of Johnny's effort went into concentrating just on staying awake. He had the idea that if he could somehow stay conscious he would have a better chance of staying alive. Yet, in order to do this, he had to spend the night listening to his dying comrade. These screams were to become the metaphors by which Johnny personified his agony.

Johnny survived to return home paralyzed. During an extended stay in a hospital he developed a strong conviction that he would do well in spite of his injuries. He was officially retired from the army and returned home to live with his mother and father.

This is Johnny's story. For us, the questions of where, how, and by what processes, we are to begin work with him now arise.

THE SEARCH FOR A PRINCIPLED SELF: A FRAMEWORK FOR PRACTICE

Cognitive-humanistic practice begins with the assumption that the goal of any practice situation ought to include a search for the principles by which the client may be enabled to live a better life. What follows, then, is a framework conceptualized as a series of "searches," through which the worker may help the client begin to order his experience, put it into some kind of context, make sense of it, and move on toward the living of a moral life.

This search begins with the often-overlooked question of where to begin, and is rooted in the principle of starting where the client is. The search for principled meaning is then addressed with particular attention paid to cognitive and moral styles, as well as the need for reflective morality. Four questions aimed at eliciting principled beliefs are suggested and, finally, the search for a principled quality of living is discussed. This search pays attention to the differentiations between "doing" and "being." The roles of personal confrontation and autonomous action are explored in the context of commitment and personal responsibility.

The search for principled beginnings

For a principled beginning to take place, it seems to me that there are two things that must happen simultaneously: practitioners must become aware of their own moral point of view in relation to what their client is saying while, at the same time, enabling their client to gain some sense of *his* own moral point of view. It must be understood that something critical happened in the client's life which fundamentally altered his perception of self and world. In Johnny's case, he endured certain appalling events, his life changed, and he felt "something" had gone wrong. This "something" affected not only his worldview, but his moral character as well.

The moral point of view

William K. Frankena suggests that one's moral point of view can be discerned by the facts used in order to create one's reasons for making moral judgments. He believes that "moral reasons consist of facts about what actions, dispositions, and persons do to the lives of sentient beings" (Frankena 1973: 113). Of singular importance, then, is the question of how to come to know what the "facts" are in any given client situation. Ordinarily, facts are understood to be objective. That is, they should stand apart from the person, untainted by subjectivity, and agreed upon by others as true representations of what "is." From the cognitive-humanistic standpoint, however, we argue that facts cannot escape the perceptual field of the person holding them. For the moment, it is enough to say that the facts are subjective creations, and thus, the search for a moral point of view is a search for what values people assign to the "facts" that they employ to support their reasons.

The central point of this discussion that bears on work with people is this: if we do not deny that we own a moral point of view, then we must acknowledge that we are constantly in the process of making moral judgments — or at the very least, judgments of values. These judgments are about our own internal attitudes, as well as our outward behavior. They are judgments about other's intentions and behaviors, as well as the interactions between all parties involved in the moral and social situation.

Now, the question of making moral judgments in social work is a sticky one. Traditionally, we have not only tried to avoid making such judgments, but we have also converted the principle of non-judgmentalism towards clients into a credo (Biestek 1957). Yet, as humans, it is impossible for us not to make judgments about our clients. As Rollo May points out, "No matter how much the therapist or counselor might protest that he assumed no values in his practice, the patient or counselee knew ... that the protestation was not true" (May 1980: 169). Such protestation on the part of the social worker may result in the modeling of inauthentic behavior, a demonstration, in effect, that lying is acceptable.

When we make normative judgments and take on a moral point of view, we then think of one's actions as having some purpose or intent. Moral decisions are not reactive to antecedent conditions in a deterministic sense, but are instead proactive in their attempt to achieve a particular aim or objective. The intent may be to bring about what are believed to be "good" consequences, or to follow the maxims of duty or obligation. In any case, we must inevitably ask ourselves the question: "For the sake of what am I making this judgment or taking this action?" Even the tentative answers derived from such questions will urge both worker and client to begin to sort out for themselves the essential elements of their particular moral points of view, as well as to help them identify more clearly their intentions in their work together.

Starting where the client is

The second aspect of a principled beginning involves the principle of "starting where the client is"; and where the client happens to be may be understood by careful listening to the explicit and covert messages clients convey as they talk about themselves and their circumstances. To do this requires that we must set aside our preconceived notions as to the nature of the client or his or her "presenting problem" and resist considering which aspects of the client's picture might be fitted into this or that conceptual scheme. While certain "facts" of a specific client's life may mesh well with our statistical and technical knowledge *about* a general problem or population, this mesh is but an abstraction. Such mental constructs could, as May (1983) points out, get in the way of our ability to *know* this particular person confronting us at this point in time.

To begin where clients are means paying close attention to the values that they ascribe to the facts as they speak of them. Here we are listening for the subtle or even blatant concepts that clients use to construct and communicate their implicit moral point of view. An obvious example is Johnny's judgment of his company commander as "stupid." Consider that another veteran might judge the same person as "gutsy," "shrewd," or "doing his duty." They are the metaphysical red flags that ought to draw our attention to how clients discriminate between the various aspects of their lives, i.e. their personal and social values as well as their sense of the morality about their past, present, and future behavior.

What we call the principled self is fundamental to the life philosophy of clients; as such, it may be so natural to them that they are for the most part unaware of its power in their lives. Hence, the client's philosophy is more often couched in metaphorical terms than in straightforward expressions. It is these metaphors that symbolize and communicate the moral concepts which hang on the client's decision-choice wheel. Such metaphors may or may not be deliberately selected or remembered by the client. But whether deliberate or not, they are the presentations of his personal meaning structure to others. It is through this process of listening to, and exploring with the clients, their metaphors that we gain some awareness not only of how they basically feel and think about themselves, but the grounded beliefs that shape their moral point of view.

Beginning with Johnny

A principled beginning with Johnny is made somewhat difficult, as it is with many veterans, by the content of the story Johnny tells. In many respects, it is the story of an atrocity. Haley, in her article "When the Patient Reports Atrocities," suggests that the first task is for "the therapist to confront his/her own sadistic feelings, not only in response to the patient, but in terms of his/her own potential as well" (Haley 1974: 194). For the cognitive-humanistic practitioner, this means assessing one's own moral point of view. For example, the practitioner might ask him- or herself if it is within the realm of possibility that he or she would have pulled the trigger that killed the wrong man, as Johnny did.

On approaching Vietnam veterans, the practitioner must be willing to come to terms with the issues raised by such questions. One must have some sense of how one would respond to similar situations. It is only when we have established for ourselves our point of view in relation to "the facts" a veteran like Johnny presents to us that we can either withdraw or begin to help him order his experience for himself in an honest way.

Through our receptiveness to the words and feelings Johny expresses in the interview, we may begin to formulate some questions, the answers to which may bring us closer to his world. During this beginning, a frequent checking with the client regarding how he is using words and what he means by them serves two purposes.

First, the attempt to clarify and comprehend, by definition, engages the practitioner in a true dialogue with the client that is based on a shared understanding of the subjective perceptions of the situation and leads to trust in the relationship. Second, the process allows for and encourages the raising of some real and meaningful questions in the minds of both persons: both may gradually feel more free to ask each other about the various and subtle meanings of the words they are using. It is in this mutual search for a principled beginning, in this search for the best questions, that much of the therapeutic groundwork is accomplished.

The search for principled meaning

Before we can consider the qualities of principled meaning, we need to say something about meaning itself. Polanyi has suggested that words in and of themselves mean nothing, that it is "only a speaker or listener [who] can mean something *by* a word" (Polanyi 1962: 252). While there may very well be agreement on the explanatory functions of a word or concept, the *meaning* of the word will remain elusive because it is determined by the user. Meaning, then, speaks of the individual's personal, tacit, and perceived definition of the situation.

This is not difficult to demonstrate. Ask any ten people to write on a sheet of paper how they would define a particular word. A brief analysis of the responses will yield at least two classes of answer. On the one hand, there will be explanatory uses, which refer to what a thing is. On the other hand, we will find statements that go beyond such descriptions and enter the world of meaning.

For example, if we were to use the word "guilt" in this exercise, we might find consensus about its explanatory function, such as "the feeling of having done something wrong." The subjective meanings of the term, however, may be quite different and go very far beyond the explanatory nature of the word. Used as a class exercise, "guilt" elicited such broad-ranging responses as: "It hardly ever leaves you," "A feeling that festers inside," "A feeling you can't talk about," "A manipulative, mind-controlling mechanism," "Shame, doing something you want to make amends for."

It is these uniquely personal meanings that provide the practitioner and client with a basis for discovering intent. This intent or purpose, as indicated earlier in our discussion of the moral point of view, may be viewed as either reactive or proactive.

A second dimension of perceiving meaning may be seen in how we conceptualize the thinking processes of our clients. Goldstein has suggested that the patterns or styles in one's thinking processes take on a direction: convergence — the tendency to narrow down, focus, and problem-solve; and divergence — the tendency towards expansiveness of thought, a poetic and/or associationistic style (Goldstein 1981). In an interview with Johnny, he said he had to find some way of stopping the screams in his mind. Clearly, such a statement is a request for a solution. The convergent thinking here narrows the scope of the problem to a simple prescription — "Stop the screams and I'll be OK," or "Maybe some drug will help."

On the other hand, we may understand Johnny as a divergent thinker as well. His initial reason for seeing a social worker had something to do with a sense that his failed relationships were connected in some way with his inability to express feeling. However, in the next moment, he quickly expressed a great deal of emotion about the war. Although he could not define the connection, Johnny associated the pain of his torn relationships with the tearing anguish he continues to feel about his part in the death of a comrade. It may seem as if Johnny is reacting to events which occurred a long time ago; yet, these reactions also contain an intent, a purpose, if we choose to see them that way. Although it may, at first, appear to be an outrageous question, the practitioner could urge Johnny to think about the possible purpose that these screams might serve in his current life situation. Such a request doesn't necessarily seek an answer; rather, it asks Johnny to begin to think about himself as a person having choice and intention, rather than as merely a victimized reactor.

The four aspects, expressed by the client's words and actions, and revealed in the search for their meanings, provide the conceptual tree and the many stems that represent the client's moral outlook. Yet we also need to understand how the individual arrives at moral choices. Just as one has certain cognitive styles, one also exhibits certain moral styles or modes of making critical choices. The point for us to consider in our approach to understanding the moral groundwork of our clients, is that there are two basic sources of knowing what is right and good: reason and emotion. From a cognitive-humanistic standpoint, these two sources cannot be separated. As noted in the introductory chapters, both reason and emotion are part of cognition and through a dialectic interplay are two aspects of a whole.

Moral theorists are also divided on the issue of whether or not morality ought to be judged on the basis of the *intention* of an action or decision, or on the basis of the potential *consequences* of the action or decision.

Traditionally, from a philosophic perspective, the dimensions of intent and consequence, cognition and emotion, were used as the beginnings, or basis of ethical theory building. Yet, the practitioner must deal with the whole person in context with his or her real-life situation. Rarely do we, as human beings, behave or decide by recourse to only one of these dimensions. Typically, our moral decisions are blends of both reason and emotion as well as concerns about what our decisions intend to achieve and how they turn out.

We also need to consider John Dewey's argument that there are periods in history when traditional theories or sources of moral choice are not relevant. It is at these times when we are forced to turn inward to ourselves as the source of authority for our choices; this Dewey calls "reflective morality" (Dewey 1960: 7). Such a morality is a synthesis of what we actually do know about right and wrong, about duty and obligation, as this knowledge is applied to uncertain and ambiguous circumstances.

In Johnny's case, the enormously ambiguous circumstance he has to wrestle with is the fact that he has killed a fellow soldier. As I want to show, it is in this type of circumstance (where there is an insoluble conflict between intention and consequence) that the need for reflective morality is essential.

Consider that in Vietnam, traditional rules of warfare (and whatever kind of morality such rules imply) did not apply. Anyone could be the enemy — including women and children. It was in this broader context that Johnny came under fire — and in the middle of the night when the threat of being killed was the greatest. Added to this was the fact that the figure coming toward him was unidentifiable. What is the morality of this situation? Ought he to have pulled the trigger of his weapon?

It can be argued in a reasonable and logical fashion that Johnny perceived the threat of losing his life. In this view, his behavior was intentional: it was *for the sake of* survival, and *in order to* protect himself and possibly others. Considering only the intentions of his act and the possible consequence of his being killed, his choice to pull the trigger was morally correct. But the consequence proved to be devastating, even though he could not anticipate it. As a result, even though he made a decision that was situationally and morally proper, he is left with the anguish of knowing that the consequences of that choice are, without question, morally wrong.

Johnny's painful moral dilemma is not unique, though it may differ in intensity and detail from those of other clients we meet in practice: the parent who attempts to discipline his or her child but, by some accident, severely injures the child, is one example; the employee whose sincere honesty results in the firing of a fellow employee and friend is but another.

When we, as practitioners, find ourselves in this domain of ethical and moral dilemmas, what do we do? Actually, there is very little we can do if by doing we mean resolving. The message that I wish to convey here is that working with moral anguish means, essentially, that we are *being with* that anguish and not "relieving," "resolving," or "curing" the suffering of the client. If we assume that we are entering into our client's life in order to be "effective" by somehow solving his or her moral problems then we are truly fooling ourselves and perpetuating a hoax at the client's expense. The best we can do can be stated in existential terms: to help the person "come to himself" and realize that "[M]an acts, man chooses, man makes himself" (Barnes 1978: 294–98).

In our *being with* we are helping clients discriminate meanings, identify their intentions, and explore the consequences of their actions so that they may be able to develop the rational moral principles that they require in order that they can come to themselves. In the shared experience, it is necessary for practitioners to be supportive as clients confront their need to choose, to risk action, and to begin to "make themselves." This nurturing role cannot be understated. Particularly for the helper who sees him- or herself as an "expert," it is probably the most difficult and complex role to enact. For, in essence, it demands that we relinquish our authority and give back clients their full responsibility and the autonomy for their own choices and actions.

Recalling the previous discussion of the four aspects of any moral choice, this provides us with some guidelines for offering the client some reasonable ways to grapple with the dilemma. We need to ask clients to deal with their feelings of anguish as openly as possible. They need to be encouraged to use their minds — to think about the problem by using their rational, imaginal, and divergent thought processes. They should be urged to explore their intentions in making the critical choice to consider what they really wished to achieve. And finally, the consequences and their meanings and implications require careful scrutiny. To be sure, these are not a set of questions that can be posed in a cookbook manner; they would be rendered meaningless and counterproductive by such an approach. They are suggested only as a guide to the practitioner who finds him- or herself caught in the maze of moral ambiguity and perplexity. The intent is to bring to light the subjective meanings contained within the client's anguish in such a way as to free the client to create the foundational concepts upon which he or she can erect the principles for an ongoing moral life.

THE SEARCH FOR PRINCIPLED LIVING

These were the questions that guided practice with Johnny and that enabled the worker to forego any of his own assumptions that he might know what was best for his client — and more important, how Johnny's moral guilt might be used. Out of the dialogue, Johnny dealt with the fact that he was the one who committed the act and that the act was inevitably an expression of his choice. In turn, he came to accept that his choice to kill was not something that he could ever dismiss or forget for it had become a part of his understanding of who he was. And who he was, he came to understand, included the capacity as a human being to act in a particular way when caught in a dangerous situation. These revelations that are part of an ineradicable past would continue to impinge on his present.

In his succeeding interviews, Johnny continued to search for meaning and value. This was a painful task since the question of meaning was always elusive: at the bottom of things, he always had to ask himself what meaning could there be in the death of an innocent man? Yet, paradoxically, it was this confounding question that gradually pressed Johnny personally to confront and take responsibility for what he had done and what it all meant. For the other side of the guilt and pain that he endured about the death of his companion was the recognition that he valued life above all else. There were his meaning and principles: caring for people became something that he could actually do something about in a meaningful way. Soon after, Johnny returned to college with the goal of entering one of the helping professions.

The choice to confront one's anguish, one's personal moral pain, and to choose to "make new" the self requires that the client comes to terms with his or her autonomy; this, in turn, invokes the principle of self-determination. This principle is fundamental not only to cognitive-humanistic practice, but to the profession of social work itself. Yet, this is, in itself, only a *statement* of moral principle. Without an active commitment to it, the moral content becomes meaningless; without the expectation that our clients accept its consequences, it becomes just another attractive phrase. The principle only proposes that our clients have the right to choice in their decision-making. It says nothing about what these possible choices might be, nor does it spell out the intentions behind these choices or their consequences. In short, it obliges us as helpers to allow clients to act on their own behalf without offering our directions about what that act ought to be. The value in the principle of autonomy or self-determination is an end-in-itself rather than a means to some other end.

CONCLUSION

Throughout this chapter I have stressed that the searches for principled beginnings, meanings, and living must begin within the personal dimensions of the client's life. These searches are carried on through an intimate and open dialogue between the veteran and the social worker. I have suggested that a reflective morality is necessary in order to come to terms with the moral ambiguities of the veteran's experience in living. If living is, in effect, a moral activity, a primary task for the worker may be defined in terms of enabling the client to create new choices and that the singular choice is that for the sake of authenticity.

More often than not, our role as helpers is not construed as one that encourages joining with the outsiders of society in order to support them as outsiders; rather, our role is more often seen as one designed to bring the outsider back into the fold, making him, as best we can, an insider.

The tragedy is, that through our joining with the veteran we cannot avoid hearing his message — in Johnny's case, the death-screams of his conscience. If we follow the more common path, we may at best ignore the importance of his metaphor. At worst, we may choose to dismiss his metaphor as just another symptom of his illness.

If we are to take a step toward the living of a moral life we must confront directly this conflict in roles. It remains for us only to discover for ourselves our own principles for beginning, meaning, and living. My hope is that we will not only choose wisely, but with authenticity.

NOTES

1. From correspondence of Ruth Wilkes to Howard Goldstein.

REFERENCES

American Psychiatric Association (1980) *Diagnostic and Statistical Manual of Mental Disorders 3rd Ed.* New York: American Psychiatric Association.
Barnes, H. (1978) *An Existentialist Ethics.* Chicago: University of Chicago Press.
Biestek, F. (1957) *The Casework Relationship.* Chicago: Loyola University Press.
Blank, A. (1982) Apocalypse Terminable and Interminable: Operation Outreach for Vietnam Veterans. *Hospital and Community Psychiatry* 33(11): 913–18.
Dewey, J. (1960) *Theory of Moral Life.* New York: Holt Rinehart & Winston.
Egandorf, A. (1982) The Postwar Healing of Vietnam Veterans: Recent Research. *Hospital and Community Psychiatry* 33(11): 901–08.
Frankena, W. (1973) *Ethics.* Englewood Cliffs, N.J.: Prentice Hall.
Goldstein, H. (1981) *Social Learning and Change: A Cognitive Approach to Human Services.* Columbia: University of South Carolina Press; pbk edn 1984, New York and London: Tavistock.
Haley, S. (1974) When Patients Report Atrocities. *Archive of General Psychiatry* 30: 191–96.
MacIntyre, A. (1981) *After Virtue: A Study in Moral Theory.* Notre Dame: University of Notre Dame Press.
Marin, P. (1981) Living with Moral Pain. *Psychology Today* November: 68–77.
May, R. (1983) *The Discovery of Being.* New York: W. W. Norton.
—— (1980) *Psychology and the Human Dilemma.* New York: W. W. Norton.
Morison, R. (1980) On Ethics, Gyroscopes, and Radar Sets. *Hastings Center Report* 10(1): 26–8.
Pilisuk, M. (1975) The Legacy of the Vietnam Veteran. *Journal of Social Issues* 31(4): 3–11.
Polanyi, M. (1962) *Personal Knowledge.* New York: Harper & Row.
Rychlak, J. (1981) *Introduction to Personality and Psychotherapy,* 2nd edn. Boston: Houghton Mifflin.
Shatan, C. (1973) The Grief of Soldiers. *American Journal of Orthopsychiatry* 43(4): 640–53.
Wilkes, R. (1981) *Social Work with Undervalued Groups.* London: Tavistock.
Wilson, J. (1980) Conflict, Stress, and Growth: The Effects of War on Psycho-social Development Among Vietnam Veterans. In Figley and Leventman (eds) *Strangers at Home.* New York: Praeger.

PART III
Conclusion

Chapter 11

Summing Up: The Integration of the Philosophy, Theory, and Practice of Cognitive-Humanism

HOWARD GOLDSTEIN

The substance of this book is made up of the ingredients that, together, mold a responsive and cogent approach to working with people and their problems of living. As they are developed in the first two chapters, they include a social and moral philosophy (humanist), a theoretical perspective on mind and behavior (cognitive), and a framework for practice that translates these metaphysical and theoretical principles into action. The three dimensions are essential if practice is to have integrity. A philosophical grounding ensures that professional action will be rooted in the helper's secure and consistent assumptions about humanity and, accordingly, that explicit moral, value, and ethical principles will serve as dependable guides to his or her interventions. A sound conceptual base, derived from and expressing these principles, predicts a form of practice that will not be capricious or aimless. Altogether, they offer the vulnerable client a measure of security and respect — and, at the very least, a promise that his or her life will not be meddled with.

The discussion in the two introductory chapters is necessarily abstract — as is any theoretical discourse *about* the human experience. It proposes a logical consistency and order that cannot represent the vicissitudes of practice *as* a human experience in and of itself. The succeeding chapters do capture the more vital and kaleidoscopic picture of practice with an array of personal and interpersonal problems. Now, in this final chapter, the intent is to bring the two sections into alignment and summarize the nature of what we call cognitive-humanistic practice.

An orientation to practice

Even a cursory review of the preceding eight chapters should show that, however cognitive-humanism is defined, it is neither a doctrinaire, a prescriptive, nor a rigidly systematized approach. More of an orientation to practice than a school or method, it does not offer a set of rules and structures for defining and dealing with these problems. To the contrary, this approach strives to remain open-ended, aware that equations or laws cannot enclose the remarkable and unpredictable variabilities of the human condition. We saw, for example, that families that commit violence (Chapter 3) may appear to manifest some outwardly common characteristics. Yet, as Sturkie so perceptively shows, beyond the same egregious behavior lie very different personal needs, intentions, and outlooks. Similarly, we would be overlooking some very critical differences among people if, as the chapters on the battered woman and the alcoholic show, we assumed that the label implied a common understanding or approach to helping.

This being the case, cognitive-humanism offers few recipes or instructions about what to do or when to do it. To be sure, there are many useful generalities and broad theories that offer some outlines for comprehending a nominal problem area; yet, each specific human event must be understood on its own ground at its particular moment in time. The adversity of chronic illness (Chapter 4) is a case in point. As Bohnengel-Lee points out, despite what can be said generally about a specific illness, its different stages and trajectory will present different challenges that the patient must cope with. And even within the same stage of the same disorder, the meaning and even the worth of life will be interpreted differently by different patients.

Even if it were possible to organize our observations of our client's situation into some fairly uniform psychological or diagnostic categories, there are certain implicit layers of that situation that would tend to distinguish it in important ways from most others. These include the substrata of the individual's ethical, moral, and often, spiritual values and their telling roles in the affairs of living. This point is vividly illustrated in many of the chapters — among them, H. Hilbert's depiction of the painful and virtually irresolvable moral dilemma of the veteran (Chapter 10); the role of faith and the ultimate recourse to a divine being as the solace and strength of the desperately ill patient (Chapter 4); and, on another dimension, the effects of the moral outlook of society on the way mental patients are treated (Chapter 9).

When the notions of formula, prescription, or system are subtracted, what is left in the concept of a cognitive-humanistic orientation to practice? What is left, to start with, is an unpretentious way of working with other human beings as colleagues and not as experts. The primary intent is to enter into and attempt to fathom the subjective world of our client; it is in that realm that we can, with some humility, begin to appreciate what is of consequence and value to that individual as well as the kinds of beliefs and ways of thinking that both aid and detract from his or her well-being and worth. This intent is keenly illustrated in Taylor's account (Chapter 9) of the elderly patient who was written off as "delusional" by institutional staff. Only when a caring and curious student took the time to inquire, almost naively, about what this woman's inner world was like to her, could she disclose that, in terms of her own survival and worth, the people that inhabited her mind were indeed quite real.

This is not a haphazard or random enterprise for we are assisted in our understanding by what the cognitive sciences are now beginning to reveal about the enigmatic workings of the mind. Yet the term "science" as it is linked to cognition is somewhat misleading since our growing knowledge of mind, brain, and behavior is not restricted to the kinds of facts and laws that ordinary science produces but embraces as well the studies of philosophers of the mind, the communication theorists, social psychologists, linguistic theorists, and other disciplines that contribute to the field of modern cognitive science.

To put this another way, our attempt to comprehend our client's subjective experience as a basis for helping calls for a blending of science and art, or a familiarity with what we do know about the human state coupled with a willingness, if not an eagerness, to grapple with all that is unique, intimate, and arcane within that experience. What is required, then, is not technical expertise or a set of dependable skills but rather what Schön calls "reflection-in-action" (1983: 49–69). Schön's study of professionals in action reveals that technical expertise is not sufficient to effect successful results. To the contrary, such presumed expertise can lead to selective inattention, to the creation of arbitrary categories that are considerably removed from the actualities of the client's experience, to situational control, and inevitably, to methods that are designed more to

280

preserve the constancy of what the professional already knows and believes than to be of assistance to the client. In contrast with the essentially convergent nature of technical expertise, reflection-in-action is divergent in character. This sort of divergent thinking is clearly evident in Sturkie's first-person reflections about his ongoing exchanges with the two abusive families (Chapter 3). Constantly open to new ways of understanding, the helper engages in an unending dialogue with the problem; each moment, each situation is explored for its own existential and special meanings. As theories are selected in the attempt to explain what is happening, the worker is unceasingly alert not only to how they fit the situation, but also to the norms and values that the theory expresses. In this unfolding process, the helper rejects control and works as a colleague with his or her client in the pursuit of a solution that, in the end, is of the client's own making.

Making sense and finding meaning

As the various chapters show, this pursuit may be initiated in any of a number of ways: by the client's own request for assistance, refuge, or relief; by the crisis that has befallen the client or that has been created by him or her; by the influence of an official authority; and, at times, by chance alone. We have also seen that, in some instances, the idea of the possibility of a solution may seem rather irrelevant to some clients since, first of all, they don't define themselves as clients, and second, they aren't convinced that there is a problem requiring a solution.

Two concepts are useful in organizing our impressions of the encounter between client and professional, and how the client feels about it: one, "problem," gives us a way of organizing what we can learn *about* the client's current state of being; the other, "solution," brings us a step closer to an understanding *of* the client him- or herself.

PROBLEMS Since it is necessary to attach a name to a phenomenon before we are able to deal with it in a sensible fashion, the concept of a problem (used in its generic sense) is useful insofar as it directs our attention to the kinds of obstacles that stand in the way of a more harmonious existence. Not only do we wish to know something more about the obstacle itself, but if we can define it even in elemental terms, we might also learn something about its more extensive implications.

Obviously, it is important to know how clients themselves define their circumstances — what, if anything, they see as the problem. Here clients are telling something more than "what's wrong." However they account for their troubles, they will, by inference or declaration, disclose where they place responsibility, what they believe they can or cannot do about them, what they anticipate as a solution, their feelings of hope or demoralization, and so on.

If, as we have argued, motivation is seen as a continuum rather than as a judgment about the client's readiness or acceptability for service, then one extreme, the voluntary, would include those individuals who feel troubled about, or even responsible for, some misfortune or unhappy circumstances in their lives. For example, we saw that many of those who seek out or form self-help groups are already aware that there may be alternatives to their suffering, expect that the group will be helpful, and, to one extent or another, are willing to consider what they might need to do or change to realize these alternatives. At the other extreme is the individual who, like the alcoholic, has set him- or herself on a cataclysmic course of resignation and failure. Although it is this course that may eventually propel such clients into the helping setting, it is apparent that before they can even begin to entertain the possibility of change, they will need to be helped to deal with their reactions to finding themselves, perhaps against their will, in this situation.

It seems safe to say that most clients fall somewhere between these extremes on our metaphorical continuum — but for very different reasons. The chronically ill, although despairing of their fate, are first and foremost likely to see themselves as medical patients — those whose bodies are to be tended to and treated by experts. Not only might they be unaware of the availability of social services, but they may not yet not be conscious of the possibility that they, as thinking, feeling, and valuing beings, can be enlisted in the endeavor to cope with the consequences of their infirmities. The abused wife, on the other hand, may dramatically seek assistance; however, as J. Hilbert observes, this may be more of a search for relief or refuge than a press for a more promising existence. The poor, rural or otherwise, and in similar ways, the ex-mental patient, may have long ago resigned themselves to a life that is bereft of quality or security. Quite possibly, the well-meaning but ineffective efforts of previous helping professionals may have even reinforced their shrunken expectations. The concept of problem, then, helps us become more sensitive to clients' conceptions of their state of being and alerts us to how we can best join forces with them in that state.

In more abstract yet no less relevant terms, this concept may also provide some clues about the client's status within the social order. This knowledge is important: beyond the intrinsic meaning of the problem itself — that is, the implications that it has for the individual — an awareness of its social ramifications tells us something about the other external obstacles we may need to grapple with along the way. For example, how is the problem (and therefore, the person) defined by the client's community? What labels or classifications stand in the way of the client achieving a more independent, dignified, and less deviant role? These questions are most salient in many of the previous examples. Taylor's account of the "career" of the mental patient makes this point quite clearly. The abused wife might be pitied by those around her but she may also be blamed as the "victim" who, in some insidious way, has brought about her own misfortune. If the poor family comes to be defined as "chronically dependent" and therefore hopeless, then the attempt by any member to improve their lot could be dismissed or demeaned. The problem of the Vietnam veteran, at least up to recent times, is, in itself, a derivation of the public's discomfort and abhorrence. And the alcoholic is seen as someone afflicted with a disease.

Similarly, we may learn something about the kind of social or political institutions we may either need to call on or contend with. It makes some difference to our practice whether, for example, we are working within the legal system when it comes to practice with the violent family or the abused wife, the medical establishment in relation to the chronically ill, the welfare system with regard to the poor, veterans' organizations in relation to the Vietnam veteran, or the mental health organizations. This reminds us that the helping professional does not work within a social vacuum. The desire to regard and respond to the client in holistic rather than categorical terms means that we are not concerned with mind, body, and behavior alone, but also the transactions within the larger world in which our clients dwell.

Finally, the concept of problem directs us to the existing body of literature and research that may be pertinent to the dilemmas we are attempting to understand. As our various authors have shown, this cumulative knowledge provides the kind of generalities about personal, interpersonal, and social problems that lend themselves to testing against the specific characteristics of the unique case.

Creative change

SOLUTIONS Vaughn's chapter on the rural poor is helpful in illustrating the complementary relationship of the concepts of problem and solution. The former gives us a three-dimensional but descriptive perspective on the client's circumstances. These may include not only the trouble itself, but also clients' interactions with their physical and social environment, the strengths or lacks in their support network, who the problem identifiers are, and so on. The concept of solution, however, draws us somewhat closer to the client's subjective and inter-personal world as well as the personal meanings that are ascribed to the difficulty.

Putting this another way, the notion of a problem is relatively meaningless until we gain some appreciation of where it fits within the pattern of the client's living, how it is understood and what it means to him or her, what is at stake either in perpetuating or changing the problem, and whether a solution is possible. As a "problem," the abuse that the battered woman has suffered for so long takes on radically different meanings when she finally concludes that all hope for the future of the relationship is lost and that an alternative way of life is either necessary or possible. The alcoholics' "problem" really doesn't exist as far as they are concerned until their illusions no longer serve them and another solution is called for. This reaffirms the major principle that our concern is not solely with the nominal troubles people are enduring, but with the means that they rely on (the solution) to resolve the dilemma.

Our concern with the existential meanings and implications of the client's way of dealing with his or her problem is expressed in three questions that, in partnership with the client, we need to explore. First, we need to ask, "Why now?" Assuming that clients' troubles did not spring up overnight, why, then, do they now find themselves face-to-face with a helping professional? Second, what is the autobiographical nature of the problem and the solutions attempted? The last question is bound to elicit far less of specific response since, in this instance, we are curious about the *purposes* the client's solutions may serve for him or her. Let us consider these questions in greater detail.

Some understanding of "Why now?" or the precipitant of the client's first contact with the helping professional (whether voluntary, at the behest of others, or by the initiation of the professional) begins to say something about how clients define themselves and their capabilities, needs, and goals at this time. In the case of the voluntary client who seeks out professional services, the press for assistance could be a new perception about the source of his or her troubles or the acute realization that "I can't handle it alone anymore." But even in the instance of this "willing" and "motivated" client we need to get some idea as to whether this perception or realization signals a feeling of hope and belief in his or her ability to cope or a sense of failure and helplessness. Blauner captures the range of these attitudes in his discussion of people coming into self-help groups. In the case of the non-voluntary clients, exemplified here by the violent and abusive family and the rural poor, the precipitant is typically some pernicious behavior or conditions identified by others — neighbors, community, relatives, for example. Hence, the client in this instance will be unable to answer the "Why now?" question (however it is phrased) other than in self-protective or defensive terms — for example, James Boykin's removed silence or Margie Jackson's question: "Do you have to keep referring to this as abuse?" The fact, however, that the precipitant was of someone else's making may tell us a great deal about how the client is defined by others and, in turn, how the client defines him- or herself.

Amidst the two groups are those persons who are undergoing a special kind of anguish but whose suffering stems, in part, from the fear, confusion, or uncertainty about help-seeking. The precipitant may, on its surface, appear blatant — Mary's blackened eye and bruised body, the sudden signs of rejection in the kidney transplant patient, Jay's vision of himself in the mirror following another alcoholic binge, or the nightmare of the veteran, for example. Yet, as has been shown, what needs to be sought out is the meaning that the client attaches to the space that he or she shares with the helper at that moment. How is it for him or her to be cast in the role of "client?"

The second query attempts to get a first-person account of clients' past attempts to make sense of and find a solution to their troubles. Their narrative may indeed disclose the values and standards that they have set for themselves, ideas about what the quality of their lives ought to be, related expectations, their level of self-esteem and the like. But their stories may also reveal some fairly straightforward lacks of information or distortions of facts, the absence of opportunities or the material things they require to resolve their difficulties, or the inability to envision other alternatives. It was shown that it is the personal awareness that something is lacking that prompts some people to enter a self-help group; they do so in order to learn what needs to be known, to correct their misconceptions, and, through the experiences of others in the same

285

predicament, to find fresh solutions. But others, some abusive families, for example, and often, the isolated poor who have had little exposure to the more psychologically sophisticated world, sincerely believe that "We are doing the best we can with what we got," and remain unaware that there are indeed other pathways to follow. The point to be made is that the worker must resist the reflexive tendency to limit his or her explanation of the client's unproductive solutions to purely psychological reasons.

The last question to be considered concerns the way the solution may serve some particular purpose for the client and/or others in his or her system. To repeat, a fundamental human purpose underlying the way we attempt to make sense of and somehow manage our daily existence is to preserve a measure of integrity — a sense of "rightness" or better, "uprightness" — as good, worthwhile, and credible beings. The individual is rare indeed who cannot offer some sort of explanation for his or her actions — no matter how obviously wrong or patently reprehensible those actions might appear to be. Hence, whatever solution the client has attempted or is attempting must be respected as an expression of a vulnerable self. (Consider how Margie Jackson's abuse of her teenaged daughter was, to her, partially justified by her perception of her daughter's actions as personal betrayal.) By no means does this imply that the solution must be admired or accepted as the best that the client can do about his or her life; nor does this impede the helper's freedom to challenge or, as in the case of the abusive family, to block the client's tendency to fall back on destructive tactics. But before clients can move forward to learn and own new ways of problem-solving, regard must be given to what they have personally invested in their ownership of the old ways.

The chosen solution may also serve other more complex adaptive purposes. For that matter, even the repeated failure of such motives may, in itself, serve a purpose. We find examples of this scattered throughout the previous chapters: the metaphor of the double helix explains the alcoholic's sense of personal failure which serves to justify his or her abuse of alcohol which brings about more failure — and so on; the ex-mental patient's reluctance to risk anything more than playing the "sick role" since that role demonstrates that he or she is incompetent and could not be expected to do any better; or the battering relationship that "proves" to the woman that she doesn't deserve anything more than the abuse that she continues to receive.

Turning to a theatrical analogy, as helpers we are the audience wanting to make sense of and find meaning in the behavior of the actors whose life-drama we are witnessing. As in any good theatre, this drama doesn't unfold in an obvious or transparent fashion; rather, a pact of sorts is established in which the good audience allows itself to be vicariously drawn into the enigma that the actors create onstage. Similarly, the good helper becomes an active participant in the client's real-life quandary. If I may be permitted yet another analogy, the concepts of problem and solution help, in a manner of speaking, to part the curtains that separate actors from audience. They provide a first-hand way of beginning to make sense out of what may at first appear to be confusion: if nothing more, these concepts begin to illuminate who the protagonists and antagonists are, what it is they are grappling with, the social scene that they occupy, the roles that they are playing out, the script that they rely on, and their motives and purposes. This consciousness now permits us to move from participant-observation towards a deeper understanding of the person as a distinct and unique self.

The self and its dimensions

As practitioners, the life circumstances that we encounter scarcely reflect the condensed existential crises and tensions that most theatrical works portray. The problems we confront often are far less romantic and intriguing.

As the prior chapters show, the lives of our clients are often marked by the seeming absence of choice, by nameless or acute suffering, by puzzlement and hopelessness. Yet, whether one is heroically struggling with one's moment of truth or is just trying to get by, at the core of either experience is the something we call self that embodies all sense and meaning.

We proposed at the outset of this book that the self as a metaphor is not a stable, enduring way of identifying any one individual. To be sure, one's self-concept retains a strong measure of consistency to the extent that one's sense of belonging, identity, and self-esteem is fairly secure. Yet, as each of us personally experiences it, we know that different aspects of who we are called forth at different times, in different places, and in different relationships. This is because our perceptions, our definitions, and our motives and intentions all take on varying complexions in these varying situations. Clearly, we cannot ever say that we surely "know" our client; but appreciating that "knowing" is a process rather than an end itself allows us to remain curious, heedful, and open to the emergence of unanticipated aspects of our clients' selves. This is exemplified in Sturkie's continuing account of his contacts with the Boykins and Jacksons. The changes in the way these people presented themselves were not representative of some personal transformation; rather, with an increasing sense of trust in and comfort with their worker, they were able to disclose aspects of themselves that they formerly had to obscure.

Unfortunately, many evaluations of people called clients or patients tend to be limited largely to the psychological realm — and at times, and to a lesser extent, the sociological. We suggest that the nature of self or person involves more than what can be incorporated in either or both of these realms of understanding. Thus, in the attempt to understand the client as a whole and integrated being, we introduced in Chapter 1 the idea of the "person of mind" to cover the inner, psychological processes and the "person of community" to account for one's ongoing transactions with one's social and cultural milieu. But in addition, we called attention to the "person of principle" that embodies the influence of the client's ingrained values, ideologies, and moral and ethical commitments, and the "person of faith" that reflects the weight of one's spiritual identifications and beliefs.

An argument can be made for the claim that, in the final analysis, all of these "persons" are really variations of one psychological state. From a cognitive standpoint, we would agree that one's cultural identity, conceptions of environment, ethical standards, or religious affiliation are indeed centered in the mind of the individual. For this reason, the various chapters all have given particular attention to the person of the mind. Our intent, however, is less concerned with creating a theory that is conceptually sound or internally consistent but, in its abstractness, is somewhat removed from life as it is experienced; rather, we want to achieve some sense and understanding of how that life is actually lived — and that "how" can scarcely be squeezed into neat conceptual categories. Hence we want to move beyond conceptual constraints to give deserved attention to all of the "persons" — the moral and spiritual, as well as the psychological and social.

Vaughn's account of practice with the rural poor, for example, does not overlook the way these clients define themselves, their existence, and their hopes for the future. At the same time, it is evident that the *person of community* must be reckoned with since these people also need to be understood in terms of their status and their identifications and interactions with the people and institutions about them. This way of finding sense and meaning encourages the kind of practice that is focused not on the individual *or* the environment but, rather, on the transactions that shape the whole of living. The notion of community takes on a different coloration in Blauner's discussion of self-help groups. Here, a spirit of community is created (and abetted by the presence of the helper) by what was formerly a random collection of strangers. It is the sense of belonging, interdependence, and power emerging from the communal experience that enables each member to find the hope and means to cope with his or her adversities.

The plight of other clients that we find in these pages is further crystallized when we pay special heed to the part that the *person of principle* plays. In the case of the battered woman, it may be palpably clear to the observer that she must take some kind of action for her own safety and well-being. Without contradicting this imperative, however, it is apparent that she will be less likely to take effective action if the values and ideals that regulate her style of life or that create dissonance are not addressed. As we have seen, this woman's commitment to caring and responsibility may, on the one hand, dilute her efforts to separate herself from her dependent mate; on the other hand, her ability to take assertive action may be impeded by the possibility that her basic values and sense of what is right and wrong have been diffused by years of denigration.

By the same token, how can we make any sense out of the "readjustment" of the Vietnam veteran without exposing ourselves to the vestiges of moral outrage and crumbling virtue that continue to distort his attempt to create dependable meaning in living? We cannot assume that we can truly understand his experience since it is so far removed from the moral order that more or less characterizes our more ordinary lives. Yet, we need to try to hear his story — if only to discover within it the confusion about what might be dependably "right" or "good" in his beliefs that will enable him to move beyond a dilemma that essentially defies solution. This imperative applies equally to our work with alcoholics who, in ways of their own making, have not only lost faith with their standards and ideals, but have come to twist or deny them in such a way as to be able to now define themselves as the "noble martyr." And perhaps in more fundamental terms, the violent family needs to be helped to regain, if not learn anew, the moral and ethical obligations that are essential to the basic functions of family life.

In these or other cases, questions about all that constitutes a principled way of life cannot be ignored because, to do so, the worker would have to be blind to his or her own beliefs and principles. We must assume that people who choose a career within the helping professions do so out of compelling concerns about needs, rights and injustice, caring, personal obligation, and other ethical convictions. In practice with clients who are already burdened by the guilt or shame that is a consequence of their own transgressions, the helper's personal ethics and morality may, to some extent, be held in abeyance. But upon confronting situations like those just noted or others in which the client has been subject to unconscionable wrongs (the mental patient, for example), would it be possible for the worker to deny his or her own principled beliefs in working with these clients without coming across as a shallow technician? This question is clearly addressed in H. Hilbert's discussion of practice with the veteran.

It is difficult to be sure about the role of the *person of faith* in many of our clients' lives. From one perspective, unless clients have some missionary tendencies, they are not likely to speak of the deeper spiritual beliefs or commitments that dignify and enlarge their existence; for that matter, they might be embarrassed even to admit that they pray from time to time. Complementing this tendency, the professional may be uncomfortable, if not wholly reluctant, about probing into this dimension of the client's life — although, paradoxically, he or she may have no hesitation about inquiring into other intimate areas. Yet we should pay heed to the chapter in this book that does illuminate the significance of spiritual belief — that concerning the chronically ill patient. What we find here may express the unspoken deeper feelings of many clients who find that the control over their lives that they once believed was secure is now stripped away from them.

From the studies of the other clients that appear on these pages, one could surmise that, if nothing else, they could maintain at least an illusion of control: the battered woman could lean on the hope that "next time" her husband would control his rage; the alcoholic could protest that "next time" he or she could refuse to drink; the veteran could risk the wish that maybe "next time" his terrifying dream will not startle him awake. The realization either that there may not be a "next time" or that, if there is, it is likely to be worse than this time, is, as Bohnengel-Lee emphasizes, something that the seriously ill battle against, resign themselves to, or accept. And in the latter case, all that they have left to turn to is what was there in the first place: proof that they are indeed mortal, and a faith in some greater force or purpose which, in some important ways, gives meaning to one's mortality.

It would seem reasonable to surmise that a greater faith in something — whether it be in the intervention of a divine being, a larger order of things, a spiritual sense, a creed or cosmology of some sort — serves as a dependable refuge and source of support even for those clients who do not have to confront directly their impermanence on this earth. All too often, we become so preoccupied with the seriousness of the client's problem and the dreadful despair of his or her way of life that we lose sight of the fact that, amidst all this debris, the client still has the strength and desire to persevere — to go on living at any cost. It would require another treatise even to begin to explore the place of faith in this choice — or for that matter, whether it is the giving up of the power of faith that allows other people to consider death as an alternative. Nonetheless, on encountering clients like Gracie, the mental patient, Jay, the alcoholic, families living amidst grinding poverty, or Johnny, the veteran, whose lives — to understate the matter grossly — are something less than rewarding, we need to retain our innocent sense of awe and regard for their wish to strive and persist. Out of this regard we might, perhaps, even gain some understanding and appreciation of the depth of belief and faith that verifies the worth of their existence.

We have used the metaphors of "self" and "persons" as a vehicle that enables us to at least glimpse something in the client's way of life that offers a measure of sense and meaning. It bears repeating that these notions are not analytic categories but, rather, facets of an irreducible whole: although one "person" or another may take precedence at one time or another, maintaining the integrity of the self is the pressing need of the individual. Perhaps because it involves a question such as, "What is it like to face a life-threating condition at thirty-seven?" (Chapter 4), what is meant by the integrity of the self is poignantly illustrated by the instance of Mr S., the patient enduring a sickle-cell crisis. A re-reading of this episode will disclose how his sense of community gave him purpose and direction. At the same time, his principled self enabled him, albeit with great pain, to make the choices that had meaning for him and others. The quality of his faith lent strength to the life pattern he chose. And his reflective mind allowed him to find the order and will necessary to accomplish that which he deemed essential. Clearly, it was his worker's regard for and sensitivity to the integrity of these selves that allowed Mr S. to finish his life in the way he thought best.

SENSE, MEANING, AND THE PRACTICE OF COGNITIVE-HUMANISM

The kind of understanding that derives from the ideas of problem, solution, self, and person sets the conceptual ground for direct practice. This understanding tells us something cogent about the cognitive processes that link the subjective inner person to his or her objective physical and social world as well as the resonance that is created between both.

When we speak, for example, of the person of community or the person of faith we are also alluding to the interpretive functions of the mind or the schema. It is this cognitive function that makes ultimate sense of and imputes meaning to experience — whether actual or imagined. In these terms, we can see that the elderly mental patient (Chapter 9) found her identity and worth in her own "delusional" Polish village that she recalled in her mind; here in this very private recess she found her refuge from the perceived threats of the "real" community that she was forced to inhabit.

In a continuing, spiral-like fashion, how we define and interpret our experiences depends on how we perceive and think about them — and ultimately act. The metaphor of the screaming, dying soldier that froze Johnny's attempt to find a place in his world (Chapter 10) shows how this process can constrict one's existence. By the same token, one's schema may be sufficiently ample to incorporate all sorts of possibilities and vistas as was the case with Mr S., the dying patient (Chapter 4).

It is this perceiving self (described in Chapter 2) that is the focus of practice. However, as we have seen and as we have noted before, the concern and care that we extend to the client's constructions can create a paradox of sorts — or what J. Hilbert, in her discussion of the battered woman, calls a "delicate balance." The point has been made that what one knows and believes is the reality that substantiates one's existence. At the same time, however, we have speculated that the cognitive scheme that characterizes the client's approach to his or her problems of living may be so solipsistic (i.e. circular and self-verifying, devoid of essential facts, or otherwise distorted) as to ensure that the client will not arrive at a proper solution. The twofold question, then, that confronts the practitioner is: "How can I respect the client's basic need to conserve his or her rendition of reality while at the same time create the conditions that will encourage modification of both reality and behavior in ways that are more rewarding for the client?" Basically, can we begin with error to achieve accuracy?

292

The answer is contained in the question. As our many examples show the process of change does not begin with the worker's private assumptions about what is wrong, what needs to be worked on, and what needs to be rectified. Rather it starts within the area of the client's real world of beliefs and patterns of adaptation — no matter how specious this ground may be. Helping, as the familiar aphorism puts it, "starts where the client is."

The helping process, as it unfolds, is a creative experience both for the worker and for the client. The helper cannot fall back on tried or true methods and schemes, nor can he or she resort to a kind of psychological atlas that will determine the route that will be taken. With the client, he or she embarks on a search for meaning and substance in which they will encounter not only the hard facts, the iniquities and the hazards of living but, as well, the metaphors, ambiguities, and absurdities that give each life its peculiar hue. But, as we have observed, creativity cannot emerge without some sense of purpose or a compelling intent: the search for meaning is compelling enough.

Many of the welcome voluntary clients who appear in the waiting rooms of social agencies and mental-health centers have, by definition, a purpose — even though it may be as simple as the desire to find relief from discomfort or anxiety. In contrast, many of the people in these pages that we have come to know are best characterized by their sense of *purposelessness*: to them, meaning, ideals, or destinations have become scattered and confused. Gracie, Jay, Johnny G., the Jacksons, the Boykins and others vividly express this emptiness.

We have seen that creative change is set in motion with what we have variously called consciousness-raising, problem-setting, or discrimination-learning. How this phase develops, however, depends on the particular client's needs and circumstances. Hence, in the case of the abusive families, the worker collaborates actively with the family to help them, as Sturkie puts it, re-examine and re-order their priorities. In the case of the mental patient or the veteran, the helper encourages the client to tell his or her story in a way that may allow new meanings to emerge; even as we hear a narration of chronic failures, we are being told something about what the client might value as success. For example, the value that is placed on closeness is revealed in Johnny G.'s tale of the series of foundered relationships; the yearning to be attractive and desirable is expressed in Gracie's account of the ridicule and rejection she felt she endured. And finally, in the case of the dependent "multi-problem" family, the ill patient, or the battered woman, we enable the client to tell us not only what is or has been chronically wrong, but, more important, something about his or her strengths, effectiveness, and capabilities.

The extent to which clients begin to perceive their circumstances more keenly, find that there are some gaps in their conclusions about how things are, discover the need for more information, or otherwise increase their awareness by a few degrees, would create the need or the prompting to risk taking another look at their version of reality. It needs to be said again that this heightening of consciousness is effected not by a "doing to" but by a "doing with." Respecting the client's frame of reference invites the client to tell his or her story; as the story unfolds, the helper, in the Socratic sense, raises questions the client could not ask him- or herself; and the answers lead to yet other questions which open new cognitive pathways of understanding.

What we call redefining reality or concept-learning directs attention to the reflective and thought processes by which one can make better sense of one's life and experience. For example, Mr Allen is helped to see that it is his strengths and his caring for his children that, amidst the morass of his other problems, will sustain his pursuit of fresh, alternative solutions. The battered wife who comes to rethink the history of her marriage in less self-blaming ways may now be able to ponder her future in more hopeful terms. The alcoholic who begins to accept responsibility for his or her muddled life must now devise a new scheme of living. And without exhausting the rich array of instances of new learning described in the prior chapters, we must consider the combination of new-found inspiration and practical methods realized by members of self-help groups: out of what they gain from their interactions with the others, these people can now define themselves in new ways that allow them to have some say in their destiny and to cast off their former role as reactive sufferers of an uninvited fate.

The type of reflection and thought that leads to more rewarding redefinitions of one's version of reality is closely bound to what is termed principle-learning. It is probably timely to reiterate that these phases do not proceed in a logical or linear fashion; to the contrary, cognition is a rough and uneven weave of recollection, anticipation, emotion, association, action, and imagery that takes its shape in somewhat unpredictable ways. As we have seen, principle-learning addresses the moral, ethical, and spiritual substrata of our being. Action without thought is, of course, random or impulsive. Thought without action is a hollow intellectual sham. But thought and action that are not founded on our value premises and ethical and moral commitments are bound to be dishonest and inauthentic.

Despite the outward differences that distinguish the clients and problems covered in this book, the idea that, in one way or another, serves as a common bond is that life needs to be lived in a principled manner. This does not propose that these or other people instinctively or naturally gravitate towards or are regulated by some inner rules of conduct. All too often, other priorities diminish the importance of one's values and commitments; in these instances, if any vestige of morality or spirituality remains, anguish is bound to follow.

Putting this another way, if our lives are more or less unthreatened and, thus, seemingly manageable, we tend to give little attention to the metaphysical implications of our daily activities. As H. Hilbert argues, however, it is that time when we are faced with a moral or ethical choice that has no quick solution, or when we cannot evade the fact that we have erred seriously in our choice, that serious and painful questioning arises. Hence, it is precisely this point in the helping experience — the moment when the client actively ventures an initial creative solution to his or her difficulty — that questions about his or her principles become critical. For example, we have to ask the batterred woman who decides to reunite with her husband if she is succumbing to the value she places on predictable misery or is this decision a reaffirmation of her belief that she is strong enough to forbid further abuse. Jay, like many other alcoholics, reaches a point in the helping process where he believes: "Now we are cured!" Is this assertion a sure sign that he has come to terms with his honest values or is it yet another means of escaping personal responsibility? But these questions, critical as they are, seem to pale when the client's moral choice (as in the case of Mr S.) is a matter of life or death.

It should be evident that the helper cannot resort to any easy answers to these dilemmas; standard practicetheories offer no "how to do" solutions in these cases. To be sure, the helper can ignore these troubling issues completely by restricting his or her concern to some sort of concrete assessment of progress (e.g. measurements of psychological change, task completion, movement, behavioral change, and so on) that will guide intervention. But in gaining only objective data, what the helper loses sight of are the subjective and existential meanings of the client's new-found courage to risk action. In the final analysis, the helper is cast back upon his or her own ethical/moral convictions relating to the right to intervene in the first place, the question of where responsibility for the client's self-determination and well-being ultimately resides, the impact of the client's actions on others, and other enigmas that each unique relationship generates.

CHANGE

Given that change is what this book is all about, it may seem odd that discussion of this concept comes at the very end of this book. Yet, if change is the consequence of a complex and often enigmatic process, it seems justified to give it its due attention only after something substantive has been said about the process itself.

Since it is a rather elusive concept that can have many meanings and implications, let us first talk about change in rather basic terms. It is, of course, the generic term that refers to the outcome of an endeavor that might be called counseling, psychotherapy, family therapy, group work, social action, re-education or just plain helping. In the first chapter, we spoke of the general intent to "free people to search for, define, and risk fresh, creative, and ethical solutions to their problems of living." Essentially, a process is set in motion whereby, at the client's or someone else's behest, a professional enters into the current of an individual's, a family's, or a group's life. The obvious should be noted: this entry occurs at a particular point in time — a time preceded by a multitude of life experiences and, quite likely, a time to be followed by a good many more. Irrespective of the professional's school, theory, or orientation, his or her basic intent is to *make a difference* in the client's way of life. Without wishing to be facetious, we need to ask: what difference does it make? What is its meaning? What is it that changes and what is the change itself?

Parenthetically, it is worth observing that these are questions that are more frequently and anxiously asked (usually of oneself) by the student and beginning practitioner who, in the face of the uncertainties about his or her role and skills, seeks some reassurance. He or she wants to be sure not only that "it made a difference," but more important, that "*I* made a difference." Unfortunately, some of our more seasoned workers, feeling greater security about their expertise or caught up in what has become the routine of daily practice, neglect to ask this pivotal question and therefore cease to reflect on the numerous meanings of the profound experience of change. It is indeed a painful question to keep asking oneself, yet faithfully doing so will help avoid the risk of the client becoming

296

objectified into a case that poses a problem to be treated by one technique or another. What can be forgotten amidst this glib routine is that this is not how clients wish to see themselves, nor is it how they wish to be treated. The account of Gracie, the former mental patient, tells us quite persuasively what it is like to lose one's life-long identity and become another diagnostic category, a deviant, a patient — a case.

The previous chapters suggest what change and the difference it makes might mean within the client's viewpoint and experience. We find that it is not likely to be a "happily ever after" outcome in which the problem has been fixed or cured for all time. Even if we, as professionals, were that adroit, we could not anticipate the problems of living that are yet to come. Neither does change mean that behavior has been changed in the manner of adjusting a timing chain or brake pedal so that the rest of the machine can function more smoothly. Nor do we enable people to return or move ahead into what is really an illusion of homeostasis or stability. Many of our examples show that, in fact, cognitive change may mean that the client has forsaken some cherished hope for harmony and security — the anticipation that, for example, my husband will stop beating me and love me again, that I can stop drinking any time I want to, that I'm not really as sick as the doctors say, that if the kids will change, I will be a better parent, and so on. And in many situations, the conditions really don't get any better: poverty remains constant; the unpredictable horrors of trying to make it alone are not allayed by just talking; the remission from a chronic illness doesn't last; the abusive family never quite models the happy families we see on television.

What is different is not some dramatic change — and probably not a quantitatively measurable outcome. What we refer to as creative change is, in effect, the new-found ability to risk stepping outside of the well-worn, even dependable, pattern of thinking, feeling, and acting so as to create and choose for oneself, and for one's relationship with others, a more authentic, caring, and assertive way of life. It needs to be said that, in some instances, this is a bitter-sweet experience as we found in the case of Mary, the battered wife, Mr S., the sickle-cell patient, and Sarah Boykin, the wife of the child abuser. Giving up the role of the suffering victim does not promise a bright, new, and joyous future.

In general terms, change implies that a number of new cognitive patterns have taken the place of the old. For one, the client may relinquish his or her former linear, cause-and-effect way of explaining and justifying his or her circumstances and adopt a more dialectical outlook. Here we find Jay who came to accept a more resonant view of himself in his relationship with his world in place of his over-elaborated and irresponsible "reasons" for his drinking. Second, clients may stop defining themselves as an assortment of pieces and parts and, instead, settle for nothing less than their integrity. Here the various persons of mind, community, principle, and faith coalesce, as was evident in the account of Johnny G. Third, change may be the consequence of new information gained. In the discussion of self-help groups we saw that information is not just a compilation of facts; what is important is that this new knowledge is supported by a climate of acceptance, respect, and, to some extent, the expectation that the client will use it productively.

The most creative and imaginative expression of change, however, is the client's ability to transfer what he or she has learned and tested in living. Although the client may long for freedom from fear and uncertainty, he or she learns that stability and adjustment are really fictions that do not prepare one for the challenges of living in an incalculable and baffling world. Rather, the client discovers, first within him- or herself, the remarkable inventive skills, the imaginative solutions, the metaphorical visions, and basically, the trust in his or her own moral principles and values, that encourage one to manage these inherent unpredictabilities of living. This is truly creative change — the metamorphosis that inevitably deepens one's sense of personal worth and esteem and that makes possible the ability to love, care, and return something of substance to one's community.

Finally, the pages we have covered thus far should suggest that change, in the way we have considered it, is made possible when we are no longer objectively "professional" and when we can relate to our clients in the same ordinary and egalitarian ways we relate to other human beings whom we value. We are at our best as helpers when we can cast off the pretentious role of expert or technician and join with our clients as colleagues and companions in the pursuit of all that is of consequence for a more reasonable life. Perhaps the words of the poet, Rainer Maria Rilke, are fitting here:

At the bottom, and just in the deepest and most important things, we are unutterably alone, and for one person to be able to advise or even help another, a lot must happen, a lot must go well, a whole constellation of things must come right in order once to succeed.

(*Letters to a Young Poet*, 1903)

Index of Names

Abram, H. 106
Adams, J. 59
Allport, G. 17
Angrosino, M. Y. 218

Bachrach, L. 235
Barnes, H. 272
Bassuk, E. 235
Bateson, G. 85
Beattie, O. 45
Beavin, J. 77, 85
Beck, A. 93
Beels, E. 94
Berdie, J. 80
Berenson, D. 74
Biestek, F. 267
Birch, D. 49
Blank, A. 262
Blauner, M. L. ix, 213, 285, 289
Blythe, B. J. 220
Bohnegel, A. ix, 102, 279, 290
Bowen, M. 77, 93
Bruner, J. 22
Buber, M. 19, 221
Bulman, R. 111
Burnes, A. 235
Bybee, R. 88

Chomsky, N. 42
Chu, F. 235
Cole, S. A. 216
Combs, A. 17
Coplon, J. 216
Crane, J. G. 218
Csikszentmihalyi, M. 45

Daly, M. 161
De Bono, E. 59
Dewey, J. xv, 47, 74, 271
Doll, W. 236
Dunkel-Schneider, C. 220

Egandorf, A. 262

Farley, W. 193
Farrer, A. 24
Ferber, A. 94
Fisch, R. 60, 87
Fischer, B. 80
Fitzgerald, F. S. 132, 142
Flanzer, J. 74, 76, 80, 83, 88, 93
Frank, J. 85
Frankena, W. K. 266
Fromm, E. 17, 157

Gabriano, J. 79
Garbarino, J. 219
Garvin, C. 214, 216
Geller, J. 179
Gelles, R. 157, 163, 184
Gennep, A. van 220
Gerson, S. 235
Gilligan, C. 178
Ginsberg, L. 193
Goffman, E. 242
Goldstein, H. on concept-learning 57; on
   convergence and divergence 41, 87, 270;
   on culture-boundedness 8; on discri-
   mination-learning 54; on family struggle
   85; on framework for practice 33; on

299

Index of Subjects

woman, battered 161, 166–67, 170–71
meaninglessness 42
medical social work *see* chronically ill
medical treatment of chronically ill 104,
117, 121
medically-oriented self-help groups 215-21,
225, 227–28, 230
meeting client *see* beginning helping
memory 44–5; *see also* selective memory
mentally ill in hospital and community
235–58, 280, 283, 286, 292–93; basic
principles 236–37; client's view 245–51;
daily routine of 238–41
metaphor and symbols 17, 40, 145, 220, 222
mind: action and meaning 14–17; person of
10–11, 14, 23, 288; *see also* psychological
frame of reference
minification of misconceptions 56
models of cognitive-social learning and
help-seeking, battered woman 170–74,
176–77
moral and ethical issues *see* ethical
moral anguish *see* Vietnam veteran
motivation (purpose) 26, 47–51; alcoholics,
helping 151–52; as continuum 282; loss of
113; woman, battered, work with 175–76;
see also purpose
multiproblem family 71, 82–3, 87, 293
mutual assistance and mutuality 230; *see
also* self-help

narcissism of alcoholic 136
needs *see* material needs
neurological patients' self-help group 219,
221, 230
non-self 18–19
nothingness 161, 166, 235, 255

objective view of alcoholism 133–38, 143–47
objectivity 39–40
objectivization of battered woman 172–73
"overinvolved" family 86–7

paradigms: perception and cognitive processes 38–45; self 18–24; stages of problem resolution 74–5; therapy techniques
91–5
participation, ritual *see* self-help groups
past, importance of 44–5, 52; of alcoholic
145–46; reinterpretation of 60; of rural
poor 199
perceiving self 18, 22–4, 34–6, 145, 292
perception concept 22

"peripherality," family 86–7
personal: integration 122–23; time construct
88–9; *see also* self phases and stages :
alcoholism 134–36; problem-solving 47–8,
74–5; woman-battering relationship 164–
65
philosophical and theoretical foundations
3–32; integration of 278–98
physical: punishment 80; /social context of
perception 38; *see also* body; material
post-traumatic stress disorder (PTSD) 259,
262
poverty *see* multiproblem family; rural
poor; survival level
power, distorted sense of 145
powerlessness 133, 187
practitioner, role of 119–30; *see also* helper
pragmatic solutions 64–5
pregnancy and adolescence 3–5, 7–8, 64–5
present, importance of 88, 181
pretending 92, 94
principle: -learning 171, 176–77, 184–85,
294–95; person of 11–12, 21–3, 25, 27,
288–91; person of, Vietnam veteran 260–
61, 265–74; *see also* ethical and moral
principles: of chronically ill 112–13, 116; of
clients 34; of practice 24–30; violation of
44
problem-solving, creative 282–84; abusive
family 72–84, 87–8; development of 46–8,
53–65; with rural poor 203–07
professional *see* helper
psychological frame of reference 7–10, 198,
200; *see also* mind, person of
punishment 80
purpose of life 112–13, 127–28; *see also*
motivation
purposelessnes 294

rational faculties of brain 39–40
rationalization of alcoholism 136
reality, personal 9, 36–7; in chronic illness
108–09, 111; reconceptualization of 57–9,
227–31, 296; and self-help groups 227–31;
and woman, battered 176–77, 180–83; *see
also* concept-learning
reasoning and behavior 26–7
recidivism of mentally ill 235–36
reconstitution of family 98
referrals 49
reflection: "-in-action" 280–81; in paradigm
of therapy techniques 92; woman, battered 170, 174–75

Creative Change

violence *see* adolescent abusing family;
  woman, battered
virtue, alcoholic's notion of 145
visits 92–3; home 78, 196
visual thought 40

"We-feeling" 221

"What for?" and "Why?" questions 58–9
withdrawal 130
woman, battered 157–90, 282–95; outcomes
  187–88; philosophical and theoretical
  considerations 159–69; practical approach
  176–87; theory and practice, linking
  169–76